What Is Global History?

What Is Global History?

SEBASTIAN CONRAD

PRINCETON UNIVERSITY PRESS

Princeton and Oxford

Cover art: 1746 Carte de L'Ocean
Meridional Dressée pour Servir a l'Histoire
Generale des Voyages, Bellin / Van Schley
Map courtesy of Harlan J. Berk, Ltd.

Fourth printing, and first paperback printing, 2017
Paperback ISBN 978-0-691-17819-6
The Library of Congress has cataloged the cloth edition of this book as
follows:
Cloth ISBN 978-0-691-15525-8
Library of Congress Control Number 2015953087

British Library Cataloging-in-Publication Data is available
This book has been composed in Garamond and Ideal
Printed on acid-free paper. ∞
Printed in the United States of America
7 9 10 8 6

Contents

What Is Global History?

CHAPTER 1

Introduction

———— ◉ ————

"All historians are world historians now," C. A. Bayly has declared, somewhat provocatively—only to add, "though many have not yet realized it."[1] Indeed, there can be no doubt that global/world history is currently booming. In the United States, and in the other parts of the Anglophone world, it has for several decades been the fastest-growing field within the discipline. This trend has also caught on in parts of Europe and East Asia, where global history is on the rise and finding increasing favor with a younger generation of historians. Journals and conventions are appearing everywhere, and in many settings "global dimensions" have become an almost obligatory feature of successful project proposals. But does this rise in popularity really mean that every historian is a global historian? Just what is it about global history that has made it so popular? And why is this happening now?

There are many reasons for this boom. Most significant has been the increased interest in global processes that followed first the end of the Cold War and then the events of September 11, 2001. Given the widespread fashion for seeing "globalization" as the key to understanding the present, the need to go back in time and explore the historical origins of this process seems self-evident. In many places, in particular in immigrant societies, global history is also a response to social challenges and to the demand for a more inclusive, less narrowly national perspective on the past. The shift in curriculum from Western Civ to global history in the United States is a typical result of such social pressures. Within the academy, trends of this nature are mirrored by changes in the social, cultural, and ethnic makeup of the profession. And, in turn, transformations in the sociologies of knowledge have reinforced dissatisfaction with the long-standing and pervasive tendency to conceive of national histories as the history of discrete, self-contained spaces.[2]

The communication revolution that began in the 1990s also has had an important impact on our interpretations of the past. Historians—and their readers—travel and experience more of the world than ever before. This increased mobility, further enhanced by the Internet, has facilitated networking and made it possible for historians to participate in global forums—though, admittedly, voices from formerly colonized countries are often barely discernible. As a result, historians today are dealing with a large number of competing narratives, and they see the potential for new insights precisely in this diversity of voices. Finally, the network logic that computer technology encourages has affected the thinking of historians, who increasingly employ a language of networks and nodal points to replace older territorial logics. Writing history in the twenty-first century is not what it used to be.

Why global history? Beyond Internalism and Eurocentrism

Global history was born out of a conviction that the tools historians had been using to analyze the past were no longer sufficient. Globalization has posed a fundamental challenge to the social sciences and to the dominant narratives of social change. Entanglements and networks characterize the present moment, which has itself emerged from systems of interaction and exchange. But in many respects, the social sciences are no longer adequately able to pose the right questions and generate answers that help to explain the realities of a networked and globalized world.

In particular, two "birth defects" of the modern social sciences and humanities hinder our ability to achieve a systematic grasp of processes that span the world. Both can be traced to the formation of the modern academic disciplines in nineteenth-century Europe. First, the genesis of the social sciences and humanities was tied to the nation-state. In their themes and questions, and even in their societal function, fields like history, sociology, and philology remained tied to a country's own society. Beyond that, the "methodological nationalism" of the academic disciplines meant that, theoretically, the nation-state was presupposed as the fundamental unit of investigation, a territorial entity that served as a "container" for a society. The commitment to territorially bounded containers was more pronounced in the field of history than in some of its neighboring disciplines. Knowledge of the world was thereby discursively and institutionally prestructured in such a way as to obscure the role of exchange relationships. History, in most quarters, was limited to national history.[3]

Second, the modern academic disciplines were deeply Euro-centric. They placed European developments in the foreground and saw Europe as the central driving force of world history. Even more fundamentally, the conceptual toolbox of the social sciences and humanities abstracted European history to create a model of universal development. Ostensibly analytical terms like "nation," "revolution," "society," and "progress" transformed concrete European experience into a (universalistic) language of theory that presumably applied everywhere. Methodologically speaking, then, by imposing categories particular to Europe on everybody else's past, the modern disciplines rendered all other societies colonies of Europe.[4]

Global history is one attempt to face the challenges posed by these observations, and to overcome the two unfortunate birthmarks of the modern disciplines. It is thus a revisionist approach—even if it builds on a whole series of forerunners, for issues such as migration, colonialism, and trade have long been of concern to historians. An interest in examining cross-border phenomena may not in itself be new, but now it stakes a new claim. It means to change the terrain on which histori-ans think. Global history, therefore, has a polemical dimen-sion. It constitutes an assault on many forms of container-based paradigms, chief among them national history. As we will discuss in more detail in chapter 4, it is a corrective to in-ternalist, or genealogical, versions of historical thinking that try to explain historical change from within.

At the same time, and beyond issues of method, global his-tory aims to effect a change in the organization and institu-tional order of knowledge. In many countries, what is called "history" was long equated in practice with each country's own national history: most Italian historians worked on Italy, most of their Korean colleagues studied Korea—virtually everywhere, generations of students were introduced to history through handbooks narrating the national past. Against this background, the call for global history comes as a call for inclusiveness, for a broader vision. Other pasts were history, too.

And even where history faculties are well staffed and prepared for broader coverage, courses tend to present the histories of nations and civilizations as monads, in isolation. Chinese textbooks on world history, for example, categorically exclude China—for the national past is taught in a different department. The compartmentalization of historical reality—into national and world history, into history and area studies—means that parallels and entanglements cannot come into focus. The case for global history is thus also a plea to overcome such fragmentation, and to arrive at a more comprehensive understanding of the interactions and connections that have made the modern world.

Global history is certainly not the only game in town, nor is it fundamentally superior as an approach. It is one approach among many, and it is better suited to addressing some questions and issues and less appropriate for addressing others. Its core concerns are with mobility and exchange, with processes that transcend borders and boundaries. It takes the interconnected world as its point of departure, and the circulation and exchange of things, people, ideas, and institutions are among its key subjects.

A preliminary and rather broad definition of global history might describe it as a form of historical analysis in which phenomena, events, and processes are placed in global contexts. There is disagreement, however, on how that result is best achieved. Numerous other approaches—ranging from comparative and transnational history to world and big history, to postcolonial studies and the history of globalization—currently compete for scholarly attention. Just like global history, they endeavour to come to terms with the connectivities of the past.

Each of these different paradigms comes with an emphasis of its own, and we will take up some of the most prominent variants in chapter 3. However, one should not exaggerate the distinctions between them; there are also many commonalities and areas of overlap. In fact, it has proven difficult to define rigidly what makes global history specific and unique. And if we look at the actual usage of the term, the task does not get easier. Any superficial glance through the current literature immediately reveals that the term is used, and hijacked, for a variety of different purposes; frequently, it is employed interchangeably with other terms. Its widespread use betrays both the attractiveness and the elusiveness of the concept, rather than its methodological specificity.[5]

Three varieties of global history

In this situation of eclecticism and theoretical confusion, it may nevertheless be helpful to heuristically distinguish different reactions to the challenge of the "global." Glossing over some of the specifics, they may be said to fall into one of three camps: global history as the history of everything; as the history of connections; and as history based on the concept of integration. As will become clear in subsequent chapters, it is the third approach that holds the greatest promise for global historians who aim to move beyond token gestures towards connectivity. Let's take up the three varieties in turn.[6]

First, one way to approach global history is to equate it with the history of everything. "Global history, strictly understood, is the history of what happens worldwide," write Felipe Fernández-Armesto and Benjamin Sacks, "across the planet as a whole, as if viewed from a cosmic crow's nest, with the advantages of immense distance and panoptic range." From such an omnivorous perspective, everything that ever happened on the earth is a legitimate ingredient of global history.[7]

In actual practice, this has led to very different strategies. The first is what we could call the all-in version of global history. Its most prominent variant is seen in works of large-scale synthesis that attempt to capture global reality in a specific period. The nineteenth century, for example, has found several sophisticated biographers, while other historians content themselves with a global panorama of a particular year. Yet others have extended the scope and portrayed whole millennia, if not the "history of the world" *tout court*. In the case of big history, the scale is expanded still further, covering the span from the Big Bang to the present moment. Whatever the scale, the general mode is identical: the "global" here refers to planetary comprehensiveness.[8]

In similar ways, historians have chosen to trace a particular idea or historical formation through the ages and across the planet. Particularly convincing examples of this kind are studies on the global history of empire that chart imperial formations and their strategies of population management from Ancient Rome (or from Tamerlane) to the present.[9] But in principle, any subject will do for a global biography. We now have global histories of kingship, and of courtesans; histories of tea and coffee, of sugar and cotton, of glass and gold; histories of migration and trade; global histories of nature and of religion; histories of war, and of peace. The examples are legion.

While the term "global history" may thus suggest worldwide coverage, this is not necessarily the case. In principle, anything can become a legitimate focus for global historians: global history as omnibus. This means that even subjects as diverse as South African mine workers in Witwatersrand, the coronation of Hawaiian King Kalakaua, or a village in thirteenth-century Southern France could be studied for its potential contributions to global history. Once it is established that global history is everything, everything can become global history. This is less absurd than it seems. The situation was not so different in the days when national history reigned supreme. Then, too, even when the scope of a work did not necessarily extend to the nation as a whole, it was nonetheless assumed that it did. No one would doubt, for example, that a biography of Benjamin Franklin or an in-depth study of the automobile industry in Detroit was also a contribution to the history of the United States. Once the overall framework of a national history was established, everything within that container seemed like a natural ingredient.

The same is true for the all-in version of global history. Studies on the working classes in Buenos Aires, Dakar, or Livorno can contribute to a global history of labor, even if they do not explore those global horizons themselves. This is particularly the case if historians take account of, and are inspired by, studies on similar phenomena. Examples include Dipesh Chakrabarty's book on jute workers in Bengal and Frederick Cooper's study on dockworkers in Mombasa.[10] The global history component is of course enhanced when historians conduct their studies with similar cases in mind and include books on related subjects in other parts of the globe in their bibliographies.

A second paradigm in the field puts the focus on exchange and connections. This is the most popular form that research has taken in recent years. The common thread connecting these kinds of studies is the general insight that no society, nation, or civilization exists in isolation. From earliest times onward, human life on the planet was characterized by mobility and interaction. Therefore, such movements are the privileged subjects of a global history understood primarily as the history of entanglements. This infatuation with connectivity complements, and thus corrects, what we could call the frugality of earlier frameworks in which the intellectual journey came to a halt at the borders of the nation-state, empire, or civilization.

There is no limit to the range of topics that can be studied from such a perspective—from people on the move to circulating ideas and trade across distances. Again, the reach of the networks and connections may vary and does not have to be planetary. Everything depends on the subject matter and the questions asked: trade in the Mediterranean, the Hajj across the Indian Ocean, chain migrations between China and Singapore, or diplomatic missions to the Vatican. In all of these instances, the interconnectedness of the world, which can be traced back over centuries, is the starting point for global historical research.[11]

Both versions of global history discussed so far apply in principle to all places, and to all times. The third and narrower approach is different, for it presumes, and explicitly reflects on, some form of global integration. At its core are patterns of exchange that were regular and sustained, and thus able to shape societies in profound ways. There have always been cross-border exchanges, but their operation and impact depended on the degree of systemic integration on a global scale.

This third model (it will be described in more detail in chapters 4 and 5) is the direction pursued by most of the more sophisticated recent studies—and it is the paradigm that will be explored in this book. Take as one example Christopher Hill's work on the emergence of modern history writing in France, the United States, and Japan in the late nineteenth century. In it, the author does not focus on the relations between traditional history writing and modern national narratives, as a more conventional study might. Neither is the focus primarily on the connections between the three cases. Rather, Hill places all three nations in the context of domestic changes and global transformations. All three societies faced internal upheavals—the United States was recovering from Civil War and France from defeat at the hands of Prussia, while Japan was reshaping its polity in the wake of the Meiji Restoration. At the same time, all three were enmeshed in the fundamental restructuring of world order by capitalism and the imperialist state system. At this juncture, history writing served as a way to conceptualize the different position of each nation within this larger and hierarchical order, and to make the emergence of each as a nation-state seem necessary and natural. Analytically, then, Hill's emphasis is on the global conditions that made possible and shaped the historical narratives emerging in the three settings.[12]

In much the same way, other historians have explicitly situated particular cases in their global contexts. They seek to explain "the contingencies and ground-level processes of human activity with[in] the structures that are at once the products and the conditions of that activity."[13] In this reading, the global becomes the ultimate frame of reference for any understanding of the past. In principle, such contextualization is not confined to the most recent past, but can be applied to earlier periods, though in such cases the degree of integration may be rather weak. As the world has evolved more and more into a single political, economic, and cultural entity, causal links on the global level have grown stronger. And as a result of the proliferation and perpetuation of such links, local events are increasingly shaped by a global context that can be understood structurally or even systemically.

Process and perspective

Global history is both an object of study and a particular way of looking at history: it is both a process and a perspective, subject matter and methodology. Janus-faced, it resembles other fields/approaches in the discipline, such as social history and gender history. In practice, both dimensions are usually linked, but for heuristic purposes, we can keep them apart. This will enable us to differentiate between global history as the perspective of historians, and as a scale of the historical process itself.[14]

Global history is one perspective among others. It is a heuristic device that allows the historian to pose questions and generate answers that are different from those created by other approaches. The history of slavery in the Atlantic World is a good example. Historians have inquired into the social history of the slave population, into their working conditions, and into the ways in which they formed communities. By employing a gender approach, they have been able to tell new stories about families and childhood, sexuality and masculinity. The economic history of slavery has been especially prolific, focusing on productivity rates, on the standards of living of slaves compared to those of other workers and indentured servants, and on the macroeconomic impact of slavery on plantation production. However, the experience of slavery and the slave trade can also be placed in a global context. This would underscore a different set of issues: the creation of a transatlantic space in the "Black Atlantic"; the repercussions of the trade on societies in West Africa; the connections of the Atlantic trade to complementary slave routes across the Sahara and the Indian Ocean; a comparison with other forms of enslavement, and the list goes on. Global history as a perspective highlights particular dimensions of the slave experience, while being potentially less attentive to others.

An important consequence of treating global history as a perspective, like gender history or economic history, is that research does not have to encompass the entire globe. This is an important caveat. The rhetoric of the global may suggest limitless coverage; but many topics are best displayed in smaller frames. This also means that most global history approaches do not attempt to replace the established paradigm of national history with an abstract totality called "world." The aim is not to write a total history of the planet. It is often more a matter of writing a history of demarcated (i.e., non-"global") spaces, but with an awareness of global connections and structural conditions. Many recent studies considered benchmarks in the field do not cover more than two or three locations. Global history, then, is not a synonym for macro-history. The most interesting questions often arise at the juncture where global processes intersect with their local manifestations.

On the other hand, however, global history is not *only* a perspective. A global history approach cannot be projected indiscriminately; it makes more sense for some periods, places, and processes than for others. Any attempt to contextualize globally needs to consider the degree and quality of the entanglements in its purview. The implications of the Vienna stock market crash in 1873 were not the same as those of the economic crises of 1929 and 2008—the degree to which the world economy and the media were integrated in the 1870s had yet to attain the level that would prevail in the twentieth century. In this respect, global history as perspective is often implicitly tied to assumptions about the ability of cross-border structures to have an impact on events, and on societies. We will return to this tension between process and perspective in the chapters that follow.[15]

The dialectic between perspective and process is a complex one. On the one hand, a global perspective on the tea trade makes more sense for the 1760s than for the Middle Ages, when global dynamics were of less influence. On the other hand, global connections seem to be particularly salient to us, in our globalized present, more so than they were for historians a few decades ago. To further confound matters, the resulting global perspective makes the eighteenth century appear more global than it was. Global perspectives and the course of global integration are thus inextricably interrelated.[16]

Heuristically, however, it is helpful to keep perspective and process apart. After all, the approach is much newer than the process; global history as a paradigm is of fairly recent origin, while the processes it studies reach far back into the past. As the two chronologies do not neatly correspond, it is useful to separate them analytically. Moreover, this is a field still very much in the making. For this reason, historians who attempt a global approach need to be self-conscious about methodology, and the chapters that follow will put the emphasis on this issue. Even if we assume that there is a process somewhere "out there," it is crucial to ponder the methodological challenges of uncovering it, and the implications of our choices.

Promises and limits

The global history trend is unlikely to slow down any time soon, and it has already helped to bring about some significant changes in historical scholarship. One clear indication of this is the fact that the major history journals, such as the *American Historical Review* and *Past & Present*, have increasingly published work in this new field. No longer merely a niche or sub-discipline, it has become mainstream, extending to both research and teaching. Specialized journals, book series, and conferences have created forums where scholars are encouraged to exchange ideas and discuss research. These forums do not exist merely in parallel to the rest of the discipline. They are not exotic. While "world history," the global history of earlier decades, was most often an occupation of established and generally older historians, today even dissertations may pursue a global agenda. The approach has also influenced teaching, in both specialized seminars and even entire degree curricula. It is also interesting to note that debate over this approach has made its way to very diverse quarters. Environmental and economic historians are as interested in the global historical context as are social and cultural historians. Indeed, all aspects of historical scholarship can be subject to a global perspective.

In the light of the interconnectedness of today's world, it is difficult to imagine that this trend might reverse itself. At the same time, there remain many obstacles to overcome. Institutionally, creating space for the new approach may prove an arduous process. Even in Western Europe and the United States, it can by no means be taken for granted that the discipline of history, so heavily dominated by the history of the nation, will be receptive to undertakings with a global historical scope. And even in settings where global perspectives have garnered general support, they compete with other approaches for funds and faculty positions. A new hire in global history might mean sacrificing a position in medieval history or in some other time-honored field related to the national past. Global history comes at a cost.[17]

The rise of global perspectives is unarguably an important development that helps us move away from a merely partial view of reality. As the relevance of territorial boundaries has been called into question, history has become more complex. In retrospect, some older studies may now appear to us like broadcasts of a football game that show only one of the two teams, to say nothing of other factors, such as the audience, weather conditions, and league ranking. Global history, by contrast, allows a wide-angle view of processes that were for a long time undetectable by the knowledge systems of the academy, or were at least considered irrelevant.

In important ways, then, this is a welcome and in some respects even liberating development. But as the old adage goes, change has its price. A global history approach is not a panacea or a free pass. Not every research project requires a global perspective; it is not always the global context that is most central to the issue. Everything is not linked and connected to everything else. It would be a mistake, certainly, to regard global history as the only valid approach—either in terms of its historiographical perspective or in the reach and density of the entanglements it explores. In every situation, a range of forces are at play, and it is not cross-border, let alone global, processes that are *a priori* the most important. Many phenomena will continue to be studied in concrete, precisely demarcated contexts. Likewise, we must not lose sight of those historical actors who were not integrated into extensive networks, lest they fall victim to the current obsession with mobility. That said, it would nonetheless be difficult to turn back and forsake the insights that the global turn has generated.

CHAPTER 2

A short history of thinking globally

———— ◉ ————

Today globalization rhetoric is loud and insistent, but this is not the first time that people have thought about their place in the world. Indeed, since the beginning of recorded history, humans have situated themselves in larger and ever more encompassing contexts. Not surprisingly, the range and scope of these "worlds" has varied, changing with the intensity of connections and the frequency of border-crossing exchanges. But imagining the world was never an automatic outcome of global integration; it was always the result also of a particular perspective and desire: a form of world-making. In order to better assess the peculiarities of present-day conceptions of the global, it is therefore instructive to understand how notions of the world have changed over time. As we will see, the quest to position one's own society within the larger ecumene was shared by all major civilizations. A genuine global consciousness began to take shape in discrete Eurasian regions in the early modern period; and in the age of European hegemony, a common narrative of material progress and national development emerged.

Ecumenical historiography

Writing world history is, in a sense, as old as historiography itself. The best-known historians—from Herodotus and Polybius to Sima Qian, Rashid al-Din, and Ibn Khaldun—all wrote the history of their respective ecumene while also considering the "world" around it. Describing and explaining the world was not an end in itself in these studies. Rather, the primary concern was to celebrate the essence of the own society or ecumene, whose unique cultural identity—and generally also superiority—was a given. The "world" thus served primarily as a land beyond the pale, a contrasting foil of barbarity. In the Egyptian chronicles of the Old and Middle Kingdom (c. 2137–1781 BCE), for instance, all non-Egyptian peoples were described as "vile enemies," even when peace prevailed or treaties existed with them. Egypt was equated with the rationally ordered world, while beyond its borders were only "absolute aliens with whom any relations would be unthinkable."[1]

A later example is the nine-volume *Histories* of Herodotus, which cast the Greek struggle against the Persians as a clash between the Occident and the Orient, between freedom and despotism.[2] Herodotus' famous dialectic between civilization and barbarism would play a constitutive role in historiography for centuries to come; it can also be identified in the works of many Arabic and Chinese chroniclers.

The way in which the world outside a particular society is perceived cannot, however, be reduced solely to the strategy of "othering." Even in the work of Herodotus (c. 484–424 BCE)—who himself claimed to have traveled throughout Mesopotamia, Phoenicia and Egypt—and in the writings of Sima Qian (c. 145–90 BCE), there is evidence of a move towards an ethnographic portrayal of other peoples and customs.

The peoples with whom the Greeks and Chinese, respectively, had close political and economic ties became objects of an interest characterized by more than just the desire to sharpen a sense of boundaries. Border areas were marked not only by conflict and animosity, but also by exchange and encounter. Examples of such interest in hybridity and cultural exchange abound. Abu'l-Hassan Ali al-Mas'udi (c. 895–956) of Baghdad described the world he knew in a book with the flowery title *The Meadows of Gold*. He reported not only on Islamic societies, but also on the regions of the Indian Ocean connected by pre-Islamic trade relations, which extended all the way to Galicia and India. Like that of Herodotus, his work, too, was the result of extensive travels that took him to many parts of the Islamic world, to India and Ceylon, East Africa and Egypt, and probably to Indonesia and China as well.[3]

This ethnographical viewpoint was not an end in itself, but often also aligned with the interests of power. When, for instance, Sima Qian described nomadic groups outside the fold of Chinese civilization, prospects for China's further expansion were a background concern.[4] Ultimately, the respective "worlds"—generally limited to neighboring territories and regions—were apprehended from the perspective of the own culture. To be sure, there were historians whose stated concern was to describe other societies from within and not to exoticize them by tallying their strange customs. Foreign institutions were to be explained in functionalist terms, according to their own inherent logic. The assessment and moral categorization of other groups, however, generally remained within the parameters of the own culture.[5]

These paradigms were characteristic of most of the historiographical traditions around the world. There was of course significant variation, both within and between the regions. In

Europe, Greek historiography bears little resemblance to later Christian historiography with its narratives revolving around divine providence. In non-Muslim South Asia, where a separate historiographical genre did not come into being until the colonial period, world-historical models were almost nonexistent; and the same was true in Africa. By contrast, some important forays into world history have their roots in the Muslim tradition. These were generally tied to the rise of Islam, which was considered the only religion with a universal mission. In addition to the above-mentioned Mas'udi and Rashid al Din (1247–1318), who explicitly addressed Mongolian and Chinese readers as well as an Arab audience and wrote in detail about India and China as well as the Islamic world, Ibn Khaldun merits mention. Khaldun (1332–1406), and above all his major work, the *Muqaddima* (which is actually only the introduction to his history of mankind), are considered the origin of a scientific Islamic historical scholarship based on causal explanations.

Historiographical traditions and perspectives on the world thus differed greatly. Bridging these differences, however, were important similarities. In each case, the "world" was generally constructed from the perspective of the own ecumene. Above all, this meant that the past—including that of other peoples and groups—was assessed and judged according to the criteria of the moral and political canon of values of the historian's own society. This world was not the planetary totality as we know it, but "referred only to the world that mattered."[6]

Accordingly, narratives were often formulated with a particular goal in mind—the development of humanity toward a Christian "kingdom of God," the creation of a Dar-al-Islam (literally "house of Islam," that could encompass all territories under Muslim rule), or the eventual inclusion of nomadic, illiterate barbarians in China's Confucian civilization.[7]

World-historical tableaus, the sixteenth-eighteenth centuries

The basic tenets of ecumenical historiography remained largely stable until the nineteenth century. This does not mean, however, that nothing changed. At times, particularly when exchange across regions and continents intensified, there was a corresponding increase in the awareness of other worlds, in interest in other cultures, and in the desire to understand the own society within a larger context. A number of works, produced in various places from the sixteenth century onward, responded to this demand.

One example is the integration of the two Americas, since the sixteenth century, into broad and expanding circuits of trade and knowledge. These transcontinental interactions, which brought the Americas into contact with Africa, Europe, the Middle East, and East and Southeast Asia, presented a cognitive and cultural challenge, and it was in the context of this challenge that history on a world scale gradually emerged as an alternative to traditional forms of dynastic historiography.[8]

World-historical models began to appear in many places. As early as 1580, a *History of Western India* (*Tarih-i Hin-i garbi*) was written in Istanbul in an attempt to comprehend the unexpected broadening of the horizon and the cosmological dilemma presented by the discovery of the New World. "Since the prophet Adam came into and set foot upon the world," the anonymous chronicler wrote, "up to the present such a strange and wonderful matter has never occurred or taken place."[9] In Mexico, Heinrich Martin of Hamburg, who had previously spent many years in the Baltics, wrote an explicitly American version of world history. He believed, for example, that the Americas had been populated by peoples from Asia, because the indigenous groups reminded him of the native population of Courland. The chronicler from Istanbul and Heinrich Martin produced their world histories almost synchronously, thus attesting to the impact that Columbus' voyage had on the world consciousness of the time. Their accounts, however, were radically different, informed by the worldviews of their respective communities. The world-historical process—the European discovery of the Americas—posed a crucial challenge, but the responses to this event remained in many ways incommensurable.

Both historians were by no means alone in their new planetary consciousness. Further examples include the Ottoman historian Mustafa Ali (1541–1600), whose *Künh ül-Ahbâr* (The Essence of History) localized the Ottoman Empire in what he regarded as the relevant world, but included also extensive studies of the Mongol empires and the three contemporary empires he considered most important—the Uzbeks, the Safavids of Persia, and the Indian Mughal dynasty; Domingo Chimalpáhin (1579–c. 1650), who embedded his history of Mexico, written in Nahuatl, in a broad overview of the entire world (including, in addition to Europe, China and Japan, the Mongols and Moscow, Persia and parts of Africa); Giovanni Battista Ramusio (1485–1557) in Italy and Marcin Bielski (1495–1575) in Poland, who were able to write a kind of armchair world history on the basis of the increasing frequency of reports about events outside Europe; and Tahir Muhammad in Mughal India, whose early seventeenth-century writings covered such places as Ceylon, Pegu, and Aceh, and even the kingdom of Portugal.[10]

Many of the works of this period were written by amateur historians who were not employed in any official capacity, and who therefore have received limited attention. What they do show, however, is that world-historical models emerged even before the late eighteenth century, and by no means in Europe alone. They tended to be cumulative in nature rather than focusing on connections and interactions; but they were no longer written with the primary purpose of constructing difference, even though they did generally judge other peoples' pasts against their own value standards. These world-historical perspectives drew on multiple genealogies and historiographical traditions, and their concerns, as well as their notions of the "world," differed. "Iberian globalization," Serge Gruzinski wrote, "gave rise everywhere to viewpoints that were irreconcilable with each other but complementary in their effort to grasp the global nature of the world."[11]

Over time, as commercial networks and imperial structures continued to expand, increasingly detailed and empirically sophisticated panoramas of world history emerged. Their objective was to describe, as accurately and completely as possible, all societies about which anything was known. One of the best-known examples is the vast *Universal History* published in London between 1736 and 1765 and subsequently translated into four other languages. It was essentially a massive compilation (sixty-five volumes), structured by simple juxtaposition. Its goal was chronicling the past and the present of as many societies as possible and presenting them all side by side. The work was based on the large number of travel accounts that had become available in eighteenth-century Europe.[12] In the second part of the *Universal History*, which covered the period following the Middle Ages, about half of the text was devoted to the European past, another quarter to Japan and China, and the rest was divided between Southeast Asia, Peru, Mexico, and the kingdoms of the Congo and Angola. Due to the work's encyclopedic bent, however, it was more a reference work than a narrative to be read for pleasure; Edward Gibbon regarded it as nothing more than "a dull mass [...] not quickened by a spark of philosophy or taste."[13]

The genre of world and universal history was particularly vigorous in Europe in the years around 1800. These writings aspired to report from every region of the world, creating tableaus of social institutions and developments that would amount to large-scale "histories of mankind." They include works by Voltaire (1694–1778) and Edward Gibbon (1737–1794), whose *Decline and Fall of the Roman Empire* covered the entire Eurasian continent up to the rise of the Mongol empires and the capture of Constantinople by the Turks.[14] One early center of universal history writing was the University of Göttingen, where historians such as Johann Christoph Gatterer (1727–1799) presented their overall views of human history. As a whole, these comparative histories remained bound to the concept of different "civilizations" and were written from the perspective of European culture (or, as was still the case with Gatterer, of the Biblical narrative).[15]

World history in the age of western hegemony

Over the course of the nineteenth century, a fundamental shift took place in how the past was viewed in many parts of the world. This was the age of European (and soon also North American) hegemony, and approaches to history increasingly aligned their narratives and began to conform to uniform methodological standards. Conventional historiography has seen this development as chiefly the result, and triumph, of Westernization: as the diffusion of an enlightened and rational approach to history, and as a form of progress when compared with the mythical and religiously bound approaches of the past. In many ways, this reading has been reproduced and developed in the context of recent postcolonial studies, albeit with a different emphasis. The spread of modern European historical scholarship is no longer interpreted as a contribution to the modernization of historical thought, but rather as an imposition of cultural values and a manifestation of imperial hegemony. Essentially, however, proponents of postcolonial studies have remained attached to the notion of the diffusion of a European idea.[16]

And indeed, their explanations have a point. The world order dominated by Europe forced the rest of the world to engage with European cosmologies and ways of interpreting the past. Historians increasingly took their cue from historical narratives grounded in the nineteenth-century ascendancy of a liberal world order and were predicated on the nation as the driving force of history and on a general notion of "modernization." European history was dressed as universal development and treated as a yardstick and a model. The translation of European works by historians like Francois Guizot and Henry Buckle, as well as the positivism of Auguste Comte and social Darwinism as propagated by Herbert Spencer, also played a key role. When, for instance, Bartolomé Mitre, Argentina's president in the 1860s, wrote the history of his country's road to independence, he drew on the widespread assumptions of a positivist Enlightenment historiography—science and progress, secularization and liberal freedoms—which seemed to fit naturally with the power politics of the international state system and the free trade regime.[17] The institutional export of European historical scholarship—the foundation of historical faculties, historians' associations, historical journals, and history textbooks—further contributed to a standardization of historical analyses.[18]

And yet, it would be an oversimplification to suggest that all this was only a result of the dissemination of European history writing to other parts of the world. After all, the modern understanding of history was new and unfamiliar in Europe as well. The focus on the nation, the concept of time as based on the ideal of progress, the methodology that stressed the need for a critical evaluation of sources, and the embedding of phenomena in a global context—all of this represented a fundamental challenge for many Europeans, too. This is particularly apparent in the case of the altered conception of time, which in Europe, as elsewhere, came as a profound rupture. As academic historical scholarship became established, it superseded alternative ways of appropriating the past.[19]

Moreover, the standard account of European origins and the worldwide expansion of what is European requires elaboration and, to some extent, correction, from a global history perspective. And this for two reasons. First, because historians always drew at least partly on their own traditions and cultural resources, even when adopting what was new. In Japan, for instance, a form of historiography emerged at the end of the eighteenth century that called itself the "national school" (*kokugaku*) and was dedicated to liberating scholarship from the dominance of Chinese cultural influence. It engaged in meticulous textual criticism in its quest to preserve an allegedly still "pure" Japanese antiquity from imported Chinese religion and culture.[20] At the same time, in China, the "critical school" (*kaozhengxue*) emerged. This scholarly movement was interested in a philological evaluation of written records and in establishing the facts and, where necessary, uncovering falsifications.[21] These examples demonstrate that the hallmarks of modern historiography that are generally associated with the name of Leopold von Ranke—such as its focus on the history of the nation and on the critical evaluation of sources—did not necessarily constitute an unwelcome intrusion of foreign cultural influences.

Second, and still more important, interpretations of history responded to the changing geopolitical balance of power. "It would be wrong to simply identify diffusion from the West to the rest as the only force behind the genesis of academic historiography as a worldwide phenomenon," Dominic Sachsenmaier has argued. "Many character traits of academic historiography—such as the strong presence of Eurocentric worldviews—need to be seen not merely as export products of an allegedly pristine European tradition but also as the result of the continent's expansion and many complex sociopolitical transformations resulting from it."[22]

In other words, world history writing everywhere bore the imprint of geopolitics; most especially of the integration of the globe under European hegemony. This was also the case in Europe—even if contemporaries hardly recognized that their historiography might have been impacted by global changes. But it was of course more obvious outside of Euro-America. To the extent that other societies became subject to a global order dominated by Western Europe (and later the United States), they also adapted their own historical narratives to chronicle a story of nation-states and progress. But the evolutionary conception of time, the compartmentalization of historical reality along nation-state lines, and the unity of the world were not primarily results of translation processes and intellectual transfers. Rather, in the face of global integration through imperial structures and expanding markets, many contemporaries considered premises such as these to be the obvious and natural basis for historiography. The ascendancy of modern historical scholarship, therefore, was the work of many authors around the world, responding to their various needs and interests. Historical knowledge changed in response to an increasingly integrated world.[23]

The central characteristic of most world histories in the nineteenth and early twentieth centuries—their Eurocentric conception of space and time—must therefore be understood as the result of global hierarchies and of asymmetrical geopolitical structures. The metanarrative, structured as a hierarchy of stages and pointing teleologically to Europe, was told in many variations. There was Condorcet's ten stages of scientific and philosophical development; Scottish conjectural history with its model of developmental stages and cultural evolution; and Hegel's lectures on the history of philosophy, in which the history of non-European societies was reduced to a "prehistory"—as in his infamous metaphor of Africa as the "land of childhood."[24] Over the course of the following century, interpretations of world history based on the paradigm of progress also appear in historiography outside of Europe. Some of the best-known authors are Liang Qichao (1902) in China, Fukuzawa Yukichi (1869) in Japan, and Jawaharlal Nehru (1934) in India. Their works are representative of a wide range of world-historical studies and attest to the emergence of analogous forms of global awareness, albeit with local differences, in various parts of the world.

Even more important in practice than comprehensive accounts of all regions of the world was the function of world history as a master narrative. In many countries, a stylized version of world history served as a yardstick by which the development of every nation could be measured and evaluated. Progress was mostly explained from within and its absence likewise attributed to internal obstacles and constraints. However, even when historians addressed concerns of national history alone, they generally did so with an awareness of global models. Ziya Gökalp, for example, described the transition from an Ottoman to a Turkish state as the manifestation of universal processes.

The establishment of a universally conceived world history in the late nineteenth and early twentieth centuries should not, therefore, be explained as simply a result of intellectual transfers originating in Europe, as is so often the case.[25] Even when historians and social thinkers outside of Europe resorted to clearly Eurocentric representations based on the categories of Enlightenment thought, these narratives were not mere copies, but were often in sync with the reform interests of their authors, and with their perspective on the realities of global change. Most historians assumed that the focus should be on Europe, because that was where the materially most advanced societies were to be found *at the given time*—a circumstance that could potentially change in the future. Therefore, they employed a concept of civilization that was understood as universal to be sure, but not bound *a priori* to Europe.[26]

Given the asymmetries of power, the Eurocentric narrative was, for a long time, hegemonic. However, this does not mean that it was the only alternative or that it was not subject to criticism. Liang Qichao, for instance, protested that "the history of the Aryan race [is] very often erroneously labeled 'world history.'"[27] In fact, basic challenges articulated as early as the nineteenth century employed argumentation that has, in part, remained influential to this day. They followed two main lines of criticism. Let us call them the "systems approach" and the "concept of civilization."

The first may be traced to Karl Marx. To be sure, historical materialism was also based on developmental stages and so bore traces of the Eurocentrism of its time. Nevertheless, the materialist Marxist approach put more emphasis than many others on the entanglements and interactions, i.e., on the *systemic* conditions, of social development on a global scale. The 1848 *Communist Manifesto*, written in collaboration with Friedrich Engels, expressed this view in a nutshell: "The bourgeoisie has through its exploitation of the world market given a cosmopolitan character to production and consumption in every country. [. . .] It has drawn from under the feet of industry the national ground on which it stood. All old-established national industries have been destroyed or are daily being destroyed. [. . .] In place of the old local and national seclusion and self-sufficiency, we have intercourse in every direction, universal interdependence of nations."[28] Subsequent world historiography has built on these insights—in particular the school of world-systems theory, but also oppositional forms of a historiography from "below," as well as subaltern studies.

The second approach, based on the concept of civilization, gained popularity in the Arab and Islamic world and in East Asia in the 1880s. At its heart was an emphasis on cultural difference, and on the idea that different traditions could not be subsumed under the paradigm of progress with its linear conception of time. Early proponents were Okakura Tenshin (1862–1913) in Japan and Rabindranath Tagore (1861–1941) in Bengal, who based their understanding of history, which recognized alterity, on the dichotomy between the materialist West and the spiritual Orient.[29]

The work of Johann Gottfried Herder (1744–1803) influenced some of the authors who espoused the concept of civilization. His four-volume *Ideas for the Philosophy of History of Humanity* (1784–91) postulated the individuality and uniqueness of the different cultures of the world, which were, he feared, in danger of being destroyed in the course of European expansion. Herder's texts were an important source of inspiration for intellectuals in many places, but again a caveat is in order. The global appeal of the concept of civilization was not merely a Herderian legacy.[30] It also drew on the seismic shifts taking place in the world order at the end of the nineteenth century, as the compartmentalization of the planet into discrete civilizations appeared increasingly plausible against the backdrop of imperialism, racial doctrine, and the agenda of the pan-nationalist movements.[31] This idea of a plurality of "cultures" that resisted classification as "advanced" or "backward" gained in popularity in the wake of World War I—not least in the European *fin de siècle* critique of civilization and, after 1918, with the broad acclaim for Oswald Spengler's *Decline of the West*.[32]

World history after 1945

The civilization paradigm persisted until the second half of the twentieth century, and it was given a new lease of life with Arnold Toynbee's ten-volume *Study of History*. The first volumes were published in the 1930s, but it was only after World War II that the work's impact was really felt. Toynbee divided the world into twenty-one civilizations, each characterized by specific cultural and above all religious features and each with its own internal logic that would explain its rise and fall. Following the devastation caused by World War II, this view, challenging as it did the universal narrative of progress, struck a chord with readers around the world. But while his monumental work resonated widely with the general public, Toynbee remained an outsider among historians.[33]

Indeed, the status of world history within the discipline remained uncertain in most countries until the 1990s.[34] No wonder, as in large parts of the world the postwar period was a time of nation-building. In many of the newly independent former colonies, in particular, the making of a national history was at the top of the agenda. Given the balance of political power, historians in these nations used the European past as a yardstick to measure their own countries' histories, superimposing upon them a narrative of development modeled on that of the West. The dominance of Anglophone historiography, in particular, grew. This was the context in which William McNeill's substantial work, published in 1963 and symptomatically entitled *The Rise of the West*, became one of the most influential points of reference. The book is representative of the hegemony of a decidedly Eurocentric macro perspective. In it the modern world is presented as a product of occidental traditions, a European achievement *sui generis*, which at the height of its glory was exported to other regions of the world. It is a view that gives clear expression to the dichotomy between "developed" and "underdeveloped" countries that prevailed in the period following decolonization.[35]

Of greater importance for the emergence of a tradition of world history, however, than either Toynbee's idea of civilizational monads or the modernization theory implied in McNeill's apotheosis of Europe, were Marxist works and those influenced by historical materialism. Especially after 1945, Marxist approaches became crucially influential—not only in the Soviet Union and other Eastern Bloc countries, but also in Latin America, France, Italy, India, and Japan. In the Soviet Union and in China in particular, world history was institutionalized after the communist takeover and was much more prominent than in the West. World history departments were established at many universities. In China, around one third of all university historians worked in institutes specializing in world history—a figure inconceivable for Europe or the United States at the time. To be sure, Chinese world history was of a particular kind, much narrower in its range than Toynbee's or McNeill's. Many Marxist historians concentrated on the history of just one country, framed in terms of a universal Marxist model of historical development. In the USSR, Stalin commissioned the canonical *History of the Communist Party of the Soviet Union (Bolsheviks): A Short Course*, which proposed a relatively rigid series of stages. Scholars generally proceeded deductively, seeking evidence for these universal patterns of development established in the abstract. The role of empirical research was to fit reality to a theoretical *a priori*.[36]

World-systems theory emerged in the 1970s as a reaction against this form of what might be termed "world history in one country," to paraphrase Lenin's dictum. Immanuel Wallerstein's unfinished work, the first volume of which was published in 1974, evoked an immediate and enthusiastic response in many places. Its focus was on systemic processes that invited historians to understand the past in a substantive global context and not solely on the basis of an abstract logic of development (see below chapter 3).[37]

While a Eurocentric interpretation of world history was predominant—even Wallerstein's approach presupposed a clear center, assuming that all nations and regions were gradually incorporated into the European world-system—it was by no means uncontested. The internal fragmentation and pluralization of historical scholarship played a large part in the emergence of critical perspectives. Approaches such as the history of mentalities of the *Annales*, the various forms of "microstoria" and "history from below," women's and gender studies, and the "linguistic turn," undermined macro-historical narratives and challenged Eurocentric assumptions.[38] At the same time, area studies were becoming increasingly important. While world historians drew on the empirically rich research of historians with regional specializations, area studies with their interest in regional dynamics and trajectories also functioned to some extent as a corrective to the hagiography of the "rise of the West."[39]

Of equal importance were critiques from an emphatically non-Western perspective that directly challenged the Eurocentric metanarrative of world history. These included the early "postcolonial" positions taken in the immediate post-war period, sometimes in very different ways, by authors like Frantz Fanon, Aimé Césaire, and Léopold Senghor. Their works contained what was in some respects a fundamental criticism of the assumptions and values underlying the Western civilizing mission with its belief in universal paths of development. The impact of these and related approaches grew in the wake of the conference of non-aligned nations in Bandung in 1955, the anti-imperialist protest movements in the age of decolonization, and the global protests of 1968.[40] Within academic circles, an even greater influence was the dependency theory approach. This model was first developed by social scientists working in and writing about Latin America. Like the work of early postcolonial authors, dependency theory also had a political thrust and was critical of U.S. development policy in the south of the continent. Its theoretical contribution was to view poverty and "backwardness" not as results of non-modern local traditions which had yet to be affected by the dynamics of the global economy, but, on the contrary, precisely as the consequence of these traditions' integration into the structures of global capitalism.[41]

Since the 1980s, historians working in subaltern studies have posed significant challenges to Eurocentric assumptions. As is true of many other approaches, this group, too, serves as an illustration of the transnational production of knowledge. Subaltern studies originated in India, initially as an attempt to write history from the perspective of the marginalized, or "subaltern," classes. A kind of critical "history from below," it evolved under specific social conditions, in the years following Indira Gandhi's state of emergency. The field was therefore rooted locally, but it also drew on a variety of international models, from Gramsci and Foucault to Said and Derrida. The research agenda of subaltern studies historians soon attracted attention beyond the field of South Asian history. Important representatives of the movement enjoyed successful careers at universities in the English-speaking world, but it nevertheless continued to be associated with India. Much of the force of its criticism of Eurocentrism can be attributed to the very fact of its origins outside the West.[42]

By the end of the twentieth century, then, world history writing had become highly diversified, even if it remained on the fringes of the discipline in most countries. An interpretation of the global past dominated by the rise of Europe continued to play a very prominent role, but criticism of Eurocentric narratives was on the rise, and these critiques came to occupy a more central position than they had just one century earlier.[43]

What the story of world history writing demonstrates is that the present interest in processes that transcend borders and cultures is nothing new, neither in Europe nor in many other regions. Historians had long practiced writing the world, or, to be more precise, *their* world—for as we have seen from the brief outline in this chapter, the "world" under discussion was by no means always the same. Its definition varied according to perspective, to what historians and their contemporaries were eager to find out and to prove. And it was affected also by patterns of interaction and exchange, and by the extent of global interconnectedness. The universal histories of the eighteenth century were based on experiences that differed from those that had produced the ecumenical world histories of antiquity; different, too, from the view of the world around 1900, informed by the idea of the civilizing mission; and from the discussion triggered by globalization in the present day. Of equal importance to differences in time were regional differences. For all their areas of overlap, Liang Qichao's world was not the same as that of his German contemporary Karl Lamprecht. Global history was—and remains today—a particular perspective, and this means that it is shaped by the conditions of the time and place in which it emerges.

This understanding—that ways of relating to the world, and in fact the notion of "world" itself, have a history—is an important insight, and it should serve us a warning as well. Current assumptions about the globalization process should not be regarded as timeless. Global history today differs from its precursors in important respects. The most fundamental of these are its emphasis on entanglements and integration and its determination to move beyond earlier notions, among them the concepts of discrete civilizations, of European diffusion, and of teleological narratives.

CHAPTER 3

Competing approaches

The current interest in global history is not radically new. In a number of fields—such as the history of imperialism and colonialism, the history of mobility and migration, some areas of intellectual history, and more recently environmental history—historians long ago began crossing boundaries and challenging the prevailing compartmentalization of the past. Global historians today are indebted to these precedents. While they are not the direct heirs of older traditions of world history writing, they nevertheless ask some of the same questions, and they travel some of the same roads. Here, too, a claim to radical newness would be misleading.

In the academic marketplace, global history currently competes with a number of other approaches that all attempt to come to terms with the dynamics of the modern world. From a larger pool of possibilities, this chapter presents five approaches that remain of particular valence today: comparative studies, transnational history, world-systems theory, postcolonial studies, and the concept of multiple modernities. Not all of these belong exclusively to the discipline of history; neither do they all aspire to explain global processes and dynamics in their entirety. The following sections will present each approach and discuss the extent to which global history perspectives can draw on its ideas.

Before we enter this discussion, we should note that for all the shades of difference between these paradigms, they also have much in common. They are by no means hermetically distinct and, in fact, influence one another in many different ways. Most important, they share a general concern with transcending narrowly national perspectives and going beyond the interpretative hegemony of the West. They share also the objective of exploring historical issues without confining themselves *a priori* to the boundaries of nation-states, empires, or other political entities. This distinguishes them from much of the history written over the past 150 years, when historical scholarship almost everywhere was closely linked to the project of nation-state building. When discussing the specific features and limits of each of these approaches, we should therefore keep in mind that their agendas and concerns coalesce in many ways.

Comparative history

In the long history of world historical thinking, comparative studies have a venerable tradition, ranging from ancient ecumenical perspectives (that compared one's own civilization to the barbarism of the neighbors) to the juxtaposition of macroregions that characterizes much of twentieth-century world history. Historical sociology, such as Max Weber's quest for the origins of modern capitalism and the large-scale analyses of statehood, revolutions, and social change that were fashionable in the heyday of modernization theory, has been particularly prone to take the comparative approach. In recent years, however, this method has come under assault from a literature that celebrates connections and flows and has grown skeptical of the rigid language of the social sciences. In some quarters, global history has been introduced as an antidote to comparative frameworks. However, comparative history in recent years has taken a global turn as well, and indeed there are no inherent contradictions between the two approaches.

To begin with, it is useful to remind ourselves that no historian can do without comparisons altogether. Virtually every interpretation and historical evaluation depends on a comparative judgment of some kind. Any reference to change (or stagnation), to specificities, or to peculiar characteristics relies on notions of difference vis-à-vis earlier periods, other social groups, or other societies. Much of the terminology that historians employ—think of concepts such as development and revolution—hinges on contrasting images, periods, and events. At least implicitly, it is difficult to imagine a work of historical interpretation that could eschew a comparative lens altogether.

For historians seeking answers to some of the big historical questions posed on a global scale, a comparative framework would seem mandatory: Why did the Industrial Revolution happen in England first, and not in China? Why did Spanish ships reach the Americas in 1492, and not the other way around? Did indigenous societies in Australia and Africa reshape their environmental conditions less dramatically than did Europeans? Why was Tokugawa Japan able to prevent massive deforestation, while no other early modern society undertook to do so? Questions such as these are impossible to address without engaging in systematic comparative work.

The advantages of the comparative approach are not difficult to see. It moves us beyond single cases and thus opens up a conversation between different historical trajectories and experiences. Comparisons also compel historians to ask clear-cut questions and pursue problem-oriented research strategies; they insist that researchers go beyond purely descriptive narratives and thus ensure analytical rigor in historical inquiries. Finally, comparisons are an appropriate tool for situations in which direct contact and exchange are minimal, as becomes obvious when we look at independent cases across time. For example, we can compare the rise of the first city civilizations, from Mesopotamia in the third millennium B.C.E., via Hierakonpolis in Egypt, Harappa and Mohenjo Daro in the Indus valley, all the way to the first Mayan cities that flourished approximately two thousand years later. Such a study can tell us much about the factors that allowed powerful urban conglomerates, based on the division of labor and new social hierarchies, to emerge.[1]

While comparisons can thus be of great heuristic value, they also have their limitations. Some of them are general challenges facing all comparative historians. For example, comparisons tend to homogenize the subjects under discussion and to level out internal differences. When juxtaposing Chinese and Dutch art, Argentine and Nigerian history writing, or social mobility in Russia and Mexico, the structure of the "experiment" tends to flatten the heterogeneity within each case.

When using comparisons as a tool to write the history of the world, two problems become particularly salient. First, there is the spectre of teleology. Comparisons measure against a common yardstick and gauge individual cases against a standard, even if that standard is not explicitly defined. Frequently, development in one case looks less impressive, and a rhetoric of "lack" is employed to describe various kinds of backwardness and situations of "not yet." Second, comparison—

especially in its sociological incarnation as "systematic comparison"—typically suffers from what we could call the fiction of autonomy. The two cases are treated as distinct and essentially unrelated, for too much contact would necessarily complicate—or, in the language of the social sciences, "contaminate"—the conclusions that we can draw. Many macrocomparisons have thus operated under the assumption that their subjects have developed more or less independently of each other.[2]

One product of these two characteristics—teleology and the fiction of autonomy—is the narrative of uniqueness that for a long time has populated our history books. Whole societies—most prominently Germany, Russia, and Japan—appear to have departed from some standard trajectory to follow a deviant path, a *Sonderweg*. On the other side of the same coin are narratives of exceptionalism, such as in the case of the United States. In world history writing, the case that has attracted the greatest attention is the alleged "European miracle," Europe's unique path into modernity.

It is important to be aware that such narratives of uniqueness are in part produced by the comparative approach itself. With its focus on social change generated primarily by internal factors rather than as the result of interaction and exchange, comparison tends to create and reproduce stories of national and/or civilizational particularity. This is ultimately also the case in revisionist studies that are explicitly directed *against* the Eurocentric paradigm and exceptionalist interpretations. As long as they compare more or less independent cases, similarities become difficult to explain, and such studies are left to marvel at the "strange parallels" that they discover.[3]

A number of proposals have been made to correct these shortcomings. Transfer histories, entangled histories, and connected histories are the candidates suggested most frequently.[4] Their focus is on the connections and exchanges, on the back and forth of people, ideas, and things across boundaries. Clearly, transfer histories and comparisons are not mutually exclusive. Most subjects share at least a degree of connectedness; on the other hand, it can also be instructive to compare different forms of transfer: Why did soccer travel to Argentina and Ghana but not to India and the United States? Why did some Native American groups adopt Christianity more readily than others? Why have people acknowledged some results of interaction while denying others, such as medieval Europe's indebtedness to Islamic science?

Comparative studies have benefited from the challenges posed by transfer and connected histories and have as a result become more dynamic and process-oriented. However, histories of transfers also remain wedded to the idea of preexisting entities and thus run into some of the same difficulties. The key limitation common to both comparisons and transfer studies is that they follow a bilateral logic; that is, they look at similarities/differences and connections between two cases. Such a framework is insufficient. The economic crisis of 1929, for example, had effects on many businesses around the world, even if they were not directly linked; a preoccupation with transfers and direct interactions would in a circumstance like this clearly be limiting. In the last instance, the methodological shortcomings of both comparisons and transfer/connected histories can be located in their binary structure.

In the global history field, therefore, comparisons without connections and broader contexts are increasingly rare. An influential work that attempts to fuse comparative and transfer histories is Kenneth Pomeranz's book, *The Great Divergence*. In essence, the work is a comparison of economic development in England and the Yangtze Delta. But Pomeranz complicates the dichotomic framework in two important ways. On the one hand, he seeks to avoid the issue of normativity and teleology by using a "reciprocal comparative method," by which England becomes the yardstick for China—and vice versa. The intention is not to inquire solely as to why the Shanghai region did not develop in the same way as Lancashire, but rather also to "entertain the possibility that Europe could have been a China."[5] On the other hand, Pomeranz moves beyond a "systematic" comparison by emphasizing the different ways in which England and the Yangtze Delta were connected with the outside world. After discussing the range of internal factors conventionally mustered to explain Britain's take-off versus China's stagnation, he concludes that it was Britain's imperial hinterland and its access to North American markets that made the difference. English economic development can only be explained, argues Pomeranz, when it is globally embedded. "Forces outside the market and conjunctures beyond Europe deserve a central place in explaining why western Europe's otherwise largely unexceptional core achieved unique breakthroughs and wound up as the privileged center of the nineteenth century's new world economy."[6]

For global historians, macro-comparisons can remain a useful tool. In a world of flows and exchanges, some questions require a comparative view. The old days of the rigid and "systematic" comparison of independent cases may, however, be over. Increasingly, comparisons no longer confine themselves to a binary framework but instead take into account the larger world that encompasses—and frequently structures—their object of study. In traditional comparisons the global perspective was a construction of historians, not based on concrete links and interactions, and thus entirely in the eye of the beholder. This has now begun to change. Comparative historians increasingly take global history as their point of departure, and pursue their inquiries against a backdrop of global contexts. Indeed, some of the most exciting work in the global history field has used a comparative lens, albeit with a difference. Instead of taking two units—two countries, two cities, two social movements—as separate and given, they place them squarely within systemic contexts to which they both relate and respond in different ways. By situating the two in a common global situation, the comparisons themselves become part of the global history approach.[7]

Transnational history

While many comparative studies with a global scope are large in scale, encompassing whole empires and civilizations, transnational history focuses on phenomena that are geographically much more limited. In contrast to the comparative framework, the "transnational" focuses on the fluid and interwoven dimensions of the historical process, studying societies in the context of the entanglements that have shaped them, and to which they have contributed in turn. To what extent did processes that transcended state borders impact social dynamics? In addressing such issues, transnational history gives particular attention to the role of mobility, circulation, and transfers. Albeit not unrelated, transnational differs from international, in that it not only explores a country's foreign relations, for instance diplomacy or foreign trade, but also examines the extent to which societies were penetrated and shaped by external forces. There is also a particular interest in transnational organizations— NGOs, companies, transnational public spheres—that are not limited to state actors and not bound by state borders. Transnational studies explore the ways in which a country was situated in the world—and how the world, conversely, reached deep into individual societies.[8]

Thus defined, transnational history is not necessarily new but harks back to a long tradition of works concerned with tracing flows and exchanges beyond national borders. The clustering of such approaches and the arrival of the term "transnational," however, only happened in the 1990s, when the rhetoric of globalization seemed to undermine the power of the nation-state, and historians began to look for ways to transcend the methodological nationalism of the social sciences. Since then, we can observe an increase in transnational perspectives in many parts of the world: studies that span the Indian Ocean or the Atlantic, focus on permeable border regions in the Andes or in Eastern Europe, and so on. Although the history of one's own nation remains the privileged form of historiography almost everywhere, this development attests to an increased demand for alternative spatial visions. Transnational research agendas are very much the order of the day in many countries, sometimes with the implicit goal of avoiding the vocabulary of a global history perceived as oversized or even presumptuous.

Nevertheless, the relationship between transnational and global perspectives is close. They share the objective of transcending container thinking and the compartmentalization of historical reality, and both seek to go beyond what are essentially internalist analyses. Specific to the transnational approach is a recognition of the powerful role that nation-states have played in much of the world over the last two centuries. It has helped to render national histories more dynamic and attuned to the complexities of the historical process.

Many studies that have emerged do not aim to abandon national history entirely, but rather to expand and thus to "transnationalize" it.

Thomas Bender's *A Nation among Nations* is an influential attempt to rethink and above all reframe the modern history of the United States. It will serve as an example that illustrates both the benefits and the limits of the transnational approach. Triumphantly proclaimed as a work that marks "the end of American history as we have known it," the book begins with the insight that "national histories are part of global histories; each nation is a province among the provinces that make up the world."[9] Accordingly, Bender situates five major episodes of North American history—colonial history, the American Revolution, the Civil War, empire, and the welfare state—in the broader transnational and global currents of the times. In his reinterpretation of the revolution, for example, Bender demonstrates the extent to which both the British-French rivalry and the Haitian Revolution influenced events in colonial America. Beyond the North Atlantic, Bender links the revolution to other late eighteenth-century revolts and thus connects the struggle for independence to similar events in Peru and Cairo, Brazil and Bengal. The chapter on slavery successfully takes the issue out of the civil war framework and shows the extent to which what is often seen as a uniquely American problematic was actually part of a broader movement toward abolition around the world.

Bender's book very effectively destabilizes conventional narratives focused on interior development. It moves beyond exceptionalism, as the "nation cannot be its own historical context."[10] He shows that what historians heretofore have frequently read as aberrations of the national trajectory—such as empire after 1898—was instead an integral part of broader global developments. *A Nation among Nations* thus shares with many recent works in the transnational bracket the aim to arrive at more nuanced, more fully entangled histories of the nation-state. Living up to the promises of its title, it is primarily interested in a better understanding of the national past. Bender's professed goal is a "new framing of U.S. history," and a better understanding of "the central themes of American history."[11]

In some ways, of course, this means holding fast to the very entity that this approach claims to transcend. This is a tension inherent in the term *trans-national* itself. Taken literally, it would seem to imply that this is a historical approach inapplicable to the early modern age, before the formation of nation-states. "I have to confess," admits C. A. Bayly, "that I find 'transnational' a restrictive term for the sort of work which I am interested in. Before 1850, large parts of the globe were not dominated by nations so much as by empires, city-states, diasporas, etc."[12] And also after 1850, the concept clearly works better for most Western societies than for many other parts of the world. To make it less normative, some authors have suggested alternative formulations such as "trans-regional" or "trans-local."[13]

More important, on a methodological level, the transnational approach frequently only gestures at the global, without fully confronting its challenges. Bender, for example, relies primarily on wide-ranging comparisons and emphasizes parallels, complemented by passages that stress interaction and connection; larger global structures, by contrast, appear primarily as background and are less explicitly linked to developments within the United States. This is characteristic of much work in the transnational paradigm, in which the global better serves as a foil against which to situate the national than as a context in which to address questions of cause and effect systematically.

World-systems theory

While comparative and transnational approaches take individual cases and nations as their points of departure, world-systems theory starts with the reverse assumption that larger regional blocks and "systems" are the primary units of historical analysis, and that all smaller entities are derivative of these larger structures. In the 1970s and 1980s, the history of the world-system became the most important macro-historical alternative to modernization theory as a framework for thinking about change on a global scale. Taking their cues from Immanuel Wallerstein's currently four-volume account, historians in this tradition have highlighted the systemic nature of the international state system and the capitalist economic order. Wallerstein's model, indebted to the work of scholars like Karl Polanyi and Fernand Braudel, represented a new paradigm of world-historical analysis. While in some respects it adhered to the centrifugal logic of the history of European expansion, it also sought to move away from it with an emphasis on systemic processes.

The concept of the world-system is often misunderstood. First, Wallerstein distinguishes between two different forms of world-systems, namely world-economies and world-empires. World-empires are oriented towards the political integration of extensive territories, while world-economies are based on the integration of markets. However, a "world-economy" is not necessarily a market structure spanning the entire planet. Rather, the term describes a more or less autonomous region able to satisfy most of its material needs internally. It is characterized by the division of labor and an intensive exchange of goods within a large geographic region, and across internal political boundaries within this region. Historically, therefore, multiple world-economies have often existed side by side. Braudel, for instance, speaks of separate world-economies in the cases of Russia (at least prior to Peter the Great), the Ottoman Empire, pre-modern South Asia, and China.[14]

In this paradigm, the trading system centered on Europe was for a long time just one among many. The out-sized importance acquired by the European world-economy is explained by the circumstance that it gave rise to today's globalized economy. Having emerged in the sixteenth century, the European world-system successively incorporated other regions into an interdependent nexus of core, periphery, and semi-periphery. As it grew in expanse, the core of this European world-system also shifted: from Spain via Portugal and Holland to France and, since the nineteenth century, to England and then to the United States. Other regions—first Eastern Europe and Latin America, followed in succession by Africa and the various regions of Asia—were gradually added to the European world-system.[15] The question of how far back we can trace the origins of the capitalist world-system is much debated among adherents to this approach, with suggestions ranging from the sixteenth and thirteenth century all the way back to the third millennium B.C.E.[16]

From the perspective of current global history approaches, world-systems theory has a number of drawbacks. Three criticisms merit mention here. First and foremost, studies based in this method frequently display a form of economistic reductionism that can give them a one-dimensional feel. Within the economic realm proper, the paradigm tends to ignore the dynamics and mutability of capitalism, such as the shift from the primacy of merchant capital to that of industrial capital. The concept of capitalism on which the theory is based (defined as an "endless accumulation of capital")[17] is so generalized that historical specifics frequently fall by the wayside. A more serious failing, however, is the way in which other factors of supra-regional and global integration—political rule, social dynamics, cultural interpretations and cosmologies—are treated as less relevant, ultimately only of secondary importance. As a result, too little attention is given to the degree to which the integration of markets was itself the product of an asymmetrical balance of power.

Second, one can gain the impression that Wallerstein and other historians of his school essentially presupposed the systems context rather than actually developing it on the basis of real-world examples, let alone proving its existence. The embedding of local developments in global contexts can thus seem somewhat perfunctory or even dogmatic.[18] And third, the world-systems approach has not discarded an element of Eurocentrism. This is, in a sense, paradoxical. After all, in the spirit of the Marx and Engel's *Communist Manifesto*, this was precisely the point of world-systems theory—to avoid the pitfall of explaining the rise of Europe internalistically, from within. However, even if the systemic approach sought this end, the upshot was still the successive integration of the world into the European world-system. At times one has the impression that Wallerstein has projected the economic dominance of Europe (and the U.S.) in the twentieth century back to the sixteenth century.[19]

While there are thus limits to the approach, especially in its more dogmatic and less empirical incarnations, important ideas from world-systems theory have been very influential and continue to be so today. This is true, first, of the decision not to accept political entities *a priori* as the boundaries of analysis, but instead to trace the actual scope of entanglements and interconnections and work from there. This turn against the methodological nationalism of conventional historiography also means that entities such as nation-states and societies are not simply taken as givens; rather, their genesis is itself understood as the product of global processes and the dynamics of the world economy.

Second, the concept of gradual "incorporation" into a context dominated by Europe has proven useful for understanding the dynamics of the modern world. To be sure, the terminology may appear rigid and not attuned to the complexity of specific historical situations, and the term "incorporation" may betray a Eurocentric bias. But for an exploration of one of the key questions of global development—the emergence of structures of hegemony that are not defined by political conquest alone—Wallerstein's work provides important ideas. More generally, and third, it underlines the importance of a concept of structured change on a macro-level. Not all historians will want to adopt the language of systems, in which differentiated individual elements based on the division of labor are viewed as unified wholes in their relationships to one another. But whatever the terminology, without an idea of structured forms interdependency—economically, but also politically and culturally—it is difficult to come to terms with the logic of the related and at the same time differentiated change that has shaped the world over the past centuries. Such an approach promises to override any glib talk of circulation and "flows" and to tie the discussion back to material conditions. In addition, it can guard against assuming, without closer scrutiny, that social development has an autonomous internal dynamic of its own.

Not surprisingly, therefore, the approach continues to be an important tool for many historians exploring the global dimension of the past.[20] In some fields—the history of slavery, for example—the impact of world-systems thinking has been particularly marked. Newer studies take a view of the market that differs from Wallerstein's somewhat static notion, include social and cultural dynamics, and above all emphasize local sites and subaltern agency in bringing about social change. More recent world-systems perspectives (the notion of a "unified theory" is increasingly questioned) thus arrive at much more subtle and nuanced accounts that connect macro-levels and the local in innovative ways.[21]

Beyond the world-systems approach, a broadly conceived Marxist framework remains today an indispensable tool for many interpretations in global history. Such interpretations share with the world-systems perspective the conviction that studies of social conflicts should not consider the inner-workings of the individual society alone, but need to take account as well of larger power constellations and the ways in which they generate and energize change. Historians using this approach have long discarded mechanistic models of base and superstructure and of teleological stages of development, and instead aim to grasp capitalism as a historically specific formation that structures, and is in turn constituted by, social antagonisms and cultural dispositions. The impact of Marxist theory has moved well beyond the narrow confines of economic history and has been crucial for building sophisticated arguments about cultural change as well.[22]

Postcolonial studies

While the emphasis of world-systems perspectives is generally on the macro-level and on processes of economic integration, postcolonial studies have since the 1980s made major contributions to an understanding of the intricacies of interactions across cultural borders. This approach builds on the premise that the modern world is based on a colonial order that in some regions goes back as far as the sixteenth century, as a result of the European conquest of the Americas. The colonial formatting of the world not only affected forms of domination and economic exploitation, but was also reflected in the categories of knowledge, in concepts of the past, and in visions of the future. In the wake of Edward Said's seminal 1978 book *Orientalism*, postcolonial scholars have been particularly concerned with the orders of cognition and the regimes of knowledge that historically sustained the colonial project.[23]

Postcolonial studies represented an important and productive response to many of the shortcomings of modernization theory. Much of its early work, stimulated by the subaltern studies collective, focused on South Asia, but as a paradigm it soon began to be applied to other places, such as Latin America and Africa. Global historians can benefit from its insights as well. To be sure, postcolonial scholars have not proposed any grand narratives of the history of the entire world. On the contrary, many are cautious to avoid sweeping generalizations and master narratives that culminate in the modern West, wary of a rhetoric of the "global" that they read as an imperialist discourse of domination. In this view, what is called the "global" is essentially a product of colonialism and of imperialist incursions into local life-worlds.

Nevertheless, the postcolonial critique of the modernization paradigm has provided a wealth of ideas fruitful for our understanding of the global past. Three aspects in particular deserve further consideration. First, the postcolonial approach affords sophisticated insights into the dynamics of transcultural exchange. An emphasis on the complexities of individual agency, on locally specific modes of appropriation, on strategic modifications, and on mechanisms of hybridization can function as an important corrective to macrohistorical models of world history in which transfers are often understood in rather simple terms of diffusion and adaptation. A crucial ingredient of such analysis is the recognition that many of the categories that we use to explain historical change have originated in response to the colonial encounter itself. For example, postcolonial historians have demonstrated that the construction of difference through categories such as caste, religion (e.g., Islam vs. Hinduism), and race has been in large part the product of interventions and negotiations in the context of colonialism.[24]

Second, postcolonial approaches take the entanglements of the modern world as the point of departure for their transnational historiography. They do not treat nations and civilizations as naturally existing historical entities, but are interested in the ways in which entities such as "India" and "Europe" were constructed in the context of global circulation. The result is an emphasis on the relational constitution of the modern world. Such a perspective runs contrary to a Eurocentric world historiography based on the notion that Euro-American development has taken place in isolation from the rest of the world and can therefore be understood purely from within. By contrast, postcolonial approaches seek to overcome the tunnel vision that explains the history of Europe internally.

This leads, third, to the awareness that processes of global integration need to be situated within unequal (colonial) power structures. This sensitivity to the issue of power forms postcolonialism's most important critique of modernization theory, and of the variants of world history derived from it. The increasing interconnectedness of the modern world cannot be separated from the colonial conditions under which those connections were formed. This emphasis trumps the hasty assumptions about the "naturalness" of globalization that are commonplace in many works of economic history. In this literature we often encounter anonymous processes of market convergence, the adjustment of commodity prices, and the supra-regional integration of labor markets that are made to appear almost as if they were the outcome of historical laws, governed solely by Adam Smith's "invisible hand." In reality, the integration of markets was inseparable from the very visible fist of imperialism. It depended on forced and indentured labor, on the extraction of raw materials, the forcible "opening" of markets (as in Latin America and East Asia), and on imperialist financial control such as that imposed on the Ottoman Empire and Qing China. What in many accounts appears as self-generating "globalization" was in fact structured by colonialism.

Together with world-systems theory, postcolonial studies remains one of the most productive paradigms on which global historians can draw. At the same time, the global approach must also be understood as a response to the impasse at which postcolonial studies has found itself. Since the 1990s, postcolonial studies have come under fire on several counts. Two dimensions of this critique are particularly pertinent here, as they affect the usefulness of the approach for a global analysis.

The first concerns the concept of culture. As postcolonial studies originated amid the cultural turn in the humanities, much of its work has focused on issues of discourse and representation. In one emphatic pronouncement, colonialism was declared to be "first of all a matter of consciousness" that needed "to be defeated ultimately in the minds of men."[25] Consequently, postcolonial scholars have been accused of privileging cultural explanations at the expense of political and economic structures. Related to this is the problem that postcolonial approaches were not immune to a latent nationalism, as displayed by the use of quasi-nativist notions of the "own" culture. Critiques of Western modernity often go hand in hand with attempts to rehabilitate alternative experiences and indigenous worldviews. Even though the vast majority of postcolonial historians have concentrated on the modern period, their analyses have sometimes been guided by an idealized image of the premodern, precolonial past. In this, they have not always managed to avoid lapsing from criticism of Western essentialisms into a cultural essentialism of their own.[26]

Second, the postcolonial paradigm rests on a very general and therefore not always useful concept of colonialism. The assumption that the world has been ordered along colonial lines since 1492 tends to downplay the fundamental differences between the various forms of colonial rule, which range from extractive empires of the early modern era to complex structures of informal empire-building in the present day. Applying a homogenized concept of colonialism risks leveling the spatial and temporal specificity of different forms of rule, societal differences, and varieties of cultural dynamics. Moreover, the emphasis on modern colonialism has limited the effectiveness of the approach when it comes to explaining the history of parts of the world that were not colonized by Europe or the United States. And, finally, privileging the colonizer/colonized divide as the fundamental explanatory framework imposes a binary logic that for all its insights ultimately remains restrictive. It lacks the capacity to take account of a complex globalizing world.

Multiple modernities

One of the astonishing features of 1990s political theory was the quite improbable comeback of the concept of civilization. Civilizational narratives were preeminent in the nineteenth and early twentieth centuries, but since the days of Buckle, Guizot, Nikolai Danilevsky, and, more recently, Spengler and Toynbee, the genre has seemed moribund. It is all the more remarkable, therefore, that it has recently gained a renewed currency. After the demise of the bipolar ideology of the Cold War, civilizations appeared in many places as the natural units with which to think through rapid global change and to explain conflicts in a globalizing world. The term "civilization" has proved particularly popular outside of Europe, for instance in the Islamic world and East Asia. It mediates between individual lives and local contexts on the one hand, and anonymous processes at the global level on the other. Adding to its appeal, the concept eases a move away from the Eurocentrism of much history writing as it attaches greater importance to political and cultural dynamics internal to the respective civilizations.[27]

The version of the civilization discourse with the greatest scholarly impact is based on a concept known by the convenient catchword "multiple modernities." One of its more theoretically elaborated versions was formulated by the Israeli sociologist Shmuel N. Eisenstadt. Eisenstadt builds on classical modernization theory while seeking to overcome its teleological structure. With this as his goal, he insists on the need to recognize as valid multiple modes of historical development, a diversity of visions for the future, and the fundamental normative equality of different cultural and societal trajectories. Drawing on American sociologist Talcott Parsons's structural functionalism, Eisenstadt developed a cross-regional analysis of patterns of social order and integration—without, however, equating the process of modernization with that of Westernization. His attempts to overcome the Eurocentrism of traditional modernization theory are aimed at pluralizing the paths leading to modernity.

The concept of multiple modernities also challenges a second pillar of modern social theory, namely the axiom of secularization. Accounts of the plurality of paths toward modernization gave rise to the insight that social transformation does not in fact lead more or less automatically to a decline in religious affiliations, as had been postulated in standard modernization theory. This realization led to a reevaluation of the role of religion and of the long-term impact of religious traditions. Not only in Spengler and Toynbee, but also in more recent formulations, scholars see the concept of civilization as rooted in the sociology of religion.

The catchphrase "multiple modernities" contains an explicit criticism of the notion that all modernizing societies will follow the cultural program of modernity as it developed in Europe. Instead, the term underscores the continued existence of cultural configurations and mentalities that have an influence on the transformative social processes that produce modernity. Even the breakdown of traditional authorities and "disenchantment" with customary value systems, many scholars claim, have not put an end to the variability of cultural paradigms. "One of the most important implications of the term 'multiple modernities' is that modernity and Westernization are not identical; Western patterns of modernity are not the only 'authentic' modernities, though they [...] continue to be a basic reference point for others."[28]

This critical turn away from a hegemonic Western modernity—and hence from the assumption shared by most models of social theory since the nineteenth century that cultures are becoming increasingly homogenized—has been taken up by many scholars in a variety of fields. Prominent examples include the expert on Buddhism, Stanley Tambiah, and the Confucianism expert, Tu Wei-ming, both at Harvard University. Tu has developed the notion of a (Confucian) Chinese modernity, which rejects the concept of the self-contained individual on which classical modernization theory was premised, and focuses instead on social connections, cohesion, and collectives. It is not, however, always clear to what extent Tu's is an analytical perspective that traces the influence of Confucianism on social change in China up to the present day, and to what extent it is a normative, political position calling for a renewal of Confucian humanism and claiming a leading role for China in the future of Asia and the broader world.[29]

For a global history perspective, the anti-Eurocentric agenda of multiple modernities—some scholars speak of "alternative modernities"—is an important point of reference.[30] Particularly useful are its goal of understanding social and cultural transformation as a process distinct from Westernization and its focus on the complex relationship of transfer and diffusion on the one hand and the role of internal traditions on the other. Processes of structural differentiation did not lead to identical results everywhere. Underlying this approach is the normative attempt to liberate analysis of non-Western societies from concepts such as imitation, or original and copy, and the intent to recognize, in principle, the equality of a whole host of first-hand experiences of modernization.

Heuristically, therefore, the concept can be useful. On a theoretical level, however, it is not wholly convincing. Three objections merit mention. First, the program of multiple modernities is still relatively vague and its argumentation restricted to the field of culture. It is therefore not always clear whether multiple modernities consist in a virtually limitless range of social models without any substantial connection to unifying structures. If that is the case, the question arises, what makes them all modern? More often, the program seems ultimately to be driving at the idea of a *single* modernity, defined by the usual sociological parameters of functional differentiation, rationalization, and "disenchantment," embodied in state bureaucracy and capitalist market mechanisms. If that is the goal, however, one should speak of variations on modernity; i.e., one modernity with a diversity of cultural manifestations.

Second, many proponents of the concept identify a modernization dynamic specific to each civilization, but treat each as a largely self-contained unit. The territorially fixed (national) society is thus replaced by a more or less hermetically sealed civilization, whose development is conceived as endogenous and dependent on its distinctive cultural traits. The homogeneity of each civilization is rarely challenged. Moreover, its cultural substance (and its institutional dynamics) is frequently deemed to consist in religion, an assumption that is particularly problematic when it is used to explain social continuity up to the present. The focus on cultural difference then runs the risk of turning into culturalism of a sort that harbors the danger of essentialization—the assumption each civilization has a timeless, immutable cultural essence, incompatible with that of any other.

Third, and finally: It is to the credit of this model that it explicitly acknowledges the cultural autonomy of various parts of the world, and does not equate modernity with the spread of Western ideas and institutions. However, by postulating the civilization as a discrete unit of analysis defined by autonomous processes of cultural development, the long history of its interactions is ignored. The history of the modern age is then read as consisting of analogous, autopoietic civilizations, with little regard given to the long history of entanglements or to the systemic integration of the world. Reducing complex and locally specific histories of cultural transformation to an indigenous prehistory of the modern thus tends to obfuscate the larger structures and power asymmetries that have brought the modern world into being.[31]

Global history as a distinct approach

The recent trend towards global perspectives is a broad movement. As we have seen in the last chapter, a whole range of approaches contribute, each in its own way, to our understanding of a past viewed outside the framework of the nation-state. Beyond this multiplicity, however, and building on these other variant modes of engaging the world, a more distinct global history approach has begun to emerge. In this chapter, I will introduce a number of characteristic traits that many recent forays into the field share. Taken together, they form the methodological core of what global history signifies as an approach. Special emphasis will be given to the notion of global integration, or structured transformations on a global level.

We can best understand the features of global history when pitting them against an ideal type—an admittedly oversimplified portrayal—of the older tradition of world history. We should keep in mind, however, that this juxtaposition of world and global history is a heuristic move. It suggests a clear delineation between an older approach and a sophisticated modern approach, while in practice many historians use the two terms interchangeably.

The concept of world history has a history that reaches back several centuries. Today, it remains the name of a school subject in many countries, generally designating a narrative that encompasses the entire world or that looks comparatively at large geographical regions. World histories thus usually follow a macro agenda, typically striving for a full picture of the planet's past—or, as is characteristic in many non-Western countries, they deal with "the rest of the world," with everything that happened outside one's own nation. There are also world histories of specific topics: world histories of empire, of state-formation, of courtly encounters, and world histories of sugar, of tea, and of cotton. In most cases, they trace these institutions and goods not only across the planet, but through time as well, sometimes taking the story all the way from antiquity to the present.[1]

As their points of departure, macro-perspectives of this sort operate with large-scale comparisons of societies or, more typically, whole civilizations. In most older world histories, interactions and exchange between these enormous building blocks were not ignored, but the main focus was on the different trajectories of the civilizations, whose dynamics were primarily depicted as generated from within. These parallel histories were then linked by increasing diffusion from centers of power to the periphery. In the modern period, this diffusion typically assumed the form of a transfer from the West to "the rest." A Eurocentric bias has thus been a rather common feature of world histories for a long time, as the title of William McNeill's influential book, *The Rise of the West*, made no attempt to conceal.[2]

Features of global history

The older world histories typically employed a methodology that combined comparisons of separate civilizations with a search for links between them, the latter explained by processes of diffusion. The thinking behind these histories crossed theoretical and ideological divides—ranging from modernization theory to Marxism and to narratives of civilization—but the mix of comparison and diffusion was remarkably constant. By contrast, the keyword most immediately associated with the term "global" has been "connections." A whole cascade of related terms—"exchange" and "intercourse," "links" and "entanglements," "networks" and "flows"—are mustered to convey the fluidity and volatility with which interactions take place across borders. In lieu of a rather stubborn reliance on macrocomparisons, global histories have elevated mobility to the throne.

This is why most shorthand definitions of global history have confined themselves to the happy marriage of comparisons and connections, taking the best of what traditional world history had to offer and combining it with a sensitivity for the more flexible and fluid dimensions of historical change. "Global connections and comparisons" greet us from the cover page of C. A. Bayly's seminal *Birth of the Modern World*, and the shibboleth that connections cum comparison are "the stock-in-trade of global history" is reiterated in virtually all attempts to define what is specific about the approach.[3]

And indeed, a focus on transfers and interactions is a crucial ingredient of all recent attempts to understand the global past. The mobility of goods, the migration and travel of people, the transfer of ideas and institutions: all these processes are the stuff that has helped produce the globalized world in which we live, and they are the privileged objects of study of many global historians. As we will see below, however, connections alone are not sufficient to explain the originality of the approach; connections need to be embedded in processes of structural transformation, and this on a global scale. Before we come to this point, I will first sketch a set of methodological choices that are recurrent features of current global history, beyond its emphasis on connections. They will be only briefly outlined here, as most of the issues are taken up at greater length in subsequent chapters.

First, global historians are not concerned with macro-perspectives alone. Many seek to situate concrete historical issues and phenomena within broader, potentially global contexts. The emergence of the notion of "culture" in 1880s Bengal is, accordingly, as legitimate a subject of global history inquiry as the full planetary history of the entire nineteenth century.[4] Second, global histories experiment with alternative notions of space. They typically do not take political or cultural units—nation-states, empires, civilizations—as their points of departure. Instead, they pose analytical questions and go wherever their questioning leads them—across the Bay of Bengal, to nodal points in a network, to religious and ethnic diasporas, and so forth.

This implies, third, that global histories are inherently relational. This means that a historical unit—a civilization, a nation, a family—does not develop in isolation, but can only be understood through its interactions with others. In fact, many groups only jelled into seemingly fixed units as a response to exchange and circulation. Attention to the relationality of the past also challenges long-accepted interpretations of the history of the world as the "rise of the West" and the "European miracle." Many older world history texts locate the driving force of world history in Europe and chronicle the spread of European achievements to the rest of the world: world history as a one-way street. By contrast, recent studies stress the constitutive role played by interactions between regions and nations, as well as between Europe and the non-European world, in the development of modern societies. Development in Europe and the West cannot be explained from within, as an autonomous process, but must be seen, at least in part, as the product of various processes of exchange.[5]

Fourth, as a discipline within the humanities, global history forms part of the larger "spatial turn." One consequence is that the relations of constellations in space to other locations—become more important. Global historians pay particular attention to the way individuals and societies interact with others—and less on endogenous change. As a result, spatial metaphors—such as territoriality, geopolitics, circulation, and networks—tend to replace an older temporal vocabulary of development, time lag, and backwardness. This also implies a rejection of the teleologies of modernization theory; i.e., a criticism of the notion that societies are transformed, as it were, from within, and that the direction of social change—from tradition to modernity, for example—is predetermined.

A direct outcome of this is emphasis on the synchronicity of historical events. This is the fifth point. To be sure, global historians by no means ignore the issue of continuities or path dependencies. As C. A. Bayly and others have argued, globalization in the modern age built on trajectories influenced by earlier patterns of entanglement.[6] However, by dissociating from the long-term perspectives typical of the history of civilizations and by not privileging conventional notions of continuity, many global historians suggest that greater precedence be given to simultaneity. As is immediately clear from the examples of the Arab Spring revolts, synchronous constellations and external forces are often as important drivers of social change as long prehistories and traditions.[7]

Sixth, and crucially, many global histories are self-reflective on the issue of Eurocentrism. This is one of the defining features that set this approach apart from most older variants of world history writing. We will take up this issue in more detail below (chapter 8). In practical terms, it generally means that greater emphasis is placed on area-studies expertise in history departments than was typical in the past. It also implies, seventh, that the positionality of thinking about the global past is explicitly recognized. Historians may write about the entire planet, but they do so from a particular place, and their narratives will partly be colored by the dynamics of that location. Looking back, it is obvious that a world history written in late sixteenth-century Mexico City would be wildly different from one written in Istanbul.[8] But even today, the "world" may appear very different when viewed from Accra, Quito, or Harvard Yard.

Integration and structured transformation

The final point, to which we now turn, concerns the notion of integration. This is a crucial aspect, so we will dwell on it at some length. To focus on global integration is a methodological choice that distinguishes global history from other approaches that operate on large scales. There are two important aspects to this choice: global history perspectives go beyond mere studies of connectedness by examining large-scale structured integration; and global historians pursue the problem of causation up to the global level.

To begin with the first point: Many world/global historians content themselves with studying interactions and connections.

"Connectedness is part of the human condition, at least as far back as we can trace human activity," John Darwin has recently reminded us, only to conclude: "The particular concern of the global historian is, or should be, with the history of 'connectedness'—and especially with those forms of connectedness that are oceanic and trans- or intercontinental."[9] Others have chimed in, maintaining that "the world has never been the site of discrete, unconnected communities, that crosscultural interactions and exchanges have taken place since the earliest days of human existence on planet Earth."[10]

But a focus on connections alone is not enough to make good global history. For, while exchanges of goods, persons, and ideas and interactions between groups and societies, even across long distances, have been a feature of human life on the planet from the beginning, some of the links within this global "human web" were crucial to the social make-up of a society, while others remained accidental and ephemeral.[11] The magnitude of their impact depended not least on the degree to which the world was, at the time, integrated—materially, culturally, and politically.

What does that mean? Take the example of the introduction of Western clocks to Japan. When European clocks, high-tech products of their time, were first brought to Tokugawa Japan in the seventeenth century, they were seen primarily as exotic gadgets. Their import had no effect on the social regime of time. Quite the contrary. While European clock-makers took pride in the fact that their watches ran evenly, irrespective of the cycles of the sun, in Japan the same clocks had to be converted to accommodate the traditional order of time, for the length of Japanese hours depended on daylight and consequently varied throughout the year. The mechanical clocks had to be readjusted twice a day, and seasonal dials were installed to undo, as it were, the new clocks' independence from the cycles of nature. In the seventeenth century, then, this technological transfer remained essentially ornamental.

The situation changed dramatically after 1850, when East Asia was incorporated into the political and economic orbit of the West. Now, Western temporality was seen as a central ingredient of all reform projects, and attempts were made to introduce "new times" to Meiji Japan. New technology such as trains, new factories with their novel ways of organizing production, and new forms of social organization, including schools and the army, all required a new time regime. Western watches and clock towers emerged as the symbol of the modern; punctuality and notions of progress translated Western time into everyday practices, and the introduction of the Gregorian calendar in 1873 abolished the traditional methods of time reckoning and prepared Japan for global synchronicity. If we compare these two transfer processes, it becomes clear that the difference between them lies less in the transfers themselves than in the larger geopolitical conditions in which they were embedded. The sparse trade contacts of the seventeenth century, conducted by the Dutch and carefully controlled by the Japanese, had been replaced in the nineteenth century by an imperialist world order under British hegemony. In this changed context, cultural imports were no longer incorporated into local cosmologies, but assumed the force to fundamentally transform everyday practices.[12]

Connections in and of themselves are only a starting point. Their significance can vary greatly, so that, depending on a whole range of circumstances, the same clock can take on very different levels of importance. Global historians need to remember that global connections are preceded by conditions and that it is essential to thoroughly understand these conditions before they can hope to understand the connections themselves. Exchange, in other words, may be a surface phenomenon that gives evidence of the basic structural transformations that made the exchange possible in the first place. Effective global history needs to remain aware of the systemic dimension of the past, and of the structured character of social change.

Lest this sound too abstract, let us look briefly at another example. When critical intellectuals in Vietnam, Japan, or China began to read Marx, this was, rather logically, seen as evidence of the transcultural circulation of ideas. Accordingly, traditional histories charted the translation process, studied the reception of Marxist ideas, and looked for the impact of Marx's texts on reformist thinking in Asia. While these were important facets of the problem, the more important causal links, it turned out, lay elsewhere. In this case, connectedness proved to be itself the result of social changes that had created the conditions under which reading Marx in Vietnam began to make political sense. In the last instance, the influence of Marx could not be reduced to the power of his arguments alone. Rather, aspiring young intellectuals were shaped by the forces and concerns that dominated the times, and the way in which they translated, cited, and highjacked Marx's texts was structured by these conditions. Connections—reading Marx—were thus primarily an effect of prior social, political, and cultural transformations (and not the source of these transformations).

The original mistake in this example involved, but was not limited to, a failure to take the influence of power into consideration. If issues of hierarchy and of exploitation are sidelined, a preoccupation with connections may blur and indeed hinder an accurate understanding of the contours of the global past.

Failure to note power structures confers agency on everyone who is involved in exchange and interactions, and by celebrating mobility runs the danger of ignoring the structures that control it. Cross-border movements were able to bridge differences between societies, but they may also exacerbate conflicts. European aristocrats on the Grand Tour and African slaves on the Middle Passage all crossed political and cultural boundaries, but it does not take much imagination to realize that subsuming them both under "connections" is highly ideological. Frequently the people who wielded real market power stayed put and benefited from being able to ship the huddled masses of their poor across the Atlantic and the Pacific.

This leads us to the second point that merits attention here. Unlike other perspectives on past connections, global history addresses the question of causation up to the global level. In many older world history texts, the analytical status of links and interactions was less than explicit. In some works of transnational history, too, they ultimately remain external to the core argument, and thus ornamental. However, as the world grew increasingly integrated, social development could no longer be understood without some notion of interdependence, or structured difference. "Britain and India came to have very different histories in the nineteenth century," David Washbrook reminds us, "but this was a result of the very closeness of their relationship, not their distance—social, cultural—from each other. They existed as two sides of the same coin, but each with a very different face."[13] A global history that aspires to be more than an ecumenical and welcoming repository of happy stories of cross-border encounters, then, needs to engage systematically with the issue of structured global transformations and their impact on social change.

Our use of the term "global" here should not be misconstrued as necessarily implying a planetary reach. For each issue under study, a separate determination must be made as to how far exactly large-scale processes and structures extend. In much existing work, historians have prematurely confined their inquiries to fixed containers and geographical constraints. It would be equally fallacious to go to the opposite extreme and presuppose globality in every instance. What "global" suggests, therefore, is an openness to pursuing links and the question of causality beyond conventional containers and spatial units; it denotes "simply the methodological concern with experimenting beyond familiar geographical boundaries."[14]

If "comparisons and connections" serves as the conventional shorthand for global history, then we must add a third "c": causality, pursued up to a global scale. The decision to focus on large forms of structured transformation and integration is a choice that sets global history apart from other approaches, such as comparative and transnational history. The emphasis on global integration will almost certainly raise a host of questions. Does this choice make it impossible to write global history about eras before integration, and before modernity? Will this choice narrow the range of possible topics by insisting on an identifiably global causality? Does it compel global historians to study this global level explicitly? I will take up these issues in the following chapter.

Beyond connectivity: competing narratives

In order to better understand the significance of a non-internalist approach, and of the analytical role of global integration, it may be helpful to briefly compare the perspective of global history with three influential but contrasting ways in which historians have hitherto understood and interpreted transformations on a planetary scale. Somewhat schematically, we can label them as Western exceptionalism, cultural imperialism, and the paradigm of independent origins. I will briefly sketch these three narratives and point out their shortcomings when compared to a global history approach.

The first metanarrative, still firmly entrenched in many textbooks and general overview works, assumes a general process of modernization that originated in Europe and was then gradually disseminated around the globe. The defining features of this notion of modernity are familiar: the functional differentiation of social spheres, such as the economy, politics, the social, and culture; and a gradual rationalization of all these spheres, giving birth to a capitalist and industrialized economy, the nation-state, and meritocratic bureaucracies; the replacement of hereditary estates by a class society and the modern individual; and the overcoming of traditional and religious cosmologies through what Max Weber called the "disenchantment of the world."

In principle, these were seen as universal developments, but in actual practice they emerged in Europe first and were then conveyed to the rest of the world. Such a diffusionist reading—epitomized by William McNeill's *The Rise of the West*—lay at the heart of many older world histories, especially when guided by modernization theory, but also in many of the Marxist variants of world histories. "For the last thousand years," as David Landes has summarized this narrative, "Europe (the West) has been the prime mover of development and modernity."[15] Such triumphalist formulations have become much less common, so that most accounts now replace the unabashed Eurocentrism of earlier days with a recognition of the various forms of negotiation and adaptation that attended the process. At its core, however, the basic assumptions of this narrative are still in place: Europe/the West is seen as the locus of innovation, and world history is essentially understood as a history of the diffusion of European progress.[16]

Against this formerly dominant view, a second interpretation emerged that was based on a radically critical reading of the dissemination of Western modernity. This view is associated with postcolonial, subaltern, and some Marxist perspectives. In it, modernity remains essentially European and is still equated with the march of universal reason. But the spread of modernity is seen not as emancipatory but as a process of deprivation.

There are two different, but related arguments involved. The first is the hypothesis that it was Enlightenment universalism that lay at the root of the West's expansionist urge. It was only a small step, the critique runs, from positing universal standards to deciding to intervene and to implement these standards, by force, under the auspices of a paternalistic civilizing mission. The second argument is related. The spread of Western modernity is understood as a form of cultural imperialism with the potential to eradicate alternative worldviews. Critical scholars have interpreted the spread of Enlightenment tenets in the nineteenth century as a process of coerced and often brutal diffusion, made possible and driven by highly asymmetrical relations of power.[17]

Both approaches discussed so far—emancipatory modernization and cultural imperialism—are essentially diffusionist and take the European origins of modernity for granted. What is more, they rest on the supposed absence of substantial cultural and social development elsewhere as one of their axiomatic tenets. In recent years, however, the European claim to originality, to exclusive authorship of modernity, has been called into question. Historians have begun to look for parallels and analogies to the European "march of civilization," for autochthonous processes of rationalization that did not depend on, but led to similar results as, developments in Europe. This is the third paradigm sketched here, and it forms part of a larger scholarly debate on the origins of modernity. It was born out of a desire to challenge diffusionist notions of modernization, and to acknowledge the social dynamics that prevailed in many societies before their encounter with the West. The aim was to replace older notions of traditional societies and "people without history" with a broader understanding of multiple modernities. But in the end, this approach posits an identical telos—a modern, capitalist society—even if this goal is not achieved via transformations inspired by contact with the West, but rather builds on indigenous cultural resources: a teleology of universal disenchantment, realized in each society internally, but across the globe.

All three approaches converge in their methodological bias for national and civilizational frames. Their many differences notwithstanding, all rely on internalist logics in their attempt to explain what must be understood as a global phenomenon. If we are going to take the challenge of global history seriously, we need to move beyond these three approaches and focus on the connectivities and processes of integration that have shaped and reconfigured societies globally. Sanjay Subrahmanyam has argued that modernity is "historically a global and *conjunctural* phenomenon, not a virus that spreads from one place to another. It is located in a series of historical processes that brought hitherto relatively isolated societies into contact, and we must seek its roots in a set of diverse phenomena."[18] From such a vantage point, it is less instructive to search for alleged origins—European or otherwise—than to focus on the global conditions and interactions through which the modern world emerged. This is why notions of global integration and system-like dependencies are crucial: changes in one location within the integrated world ripple through the system to affect other parts as well.

It is clear that the four approaches discussed above—world history, postcolonialism, multiple modernities, and global history—cannot be neatly separated, but overlap in many respects. They are, in other words, ideal types. For heuristic purposes, however, it is helpful to keep them apart analytically. Let us very briefly look at a few issues and see how these different paradigms may lead to very different results (indeed: to different questions)—before then using the case of nationalism to illustrate in greater detail the analytical surplus that is characteristic of a global history approach vis-à-vis the three other paradigms.

A first example is the case of human rights, on which a substantial historiography has recently emerged. A standard world history perspective would hold that the rights of man have a European genealogy that reaches back to humanism, and even a bit earlier, before coalescing into a program with global reach during the French Revolution. These rights with their universal claims then traveled beyond their place of origin and gradually gained acceptance around the world.[19] A postcolonial reading would instead emphasize the parochial and culturally specific notion of human rights and the indiscriminate way in which it was used to marginalize, and indeed efface, alternative concepts of entitlement and equality that were less dependent on the concepts of nation and the individual. A third approach, that of multiple modernities, insists on indigenous cultural and political resources that allowed multiple notions of human rights to emerge in many different places, largely independent of each other. Building on these three approaches, recent forays into a global history of human rights focus instead on the emergence of human rights as a truly global discourse. Historians have thoroughly explored the global scope of human rights discourse by placing the emphasis less on the French Revolution and more on the appropriation and universalization of a language of rights in Haiti a few years later.[20] In the twentieth century, the 1970s appear as a pivotal moment, when the decline of socialism and nationalism as political ideologies paved the way for the rise of human rights claims to the status of a hoped for "Last Utopia." The intellectual origins of human rights, in this reading, are of less importance than the synchronous global conditions of their overall acceptance, and of their fusion with local genealogies in very diverse locations.[21]

A similar case can be made in the field of international law. For a long time, historians have seen the Law of Nations, as it emerged in the wake of Hugo Grotius, as well as the subsequent development of international law, as a rationalization of international relations. Against this belief in the benevolent spread of a European accomplishment, critical scholars have pointed out the close connection between the Law of Nations and European imperialism, and have judged ostensibly universal claims to be no more than a thin veil concealing colonial ambitions.[22] Third, in their quest to identify independent origins for international law in today's global order, scholars have begun to mine the cultural and legal history of various societies to show that parts of what is currently held to be common sense are contributions from alternative non-Western traditions. A global perspective would want to address more specifically why international law emerged when it did, why it was appropriated by different actors around the world, and in what ways it can be understood as a response to a global challenge. A preoccupation with the inventors and intellectual patent-holders, in other words, would lose its primacy, while the actual practice of international law moved to center stage.[23]

We can extend the heuristic differentiation of these four approaches to virtually all fields of historical inquiry. Was the concept of race a European invention, a tool of empire, a notion that grew from various indigenous roots—or a response to global challenges? Was the Enlightenment the accomplishment of European salon culture, a Western imposition, the product of many indigenous cultures of rationalization—or rather a way in which social elites around the world came to terms with new global realities?[24] Or think of attempts to historicize the global history of fascism. World historians have tried to define the term by drawing up a laundry list of necessary features: a charismatic leader, mass mobilization, an ideology of ultra-nationalism, and so on. All of these features, however, were derived from the European experience. Other instances of fascism, in Japan or Argentina, for example, would seem to fall short of the requirements; in fact, even German National Socialism did not live up to the model set by Italian Fascism, and vice versa. By using global history as a corrective lens for this slightly myopic analysis, historians have paid more attention to transfers and direct contacts and have thus been able to reveal to what extent Italy and Germany served as models and inspiration in many places around the world.

Moving beyond comparison and transfer history, finally, a more systematic focus on global integration would begin with the shared global situation of the interwar years, and the quest, by many societies, for a "third way" between classical liberalism and communism, a quest that led many governments to experiment with new forms of social organization and mobilization. From such a perspective, the absence of this or that item on the laundry list—Was there a mass party challenging the establishment, or only mobilization "from above"? for example—is of less importance than understanding different cases as related, but differentiated ways of coping with structural transformations and a changing international order.[25]

Case Study: Nations and Nationalism in global history

In this final section, let us look in greater depth at the historiography of nationalism, as it is here that we can observe most clearly how new global perspectives have been able to complement and modify earlier ways of situating the nation within world history. In some respects, the nation is an unlikely candidate for such an endeavor. Not too long ago, in the 1990s, when "globalization" became the "in" word, some pundits were quick to predict the end of the nation-state altogether. In the realm of scholarship, its future prospects were equally bleak. Transnational and global histories were written with the explicit purpose of moving beyond the nation-state. But this moment of crisis—or was it one of euphoria?—soon abated, and gave way to the recognition that nation-states had staying power and would continue to be relevant, albeit in an altered setting. It has also become clear that global history is not about consigning the nation/nation-state to the dustbin of history, but rather about reassessing its historical role and better explaining its emergence and significance.

How do these more recent approaches compare with earlier attempts to place the nation in the world? To a certain extent, it is no exaggeration to say that the theory of nationalism operated on a global scale from its very beginnings. Thus, the explanatory approaches inspired by early modernization theory—most notably by Ernest Gellner—were universal in scope. They posited the formation of nations as an effect of the ongoing transition from traditional to modern societies. While nationalist activists typically emphasized the distinctive character of a given nation, Gellner discarded all claims to uniqueness by postulating a universal law of development: industrial manufacturing destroyed the hierarchies of agricultural society in order to guarantee the mobility of labor and thus continuous growth. Nationalist self-legitimation may have stressed a shared history, a common language, and common cultural patterns, but for Gellner, nationalism was "the establishment of an anonymous, impersonal society [. . .], in place of a previous complex structure of local groups [. . .]. That is what really happens."[26]

In this view, all nationalisms were, despite their superficial variations, essentially the same, and nationalism everywhere was an effect of socioeconomic modernization that could be explained in entirely endogenous terms. That being the case, there was no obstacle to comparing the experiences of far-flung locales with one another. By contrast, more recent approaches have instead highlighted connections and transfers. They have concluded that the worldwide prevalence of nationalism in the nineteenth century cannot be ascribed to internal factors alone, but must be understood as a result of diffusion as well.

Although Benedict Anderson has received attention chiefly as a proponent of a constructivist approach to nationalism, his most important methodological contribution has been his description of the modular character of the nation. By this he meant that after its initial creation, the form of the nation could, in principle, be transferred to other settings as a kind of template. This form developed first in the Creole societies of the Americas, and then in Europe in the mid-nineteenth century. Concepts and models of nationalism were generated there and subsequently became available globally as a kind of toolkit. From this point onward, all emerging nationalisms were shaped and influenced by this same paradigm.[27]

Compared to earlier models inspired by modernization theory, Anderson's approach marked an important step forward, since the global spread of nationalism could now no longer be regarded as something akin to a clockwork result of the laws of social development. The concrete mechanisms by which the national form spread, however, remained little examined. Anderson's interest was in the development of nationalism in Europe and the complex conditions under which this became possible. When it came to the rest of the world, he focused on how the form was used and modified. He essentially took its transferability as a given.[28] But how can we understand the dynamics of transfers if we limit our attention to the origins of the form that travelled and to the nature of that form, but do not explore the conditions of possibility that made its transfer attractive to its recipients?

Anderson's approach met with criticism from postcolonial historians, who for their part placed greater emphasis on the concrete imperial conditions under which nationalist movements developed in the colonized world. In his much-cited book *Nationalist Thought and the Colonial World*, Partha

Chatterjee argued that nationalism in the colonial world must inevitably remain a phenomenon derived from Europe, a "derivative discourse." While it was true that nationalist movements were directed against foreign rule, on an ontological level—Chatterjee claimed—they continued to be indebted to the parameters of the dominant, which is to say imperial, discourse.[29]

In addition to this, the book contains a second argument. In substance, Chatterjee claims, anticolonial nationalism is fed by opposition to the West, which often takes the form of an emphatic stress on the national spirituality of the non-Western in contrast to Western materialism. And indeed, the dichotomy of a spiritual East versus a material West was a standard ingredient of political discourse in Asia in the late nineteenth century. Chatterjee goes on to expound this argument further in *The Nation and Its Fragments*, which is to some extent a revision of his first book. Here, Chatterjee divides nationalism into a material, external sphere and an inner, spiritual one. On this spiritual level, "its true and essential domain," he sees the nation as already sovereign, long before it achieves political sovereignty. This inner domain appears as the realm of the true cultural expression of a nation. In other words, even if the "national form" (Etienne Balibar) is transferable and the national discourse remains derivative on the formal level, the substance of nationalism nevertheless is geographically and culturally specific and cannot be derived from the European imperial model.[30]

To what degree, we may now ask, is this particularity of the content of nationalism itself the product of global constellations? It is a valid question for, to a certain extent, Chatterjee's approach remains indebted to the endogenous model: while he acknowledges the transfer of the nation as a form within the context of imperial power, the specific nature of the substance of colonial nationalism is explained with reference to local cultural resources, and in particular to older, precolonial traditions. Chatterjee has been accused of idealizing and reifying these precolonial cultural resources.[31] From a global history perspective, however, two further criticisms are of greater importance. First, Chatterjee's analysis remains entirely focused on the binary relationship between the colonized nation and the colonizers. This is a limitation that his account shares with the general thrust of the postcolonial paradigm. The dynamics of Indian, Chinese, or Thai nationalism were part of a global constellation. The paradigm of a local "reaction" to stimuli from Europe and the United States, important though it is, remains narrow in scope, just as the privileging of references back to autochthonous cultural traditions fails to tell the whole story. By cleaving to a postcolonial narrative, Chatterjee risks disregarding the larger global context, and overlooking the way in which historical actors in many regions from the late nineteenth century onward increasingly made reference to a global totality. Nationalism and thinking in national categories developed within this context of global integration.

And, second, he excludes as a factor the degree to which the substance of nationalism, too, not only referred back to endogenous traditions, but was also a product of the global constellation. Rather than making an analytical distinction between a (universal, transferable) "nation-form" and the culturally specific manifestation of its content, then, the aim must be to reconstruct both levels, each in its global context. After all, the larger geopolitical reality often was a crucial factor in determining which of numerous local traditions were mobilized for national projects.[32]

What is needed, then, is a deeper embedding of the ways in which the nation was defined, understood, and put into practice in global contexts—building on and going beyond the insights gained from comparative studies, histories of diffusion, and postcolonial approaches. A number of recent forays into the global history of nationalism have shown just how fruitful such an approach can be. Let us look at two studies that exemplify this trend.

The first example is Andrew Sartori's *Bengal in Global Concept History*. From the 1880s onwards, Sartori sees Bengali intellectuals grapple with a notion of culture that has many family resemblances to Herder's concept of *Kultur*, and also to related propositions from Russia and Japan. The overall problematic is how to account for the relationship between the parts and the whole, or in other words, how to explain the similarities between these different versions of culture discourse without losing sight of the specificity of Bengali debates. To recall the ideal types outlined above: Was Bengali culturalism the result of a transfer of ideas from the West and their subsequent local appropriation? Was it the product of uneven relationships of power and thus a form of colonization of minds? Or should we emphasize the indigenous cultural resources and traditional genealogies of a specific Bengali understanding of culture?

In his global history analysis, Sartori moves beyond all these interpretations. Though his work is clearly influenced by postcolonial readings, he finds them ultimately mired in assumptions of cultural incommensurability and intent on discarding the concept of "culture" itself as a Western derivative, as a form of cultural imperialism. For him, similarities are not the simple effects of diffusion and power differentials; rather, he sees Bengal as one location, among many, in which a notion of "culture" was employed in response to global challenges. "The history of the culture concept in Bengal," he insists, "can be treated neither as a local deviation from nor as a late reiteration of an essentially Western intellectual form, but will rather be investigated as a spatially and temporally specific moment in the global history of the culture concept."[33]

The turn to culture can be read as a turn away from an earlier version of liberalism characterized by rational individualism and economic self-interest. Against this liberal gospel, the notion of culture was embraced by social groups that formulated a nationalist critique of British rule and economic hegemony. In Sartori's reading, the global structures to which these eminent intellectuals responded were primarily economic. In the wake of the financial crisis of the 1840s, trade and industry were increasingly monopolized by British merchants, while native capital was invested only in property and real estate, thus disconnecting Bengali society from the dynamics of commerce. In this situation, the notion of culture became part of a quasi-Romantic discourse among Hindu elites as they sought to affirm their organic connection to the land and to the agrarian workforce.

More generally, and much more abstractly, Sartori links the debate on liberalism versus culture to the expansion of capitalism. He argues that culturalism emerged around the world as a reaction to the particular kinds of alienation and subjectivity that labor relations and forms of production under capitalism generated in particular areas. The specific notion of culture was, to be sure, suffused with local particularity, but the alleged traditions were not only thoroughly worked over by capitalism but also pressed into the service of social practices in a capitalist regime. Thus, culturalism cannot be fully accounted for as the effect of intellectual transfer; rather, it must be understood as a series of unique responses to the same global problematic.

The second example is Rebecca Karl's *Staging the World*, a study of nationalism in late Qing China. For Karl also, the notion of China as a nation could only take hold at a specific historical moment, at the moment when China discovered the new "world" for itself. This moment did not consist merely in China's perception of regions outside the Sino-sphere, outside China's area of influence, but rather in an awareness of the world as a structured whole, increasingly made up of sovereign (nation-)states and dependent colonial countries. This new understanding of the "world" as a totality of units connected through globe-spanning forces like imperialism and capitalism then replaced the millennia-old mental dichotomy between the Middle Kingdom and barbarism.

What does this mean in concrete terms? Rebecca Karl is particularly interested in the way in which events that once appeared marginal from a Chinese perspective—the annexation of Hawaii by the United States, the partitions of Poland in the eighteenth century, the American conquest of the Philippines, British rule in Egypt, and so forth—became objects of intense debate in China around 1900. Within the traditional cosmology of the Qing court, these locations were indeed peripheral, at the fringes (and sometimes squarely outside of the reach) of Chinese "civilization." At the turn of the century, however, Chinese reformers began to realize that the political and economic threat that China faced was not so different from the plight afflicting these smaller nations. While Hawaii may have been remote in cultural terms, the modern logic of geopolitics placed it in a situation very like that of the Qing Empire. The colonization process was no longer simply a concern of distant and exotic peoples, but now threatened even China in similar ways. As a result of globally effective structures, commonalities were no longer culturally, but rather geopolitically determined. They were now the result of the colonial threat and of China's peripheral position in the capitalist world economy.[34]

The central thesis of Karl's book is that the perception of China as one nation among others and as a part of "Asia"—understood here primarily in terms of a shared marginalization within the hegemonic imperial order, and less in terms of cultural or ethnic commonalities—only became possible within the context of global integration. "China only became both specifically national (and not an empire) and regionally Asian at the same time as, and only when, China became worldly."[35] The establishment of the nation was thus equally a diachronic projection and a response to China's incorporation into the world. As the title of the book suggests, it wasn't diachronic stages of development that were responsible for the emergence of dynamics of nationalism, but a synchronic "staging of the world"—a performance on a global stage.

Both Sartori's and Karl's books are written by scholars whose contributions to global history are largely resident in their particular areas of expertise, modern India and modern China. While other global historians focus on networks of nationalists, compare nationalist movements in different locations, or aim at a planetary synthesis, these studies focus on a particular location that they then analyze through its global entanglements.

More important, both books are examples of a broader historical movement that attempts to understand global structures not only as the necessary context, but also as the necessary precondition for the emergence of particular forms of nationalism.[36] Both authors focus predominantly on political economy, and they posit a sometimes highly abstract notion of capitalism as the driving force of history. Equating a global totality with capitalism will appear too rigid to some, and critics have taken both authors to task for what they see as dogmatic reliance on overly abstract notions of capitalist expansion. But the possible shortcomings of our two examples do not diminish their value as illustrations of just how integral a nuanced understanding of the global can be. As we have seen above, we can conceive of and explain global integration in a variety of ways. In the context of this chapter, Sartori and Karl are relevant because they see the global not as an external, and additional, context—but rather as constitutive, shaping the objects of study while being shaped by them.

Taken together, the set of methodological preferences outlined in this chapter and the emphasis on the concept of integration, constitute a rejection of explanations that slight or even completely disregard external influences and factors. This is the methodological core of global history understood as a distinct approach. Conventional social theories generally operate within what can be called an internalist paradigm. In past grand narratives of modernization, historical phenomena were explained endogenously, from within, and typically analyzed within the boundaries of a society. This focus on internal change has been the hallmark of virtually all social theories to date. Whether inspired by Marxism, Max Weber and Talcott Parsons, or the work of Michel Foucault, social theories essentially treated societies as self-generating and assumed that social change was always of a society's own making.

Global history, by contrast, steps outside this internalist or genealogical framework. It pays particular attention to interactions and entanglements across borders. And it recognizes the impact of structures that extend past the boundaries of individual societies. Global history thus acknowledges the causal relevance of factors that do not lie within the purview of individuals, nations, and civilizations. Its ultimate promise is a perspective that looks beyond the dichotomy of internal and external altogether.

CHAPTER 5

Global history and forms of integration

————————————◉————————————

The last chapter offered a working definition of global history understood not as an object of study, but as a particular perspective. Global history as a distinct approach explores alternative spatialities, is fundamentally relational, and is self-reflective on the issue of Eurocentrism. We have placed particular emphasis on the concept of integration and of structured transformations on a global scale. This focus on systemic contexts is a heuristic choice that distinguishes this approach from others. It means that global history takes structured integration as a context, even when it is not the main topic. It also means that global historians pursue the question of causality up to a global level.

The focus on integration also implies that global history moves away from connectedness alone as a guiding principle. This is an important move, as a focus on connectedness is central to the shorthand definition of global history that we frequently encounter in the scholarly literature. Of course connections are important, and they will feature prominently in any global analysis. Without mobility and interaction, there is no globality. But connections are of varying quality and intensity. Some remain either spurious and ephemeral or locally confined—and their impact is thus limited. To prematurely equate trade links across the Sahara or the import of kingfisher feathers and rhinoceros horns into Tang China with "globalization" is not very helpful. Ultimately, the quality and the impact of connections depend on the degree to which worlds were integrated into more or less systemic wholes. When in 185 B.C.E., the last of the Mauryan kings was assassinated and his kingdom collapsed, this was a decisive turning point in the history of South Asia, with important reverberations in the Hellenistic world—but it certainly did not throw the whole planet into turmoil as did the assassination of the Austrian Archduke Franz Ferdinand more than two thousand years later. The relevance of links and connections—How far did they reach? And how important were they really?—will thus have to be measured against the degree of integration that was actually achieved. Sometimes a slump in trading activities in one region will hardly affect others at all; but the 1929 slump triggered a systemic crisis of worldwide proportions.

It is difficult, in other words, to disentangle global history as a perspective from an assessment of the process of global integration. As a consequence, the potential of the approach can best be exploited in studying periods when integration is sustained and of a certain density. Conversely, in historical epochs when connections remained spurious and integration is hardly palpable, it is much less productive—and possibly less efficient than other approaches, such as comparative history, which properly speaking are not global history.

As a distinct paradigm, with its focus on integration and structured global transformations, global history is a very specific approach. It is certainly not a catch-all method for explaining everything that ever happened under the sun. This chapter will further discuss the implications of choosing this paradigm. In what follows, we will discuss three major issues in some detail. First, does the emphasis on integration effectively turn global history into a history of globalization? Second, how can we understand the notion of "integration" and the driving forces that bring it about? And finally, if global history is predicated on integration, how far back in time can we extend our global perspectives?

History of globalization

To begin with the first question, does the focus on integration essentially turn global history into the history of globalization? Studies of globalization, understood as the process of growing interconnectedness, are concerned with the increase of links and complexity, and with the emergence of the world as a single system. As some understanding of structured integration is a necessary ingredient of the global history approach, the history of globalization may at first glance appear to be the natural subject matter for global historians.

And indeed, global history and the history of globalization are frequently treated as one. This is, however, inaccurate for two reasons: First, global history, as we understand it here, is primarily an approach; the history of globalization, on the other hand, denotes a historical process. And second, integration on a global level is a necessary condition for a global perspective; it is a context—but not necessarily the object of study itself. Global history inquiries thus do not have to account for the origins and causes of integration, but can focus on its impact and effects. The history of globalization is then an important subgenre of global history writing, but not the field itself.[1]

The term "globalization" is a new addition to the vocabulary of historians. It very rarely appeared in public discourse before the early 1990s; but from then on, its diffusion became almost epidemic.[2] Initially, the term was employed primarily by economic historians, but around the turn of the twenty-first century, the history of globalization became a legitimate subject for historians, and its reach extended beyond the specific question of the development of a world economy. Numerous works have made use of the term and have attempted to apply it productively to inquiries into the long history of the globalization process and other historical subjects.[3]

If, then, the term is new—how new is the phenomenon itself? According to Manuel Castells, we today are witnesses to a turning point in world history: "The material foundations of society, space, and time are being transformed, organized around the space of flows and timeless time. [...] It is the beginning of a new existence, and indeed the beginning of a new age, the Information Age, marked by the autonomy of culture vis-à-vis the material bases of our existence." Castell's assertion that this is a new phenomenon is itself by no means new. Already in 1957, the modernization theorists M. F. Millikan and W. W. Rostow found themselves "in the midst of a great world revolution. [...] The rapidly accelerating spread of literacy, mass communications, and travel [...] is breaking down traditional institutions and culture patterns which in the past held societies together. In short, the world community is becoming both more interdependent and more fluid than it has been at any other time in history." As early as 1917, American sociologist Robert Park was convinced that the world was crossing a threshold into a new era in human history, though this transition was still rooted in the technologies of the nineteenth century: "The railway, the steamship, and the telegraph are rapidly mobilizing the peoples of the earth. The nations are coming out of their isolation, and distances which separated the different races are rapidly giving way before the extension of communication. [. . .] [G]reat cosmic forces have broken down the barriers which formerly separated the races and nationalities of the world, and forced them into new intimacies and new forms of competition, rivalry, and conflict." We could go even further back, for reports of rapid and scarcely comprehensible social change have accompanied the modern world since the French Revolution. And since the mid-nineteenth century, this change has been associated with cross-border interaction. Already in 1848, Karl Marx and Friedrich Engels declared in the Communist Manifesto that "in place of the old local and national seclusion and self-sufficiency, we have intercourse in every direction, universal inter-dependence of nations. [. . .] National one-sidedness and narrow-mindedness become more and more impossible."

How is it possible to analyze, let alone periodize, a historical process that seems infatuated with the sense of novelty—continuously? The widespread conviction, constantly reiterated, that we are experiencing a radical historical shift and witnessing a fundamental turning point appears to devalue any claim to meaningful subdivisions. "How can we evaluate the claims of globalization seriously," Adam McKeown has asked, "when the only consistent fate of each transformative new age is to be regarded as a period of stasis and isolation by the next new age?"[4]

Some historians have gone so far as to suggest shelving the question altogether. In their view, whether we are looking for globalization or global integration, the project is doomed from the start, due (in part) to the fact that the concept of globalization is theoretically vague and relatively undefined. Primarily, however, their skepticism is empirical. If a process does not reach absolutely everywhere, they hold, it is not valid to call it global. Even in our seemingly globalized present, not everyone is connected to everyone else. In many parts of the world, there are people who do not own mobile phones, do not watch the Olympics, and are not hooked up to the Internet. "The world has long been a space where economic and political relations are very uneven; it is filled with lumps," writes Frederick Cooper. "Structures and networks penetrate certain places [. . .] but their effects tail off elsewhere."[5] Across the planet, there continue to be clusters of people exempt from the benefits, and from the alienations, of so-called global flows. A genuinely global integration has never occurred, and presumably never will, as long as there are exceptions to the larger trend.

This is, of course, a rather rigid and in some ways fundamentalist perspective. Ultimately, it would rule out almost any aggregate or macro-sociological terminology, as counterexamples can always be mustered against generalized patterns. But many recent exercises in global history do not fit this description. They do not equate "global" with an absence of limits and boundaries or insist on the planetary totality of historical processes. Instead, their aim is to move beyond established units and compartments, and to trace goods, ideas, and people across borders, wherever their trajectories may have moved them. These movements, moreover, did not range freely, but were typically structured and followed specific patterns.

Other studies, by contrast, have traced the origins of global integration far back into history; in some cases, very far indeed. World systems historians such as André Gunder Frank have insisted that the history of the world system can be followed five thousand years into the past. Unlike Wallerstein's and other rivaling interpretations, Frank holds that the beginnings of inexorable capital accumulation did not wait until the 1500s, but can be identified many centuries earlier.[6] From a very different perspective, one of the pioneers of the world history paradigm, Jerry H. Bentley, has proposed a history of transcultural interaction that stretches back to the fourth millennium B.C.E. and extends to the present moment. "From remote times to the present," Bentley suggests, "cross-cultural interactions have had significant political, social, economic, and cultural ramifications for all peoples involved." According to such a view, the various forms of mobility, of trade, and of empire building have created global connectivity through the ages, if in different forms.[7] Others have shifted the beginnings of global interconnection even further, sometimes as far back as the development of human language.[8]

Such radical proposals are of course problematic. It is important to explore the long history of transcultural links and routes of interaction, and to recognize the complexity of early civilizations. This should not lead us, however, to assume that the links we observe add up to a continuous story that crosses continents and continues unbroken through the ages. Most historians are more cautious, steering clear of black and white and always-or-never pronouncements.[9] In place of the dichotomy of the either-or, they have begun to ask more concretely: When did the world first show signs of cohesiveness, of a fundamental inter-relationality? When did people become so closely knit that events in one place had immediate and important effects in another? When did the world become a single system?

In response to these questions, a whole industry of studies has arisen with the goal of locating crucial watersheds and identifying the origins of globalization.[10] This literature is a reaction against the presentism of an early social-scientific understanding of globalization that applied the term exclusively to the most recent decades. Beginning gradually in the 1970s and accelerating radically in the 1990s, this interpretation held, Internet communication, the global manufacture of goods, transnational capital investment, and the emergence of global governance structures changed the world, bringing about an intensity and a new quality of interaction that was fundamentally different from earlier forms of connectedness.[11]

Historians, for their part, were quick to challenge this idea of a radical and epochal break with the past. Today, they largely agree that globalization has a much longer history that both prefigures and impacts the present. In the academic literature, debates about major surges toward global integration focus largely on two historical moments: the late nineteenth century and the sixteenth century.[12] Most historians now take for granted that by the 1880s, the acceleration of cross-border contacts had coalesced to the point that it was possible to speak of an integrated global whole. Enforcing political isolation, as Japan and Korea had done for centuries, was now virtually impossible. Labor markets and commodity prices converged across political and geographical boundaries.[13] Networks of communication encompassed the whole world and enabled the impression of simultaneity. "The conditions under which we live," Sandford Fleming declared triumphantly in 1884, "are no longer the same. [. . .] The whole world is drawn into immediate neighborhood and near relationship."[14] The moment and degree of integration of various components into this world of global simultaneity was variable; but by the outbreak of the First World War it had reached all societies and brought about a veritable re-territorialization of the world.[15]

Other historians see the early sixteenth century as the true origin point of a unified world system. Some of the processes that foreshadow greater global cohesion indeed had their beginnings in the 1500s: the European "discovery" of the two Americas, the beginnings of colonialism, and European-dominated capitalist trade connections. The conquest of the two Americas marked the beginning of the European expansion that was to change the face of the earth in the centuries to come. The creation of trans-Pacific trade networks, via the famous Manila galleon, linked the Americas to Asia and enabled the development of the world market. Many of the structures established in this period of "Iberian globalization"—global sea passages, the world economy, the growth of large states, the diffusion of technologies, and a broader awareness of the global whole—had remarkable staying power.[16]

Beyond globalization

The history of globalization has developed into a veritable subgenre of global history writing, with the search for turning points and for the origins of a global totality as its marked features. Heuristically, narratives of globalization will remain relevant to any attempt at understanding the genealogy of the present and accounting for change on a global scale. They serve also as a first orientation and help place events and processes in larger contexts. Not least, histories of globalization can enable us to address questions on a global scale and questions of long-term scope.

But ultimately, turning the past into a history of globalization creates difficulties. Some are due to the vagueness of the term; it is not always clear where connections end and globalization begins. Histories of globalization suffer, too, from the tendency to privilege one level of explanation over others. Many are based on a narrow emphasis on political and, most of all, economic history—such that the story of market integration comes to stand for global history *tout court*.

Beyond such practical issues, a globalization-perspective is fraught with several more fundamental problems. First, it streamlines history and formats it according to the single criterion of connectedness, thus slighting the manifold trajectories and repercussions of past developments, and translating them into a vocabulary of "less" and "more." In some ways, the historiography of globalization then looks like modernization theory reloaded, so that "tradition" is replaced by isolation and "modernity" by entanglement.[17]

Second, histories of globalization operate with the myth of continuity. They chart long-term developments that, as becomes clear on closer scrutiny, did not follow a straight path and were not evenly paced. Peak periods of interconnection and interaction were followed by periods of comparative disconnection and divergence. Unless we operate on huge time scales, the emphasis on convergence so typical for histories of globalization is thus highly problematic. Generally speaking, the idea of continuity is largely a retrospective fiction. It is not unusual for histories of globalization to see connections and sometimes path dependencies between earlier and later forms of entanglement, and to draw from this the conclusion that later events naturally followed from earlier ones. But this can be misleading. Columbus knew nothing of Leif Erikson who had reached Newfoundland five hundred years earlier. In China, memories of Marco Polo's visit were largely forgotten by the time the Portuguese arrived in Canton in 1517. The idea of a continuity of globalization owes more to the desires of the present than to the logic of the past.

And third, a quest for the origins of globalization presupposes that connectivities have a definite starting point, when they in fact do not. The obsession with origins threatens, moreover to force the past into one overriding and seemingly logical trajectory, which is equally fictional. Trade and market exchange, patterns of migration, the expansion of communication, the spread of ideas, the trajectory of social conflicts, the aspirations of empires and religious communities—these and many other processes follow their own chronologies and their diverse turning points, which will only rarely map onto each other neatly. The term globalization, then, obscures the reality that connections and global processes were of a manifold and multilayered quality and adhered to different and sometimes incompatible logics. To subsume all of them under the unifying label "globalization" essentializes the process and masks the heterogeneity of the past.[18]

Whether the notion of globalization will survive as an analytical concept that is useful for historians is an open question. There is much support for the idea that more specific concepts with a greater sensitivity to historical context might yield more fruitful results—even if we grant the need to periodize the past not only locally and regionally, but on a global scale. In some ways, we can even say that a global history perspective immunizes us to some extent against the encroachments of globalization rhetoric. With its preference for synchronicity and for situating events in global space, it effectively challenges assumptions of long-term continuity. Slices of time will be a more appropriate temporal unit for studying many topics than an allegedly inexorable march of globalization.

What integration? What structures?

The global history approach, then, does not simply equate with the history of globalization. It does, however, rest on the notion of global integration as a defining feature. In the next two sections, we will further explore this idea. Let us note at the outset that the concept does not carry an inherent teleology. Deep connections between Asia and Europe in the thirteenth century, for example, evaporated after the fall of the Mongols. The study of integration, of structured transformations on a global scale, does not presuppose a steady and continuous movement from less to more, from scarcity to fullness.

The notion of integration, self-explanatory though it may appear, becomes more complicated the moment we take a closer look. Its basic premise is that no society can be fully understood in isolation. Social change does not happen in any one place alone, but depends on exchange between groups. When we speak of integration, we assume that such contacts are more than ornamental, that they impact societies in important ways. We also expect that interactions are not ephemeral and accidental, but recurrent and thus able to shape trajectories in a sustained and sometimes patterned way. Methodologically, the concept of integration shares many features with the sociological notion of structure. When applied to relations between societies, other terms have been introduced, most prominently the concept of system. Some historians have resorted to less rigid terminology, preferring to speak of "circulation," understood as repetition in movement.[19]

Sophisticated as the literature on the subject may be, the concept of integration remains vague and elusive in many ways. Just what counts as "important," as "sustained," and as "patterned" is open to scrutiny in each case, as are the boundaries of the integrated whole. Like the difference between trees and a forest, the difference between a connected and an integrated world may be intuitively plausible, but it certainly requires interpretation. Even if difficult to define, however, any global history study depends on some background understanding of the degree, scope, and quality of large-scale integration. Such an understanding can help us differentiate, for example, between different forms of mobility and interaction. After all, it does make a difference whether a shipwrecked Robinson Crusoe is washed ashore on an isolated island or a steady stream of tourists flown to the island of Bali by modern aircraft as part of a global consumer economy.

Social structures, to be sure, are not autonomous entities. They are neither stable nor given. In fact, they are produced and reproduced through individual practices, and thus through human activity. They should not be treated as abstract entities with which we are merely confronted, for they are products of agency, of everyday practices, of constant transformations and modifications. This also means that there is no inbuilt opposition between connections and structure. On the contrary, as structures are themselves the product of interactions and exchange, they rely on connectivity. When addressing such issues, a set of questions immediately presents itself. How have historians dealt with the question of integration? What forces have they focused on to account for cohesion and the possibility of cross-border exchange? How can we explain the forms of systemic interconnectedness that, it seems, have put a stop to any possibility of isolated development? Where do historians locate the power that creates global structures and dictates its logic?

It is striking to observe that, frequently, historians privilege one driving force over all the rest. Sometimes, discussions are a bit muddied of course, and different factors are allowed into the mix; but for the purpose of our discussion, we can distinguish five such motors of change that dominate historiography: technology, empire, economy, culture, and biology. Ultimately, we will suggest that integration has multiple causes, multiple manifestations or consequences, and in a sense also multiple chronologies, some longer than others. But let us first look briefly at these five modes of integration that historians so often draw upon.

One of the most powerful narratives explaining the emergence of global cohesion is that of technological change and of the media evolution that has facilitated cross-border communication and interaction. This is the story of the invention of writing, of printing, of electrical long-distance transmittance, and of the Internet. It is also the story of the wheel and of shipbuilding, of the steam engine, and of air travel. Not least, it is the story of the military revolution, of swords and artillery, of machine guns and tanks, and of nuclear weapons. Just as the expansion of ancient empires depended on the invention of spoke-wheeled chariots, it is hard to conceive of the British Empire without the gunboat and the telegraph. The shrinking of the world in the nineteenth century would have been impossible, surely, without steamships and the railway. Essentially, in this reading, the shifts in global integration can be attributed to changes in hardware.[20]

A second paradigm emphasizes political decision-making and military expansion, and focuses on empires as the most powerful entities in human history. Global histories of empire alert us to the remarkable staying power of multiethnic and expansionist states.[21] Throughout the ages, empires organized exchange across great distances and facilitated the movement of people and ideas outside of their original communities. We think of the Romans and the Maurya dynasty, the Mongols, the Spanish, and the British. In the modern period, the interplay of empires coalesced into an imperialist system and fed into the globalization process of the present. Whether hailed as a beneficent model or viewed with skepticism, the forces of imperial expansion have been crucial in linking distant parts of the globe and in bringing about large-scale integration.[22]

Third, economic interactions have, perhaps more often than other candidates, been credited with the role of prime mover. There are two complementary narratives here: of trade and of modes of production. For many centuries, if there was a global arena, it was "the world that trade created."[23] Already in the ancient period, production was partly geared to faraway markets. Shards of Chinese porcelain from the ninth and tenth centuries have been found in the Arab peninsula and in Eastern Africa. From about the thirteenth century onwards, trading regions were linked ever more closely, and most economic historians agree that from the nineteenth century onwards, an integrated world market had emerged. Such market integration led to the convergence of price levels, and to the emergence of a globalized labor market. At the end of the nineteenth century, rural workers from Italy exploited the seasonal differences between Europe and Latin America, spending the European winter as harvester *golondrinas* (migratory birds) in the wheat fields of Argentina. Falling transportation costs, combined with extended commodity chains and the migration of labor to produce an integral system in which changes in one place evoked responses in another. With the outbreak of the American Civil War, cotton production plummeted, triggering the creation of new cotton fields in Togo and Egypt, as well as rising textile prices in Europe and Asia.[24]

While the trade narrative is fairly straightforward and even quantifiable to some extent, the narrative that focuses on modes of production and on capitalism is more complex. Trade networks can accommodate a huge variety of societies, the argument goes, but the capitalist transformation of the economy since the sixteenth century has entailed a transformation of modes of production and of social relations more generally. In this reading, there is a qualitative gap between circulation per se, and circulation under conditions of capitalism. The capitalist incorporation of ever-larger parts of the world—largely achieved over the course of the nineteenth century—did not merely lead to an extension of markets, but fundamentally transformed social relations. The conversion of use value into exchange value made possible the commodification of social interactions, ranging from wage-labor to relationships within the family. The argument here is that change was systemic, but not necessarily homologous. The rise of the automobile industry in Europe and the United States gave jobs to paid contract workers, but it also led to the growth of rubber plantations that operated with indentured and slave labor.[25] In this understanding, global integration became possible only as a result of capitalist penetration and is thus a rather recent phenomenon. Integration, then, is not an issue of scale (the entire planet) and quantity (the amount of trade), but of quality: the commodification of things and social relations creates a systemic coherence, as it enables compatibility and exchangeability across geographical, cultural, and ethnic borders.[26]

Many historians have reacted with skepticism against what they perceive as economic determinism. In its stead, they have championed culture as the core ingredient of the globalizing process. Some have hinted at the great religions that ever since the Axial Age—the period around 500 B.C.E. when major philosophies and religions emerged independently in China, India, the Middle East, and Greece—have powerfully linked different regions of the planet. Others have focused on ideologies and cosmologies. Sanjay Subrahmanyam, for example, has made a case for a "millenarian conjuncture on the Eurasian scale" that united many societies from the Iberian Peninsula to the Ganges plain from the fifteenth through the seventeenth century, across political and religious divides.[27]

There is no shortage of further examples. Beyond the empirical cases, what are the methodological assumptions on which the culture claims are based? Thomas Kuhn's notion of paradigm—understood as a "common body of belief that [. . . can be taken] for granted"—is a contender; another is Michel Foucault's concept of episteme that "at any given moment [. . .] defines the conditions of possibility of all knowledge."[28] Both are essentially internalist approaches, in that they see change—paradigm shifts, epistemic rupture—as generated within the field of culture. Systematic arguments in favor of the impact of cultural factors have also been proposed by sociologists of the world polity school. These neo-institutional theorists claim that the core process of globalization has been, since the nineteenth century, the emergence of a world culture. Notions like freedom, rights, sovereignty, and progress were disseminated globally and have shaped social institutions around the world. More thoroughly than either market exchange or political competition, a set of globally accepted norms has, according to this view, transformed daily life around the planet. Their effects have an enormous range, affecting everything from state institutions like public education to individual dispositions such as individuality. World culture, in this way, was able to bridge traditional cultural differences and create a world of increasing similarities and "isomorphisms."[29]

Finally, some historians have proposed biological and ecological factors as the energizers of global change. Their focus is on environmental events that impacted the human past: the Black Plague that ravaged Asia, Europe, and Africa in the mid-fourteenth century and reduced world population by one-fourth; the diseases carried over the Atlantic by the Spanish that decimated the indigenous population of the Americas; the biological exchange in the wake of Columbus' discoveries that brought wheat and cattle to the Americas, and potatoes and maize to China; the mosquitoes that helped to weaken European empires in Latin America and Africa; the Little Ice Age of the seventeenth century. The list goes on. Most recent are discussions of the Anthropocene, the period since the Industrial Revolution in which the human footprint has begun to change the geology of the planet. Historians taking this perspective see links between different groups as made possible by a continuity of human experience that is partly physiological. The biological unity of the species thus becomes one of the factors that allow us to see the globe as an integrated whole.[30]

Integration by overlapping structures

For heuristic purposes, we have discussed the driving forces of global integration one by one. They stand in for the great variety of possible structures, ranging from those "that shape and constrain the development of world military power to those that shape and constrain the joking practices of a group of Sunday fishing buddies."[31] While some have acquired a global reach, others are much more limited in scope. Structural integration may remain regional and even local. It does not have to be planetary. For many global historians, the infrastructure provided by the British Empire and the trade routes in the early modern Indian Ocean are key to explanations of global change.

We should also avoid seeing integration as a quasi-natural process. It was the work of historical actors. A variety of groups and actors pursued their own globalizing projects—projects that competed with and sometimes contradicted each other, and that differed in density and geographical reach: the network of the Dutch East India Company, Napoleon's empire, the transnational networks of anarchists, Sandford Fleming's creation of world time. Much of what we may perceive as global structures is the result of such projects, of competing strategies to generate and control circulation, and of diverse world-making schemes.

Moreover, structured integration cannot be attributed to a single cause or set of causes. One task of global history as a perspective is precisely to understand the *relationship* of different causalities operating at a large scale. There were times and places when trade relationships played a key role, and there were moments when global coherence was accelerated by technological change. On the whole, it is helpful to understand global integration not as the workings of one factor alone, but as the result of overlapping structures. It is difficult to neatly disentangle economic, political, and cultural dimensions. The convergence of markets, for example, was not a self-governing process, but influenced by cultural preferences and "facilitated" by political interventions: by the Portuguese seizure of Gujarati ships in the Indian Ocean, by British gunboats, and by the forceful opening of port cities in Yokohama and Incheon, Ningbo and Xiamen.

These processes were thus not independent. Nor were they necessarily homologous; they did not all point in the same direction and follow the same chronology. The First World War triggered the erection of economic barriers, but cultural exchange and international organizations thrived in the interwar period. Phases of economic integration could go hand in hand with political dissociation; increasing cultural openness and phases of political and economic exchange were not always synchronous. What we usually refer to as "globalization" was thus the result of a complex web of interrelated and overlapping structures that each followed its own dynamics: an "interdependent master process," Charles Tilly has called it.[32] The way in which these processes intersected differed—the structure-mix, so to say, was not the same everywhere. As a result, the impact of these larger forces was felt very unevenly.[33]

It is important to remind ourselves, finally, that the emphasis on structure does not imply that individuals, and human agency more generally, were no longer crucial. This is an important caveat. The vocabulary of structure, like the rhetoric of globalization, may create the impression of an iron cage, of overpowering macro-developments that leave no room for the individual, for events that reconfigure structures, for the accidental, for serendipity. Some surveys, in particular when they span several centuries or more, may convey the impression of a history driven by anonymous macro-forces: a history without humans, as if the earth was a depopulated megalopolis. But this is worse than misleading, for processes of structured integration depend on individuals and groups, and on their everyday activities, for duration and stability. Structures may provide the conditions under which people act and under which entanglements take place, but they do not entirely determine these actions. The originality and creativity of human actions cannot be predicted by the study contexts alone.

What characterizes global history as an approach is therefore neither functionalist, nor does it need to be macro-sociological in perspective. Causality cannot be derived from macro-processes alone. What is more, forces effective on a macro-level do not necessarily have greater impact than processes of a more local nature. While the Little Ice Age of the seventeenth century had repercussions of global proportions, for example, most events can be better explained without recourse to climate change. What remains important is to explore such problematics and to be open to pursuing questions of causality up to the global level.

When was the global?

Against the backdrop of our discussion of the multilayered character of structured transformations, we are now in a position to better address the final question: When was global history? Or, more precisely: For what periods does it make sense to employ a global history perspective? Are there periods in which it is particularly useful and yields better results than other approaches? Are there other moments when it makes no sense at all? Are there eras in the human past that remain off limits to global history? How far back can the global historian go?

My proposal is as follows. When thinking about the long stretch of human history, a global history approach, as outlined in this book, is not *a priori* off limits. It can in principle be applied in any region and to any period in the past. No historical epoch commands a monopoly on global perspectives. This may seem counterintuitive, given the strong emphasis on global integration in this chapter. And indeed, the plausibility and explanatory power of global approaches will be stronger in periods when connections are deep and interactions intense. This is particularly true from the sixteenth century onward, and with growing urgency since the nineteenth century, when the impact of such integration was felt by many contemporaries around the world.

But as a perspective, a global approach can also be extended further into the past with much benefit. For many forms of long-distance links, we can in fact go rather far back in time. Movements of people are certainly not limited to recent centuries. They have characterized the human condition since prehistoric times. And from antiquity (at the latest), production was not for local consumption only, but was intended for commercial exchange, sometimes over very long distances. Rather early on, there also emerged an awareness of the possible advantages of such links.

Excavating connections and forms of consciousness, some global historians have proclaimed a global Middle Ages, and others have begun to explore what they venture to call "ancient globalizations." When Edward Gibbon, writing in the eighteenth century, remarked in a footnote that the slump in the demand for English fish in 1328 was caused by the expansion of the Mongol Empire, he found it "whimsical enough, that the orders of a Mongol khan, who reigned on the borders of China, should have lowered the price of herrings in the English market."[34] Such astonishment and the rhetoric of whimsicality no longer hold sway. In recent years, historians have unearthed a fascinating array of interactions that did not figure prominently in many older studies, confined as they were to one civilization or society only: the spread of Buddhism throughout Asia; the trade links in the Indian Ocean, from Malacca to East Africa; the Mongol empires that lastingly transformed large parts of Eurasia; diasporic mercantile communities and the routes of caravan trade, such as those across the Sahara; or the journeys of Ibn Battuta in the fourteenth century that ranged from North Africa and Spain all the way to China and made him, in the words of Jawaharlal Nehru, one of the "great travelers of all time."[35] Some of these entanglements left a lasting imprint and markedly changed the societies involved. In the Middle Ages, in antiquity, and before, important patterns of global connectivity were established. The quest for global connections in these early periods has spawned much exciting new work, demonstrating that it is not only possible, but often very productive to extend global perspectives deep into the human past. And for some issues—take long-term studies of climate change—it would be absurd not to do so.[36]

To be sure, in these distant times links and connections were much weaker, and their impact more muted, than, say, in the twentieth century. They were not necessarily ornamental, but in many cases, their impact was limited. Frequently, for example, they affected only the elites in a few port cities rather than whole societies. And some connections were short-lived. Given the strong emphasis of the global approach on questions of integration and global structures, these limitations must be taken into account. It is not helpful to project global concerns indiscriminately into the deep past.[37]

Not all topics, therefore, will lend themselves equally to global perspectives. Let us take the example of Siep Stuurman's recent study of two major ancient historians, Herodotus and

Sima Qian. Writing in the fifth century B.C.E. and around 100 B.C.E., respectively, both interpreted the past from within their cultural ecumene, but both were interested in the societies around them and took what can be called an "anthropological turn" in their efforts to understand the societies around them—and to imagine how these strangers might see them in turn. This is a study of a broad trans-cultural subject, wide-ranging and stimulating; it allows us to find similarities where an older historiography would see only differences—of language, culture, and worldview. But strictly speaking, this is not global history in our sense of the term; on the level of method, it remains a traditional comparison. That in itself is of course not a shortcoming—given the absence or dearth of direct links between Classical Greece and Han China, and given the gap of several centuries between the two historians, a comparison is perhaps the more effective tool. But while the topic is broad and even global, the approach is not. Both cases are treated essentially on their own terms, in internalist fashion.[38]

Suppose we engaged in a comparison of state-building practices in the Roman Empire and Han China, the story might look quite different. Admittedly, there was hardly any direct contact between these two empires that each dominated large parts of the ancient world. When the government sent Gan Ying as an ambassador to Rome in 97 C.E., the envoy turned back at the Black Sea before reaching the city on the Tiber—that was the closest Han China ever came to direct interaction with Rome. Nevertheless, there were external factors that impacted both polities in different but related ways. Commercial exchange along the Silk Road indirectly linked both empires; its rhythms subjected them to related, if not identical, challenges—as for example when wars in the Asian steppe disrupted the flow of trade throughout Central Asia. Conflicts with nomadic people on the fringes of empire affected both as well, for wars in the western regions of China regularly triggered uprisings on Rome's eastern frontier.

A study of state-building techniques in both places would have to take these larger contexts into account. It might still be organized as a comparison, but it could pursue very explicitly a global history agenda. Unlike the earlier example, it would build on some form of structured integration and treat it as an important context, even when nomadic wars and the Silk Road were not the main topics of study. These contexts need not take priority over everything else; indeed, they may be less prominent than other factors. But that is not the point. It is one of the tasks of global historians to gauge the relative impact of different degrees and different forms of integration. But whatever the scope of integration may be, a global history approach also urges us to address the question of causality on this larger, global scale.

CHAPTER 6

Space in global history

———————⊙———————

Since the advent of globalization, historians have begun to challenge the spatial parameters of their discipline. Experiments with alternative geographies are only the most visible manifestations of a more general "spatial turn" that seeks to rehabilitate space as a theoretical category.[1] On a practical level, this tinkering is what has most frequently been associated with global history. The quest for innovative conceptions of space and new spatial frames that break out of compartmental thinking opens up important questions for this discipline. Does global history encompass the entire stretch of the human experience? Is global history necessarily planetary in scope, covering the whole world? What are the appropriate units—the sites, the locations—for global historians?

Such questions, of course, are not at all new. Historians have long discussed the respective merits of different perspectives, of the close-up versus the macroscopic vision. Differences of opinion were particularly pronounced in the challenge that micro-history mounted against structuralist approaches. In many ways, current concerns are heir to these older debates. At the same time, in the field of global history the question of scale poses itself with particular urgency. For one thing, global historians claim to move beyond venerable Eurocentric spatialities, thus putting the issue squarely at the center of the scholarly agenda. And second, the question of where to locate "the global" is not at all trivial. Is the global a distinct sphere of social action and of analysis? Is it a given, or rather produced through social activity and practice?

It is the professed goal of the entire phalanx of transnational, world, and global historians to write "histories for a less national age."[2] The nation-state container that the modern discipline of history has taken for granted must be left behind; and more than that—for the challenge is to break out of all established spatial units, including empires, religions, and civilizations. Here, too, historians need not reinvent the wheel. Historians of empire, trade, migration, and religion, to name but a few, have long preferred links and connections over discrete national narratives. Indeed, some have approached their subjects with an inherently transregional lens. The history of the slave trade is a good example. While the trans-Atlantic middle passage served as the central focus, equally critical were recruitment patterns in Africa, various forms of inner-African slavery, and slave markets in the Indian Ocean. This topic had the potential to open up larger vistas, for it involved a multiplicity of actors from Europe, Africa, the Americas, and the Middle East. The trajectories of trade routes and migration created new social spaces of communication as well, such as the frequent back and forth of former slaves across the "Black Atlantic." Despite this, historians often used a primarily national perspective, treating slavery as part of North American, Cuban, or Brazilian history.

Another field with seemingly built-in globality is environmental history, as pollution and climate change most definitely transcend political and cultural boundaries. For many years, however, the inherent transnationality of the phenomenon did not prevent historians from parceling their materials into national narratives about environmental movements and legislation—not least because the data available was aggregated on a national level. In principle, however, the effects of soil erosion, earthquakes, and tsunamis, as well as the spread of germs and pathogens, diseases and epidemics, and so forth, plainly require perspectives that are open to spaces constituted by the object of study, which do not necessarily converge with national and imperial borders.[3]

Does the escape from national narratives immediately necessitate a leap to the global? This is what many people commonly associate with the new approach. And indeed, the past two decades have seen a flood of publications that paint their subjects on a world-spanning canvas: global histories of the Cold War, of sugar and cotton, of state-building, of the nineteenth century, of humanity itself. These are histories of an omnivorous kind, histories of everything, of planetary totality. Some are magisterial works that are able to substantially and successfully shift the parameters of their topic. They form an important sub-field of global history. But while they have garnered much popular attention, they are not necessarily typical of global history as a scholarly approach. Unlike these works of synthesis, most research projects and most innovative studies, have not opted for a world stage, but have rather sought to locate their objects of study in alternative historical spaces.

There have been many attempts to conceive new spatialities and to explore novel geographies beyond the national, but short of the global. What is regarded as innovative will of course depend on the field and the period—broad European perspectives for example pose much less of a challenge to medieval historians than for historians of the modern period. In what follows, we will discuss in some detail four strategies for rethinking global space: constructing large transnational regions, the paradigm of "following," thinking in networks, and writing micro-histories of the global. Ultimately, this chapter will argue that, as important as the quest for alternative spatial units may be, the real challenge consists in shifting between, and articulating, different scales of analysis, rather than sticking to fixed territories.

Transnational spaces: oceans

One of the most popular strategies for moving beyond the nation-state container has been to work within larger, supranational spaces that mediate between local conditions and large global constellations. In this context, interactive spaces have moved to the foreground, spaces that—like the great oceans—facilitated exchange over an extended period of time, across different political regimes, and even over great distances. These spaces enable us to see how interaction and communication established new forms of stability.

Such perspectives are not new. Large regions designated as "Islamicate Eurasia," the Chinese-dominated world of the "Sinosphere," and, most prominently, the Mediterranean, have long found their biographers. In the wake of Fernand Braudel's classic work, other oceans—such as the Atlantic and the Indian Ocean—have generated a large historiography. The main temporal focus of such regionalist work has been the early modern period, a segment of the past not predominantly framed along national lines. Here, transcending the nation-state was not on the scholarly agenda. But even so, studying large regions and the oceans, posed a significant challenge to conventional geographies, and to the area studies. For much of human history, the great seas did not function as isolating bodies of water, but rather allowed for contacts and interconnections across political and cultural boundaries.[4]

Global historians in recent years have built on these well-established approaches. Research on the Atlantic in particular has become a veritable breeding ground for transnational and global history research.[5] This more recent work has refined the frameworks, and has introduced several modifications that by-pass the limitations of earlier studies. First, the cohesion of such macro-regions, and in particular of maritime history, is no longer viewed as being confined to the early modern period. New research has established the extent to which oceanic spaces continued to be important well into the modern period, as transnational arenas mediating between national and global processes, especially in economic and cultural fields. This temporal extension of oceanic history has helped contest the idea that national frames necessarily took center stage from the nineteenth century onward.[6]

Second, earlier forms of "thinking in large regions" (such as the history of medieval Europe) frequently had a Eurocentric bias. More recent work has complicated that traditional story in several ways. Some scholars have challenged assumptions of internal Euro-American development, complementing the venerable institution of Atlantic history with a focus on the Black and Red Atlantics.[7] Others have looked at the ways in which Europe was shaped by its connections to other parts of the world, via the Silk Road, for example.[8] These works show that European history cannot be understood as having been self-generated, but rather was itself impacted by its many entanglements.[9]

Another technique employed in undermining Eurocentric master narratives developed out of new research on regions where Europe for a long time played only a subordinate role. One prominent field of such research is the history of the Indian Ocean, sometimes referred to as the "cradle of globalization." Long before the European presence in the region, this body of water made possible cultural and economic relationships between Africa, the Arab world, the Indian subcontinent, Southeast Asia, and even China.[10] The Black Sea, the South China Sea, the Pacific, and the Bay of Bengal played similar roles.[11] A further oceanic space that has recently commanded much scholarly attention is the maritime world of East Asia, where a network of relationships spanned the Sea of Japan and the East China Sea. Much of this research, the majority of it published in Asian languages, is first and foremost a contribution to the history of East Asia. But it also provides important stimuli for global historians. For example, recent studies demonstrate that regional circumstances created the conditions under which it became possible for Western powers to expand their reach into East Asia. East Asia was not simply "incorporated" into the European trading world. Its connection to a Western-dominated world economy must be understood against the backdrop of an actively constructed East Asian order that was interlinked via the tributary system and connected via the silver economy to other circuits, extending all the way to the Americas.[12]

Exploring alternative spatialities

Beyond histories of large regions and maritime worlds, global history has also triggered more experimental ways of ordering space. In several fields—among them the histories of commodities, of global organizations, of global health, and of global labor—historians have carved out novel spatial frames for their studies. The most innovative ventures in this direction are not based on fixed territorialities, but instead begin with questions and then follow people, ideas, and processes wherever they lead. In this way, historians have been able to transcend bounded territorialities, to link locations within nations to other, supra-national levels, and to explore overlapping spaces.[13]

Such novel forays have been stimulated by discussions in neighboring fields such as anthropology. In an influential statement, George Marcus has turned "following" into a methodological mantra for doing ethnography in a global age: follow the people, follow the thing, follow the conflict, and so forth.[14] Historians have taken up this suggestion and have embarked on studies that do not have one fixed territorial point of reference, but rather move across regions depending upon the dynamics of the issues at stake. A recent example is Gregory Cushman's global history of guano. This is a book about bird shit. Though it would be more dignified perhaps and not inaccurate to describe it instead as a study of a commodity with high nitrogen concentrations that served as a much sought-after fertilizer and significantly increased agricultural yields in the industrial age. "Discovered" by Alexander von Humboldt in the early 1800s, by mid-century guano exports accounted for more than 60 percent of Peru's state revenues. It was first harvested on islands off the coast of Peru, but the author extends his story to wherever the bird droppings lead him. Instead of focusing on a particular space, he follows the guano: the trade, the people involved, and a set of ideas, along the South American coastline, into the Pacific island world, and on to the agricultural centers of Britain and the United States.[15]

Sometimes the connections studied are more imagined than real. In a stimulating book, Engseng Ho has followed the diaspora of the descendants of the Prophet Muhammad, beginning with its origins in southern Yemen and, over the following five hundred years, crossing the Indian Ocean to South East Asia. In their various destinations, the so-called *Sayyids* integrated into local societies (societies that were themselves impacted by the empires of the Portuguese, Dutch, and British), while at the same time standing out as cosmopolitan elites. What is most noteworthy is that they did not form a discernible community but instead belonged to different states, nations, ethnics, and linguistic groups. Their connection was primarily imagined, through the idea of a shared genealogy that guaranteed their social status. What Engseng Ho describes and reconstructs is in effect a "society of the absent," a virtual world that nevertheless had important real consequences, because *Sayyid* status facilitated travel and settlement.[16]

In other fields, trans-local mobility is situated more firmly within structural and institutional constraints. Global labor history, for example, charts the mobility of different types of workers—including slaves, indentured servants, seasonal employees, and "guest workers" while tying these movements to markets and to imperial infrastructures.[17] The history of commodities traces particular items—most famously sugar (in the classic study by Sidney Mintz), but also cotton, soy, porcelain, and glass—across distant geographies and across time. These are studies of interconnectedness that link sites of production and consumption in different locations and show how these commodities impacted individual households as well as larger groups and social formations.[18] Even more explicitly, historians of commodity chains emphasize the ways in which market exigencies and the initiatives of historical actors overlap, and how institutional conditions shape the trajectories of laborers and goods. This category originated as a subfield of economic history, but it is potentially also open to cultural history perspectives, as it opens up a space in which to examine the motives and worldviews of workers and entrepreneurs, bankers and traders, buyers and consumers. The reconstruction of commodity chains very tangibly underlines the trans-regional flow of labor and goods, and by focusing on specific locations testifies to the structures that make possible, and at the same limit, global exchange.[19]

As these examples illustrate, global history approaches have prompted historians to explore alternative frameworks and to experiment with spatial categories that take account of the interconnectedness of the past. In the best of cases, they are able to capture the regularities of large trans-border processes, while remaining attentive to the local level, as when the focus turns to producers and consumers. Fields like global labor history and the history of commodity chains also demonstrate that there is no inherent contrast between what some commentators have termed processes of territorialization—the regulation of space by empires and nation-states—and deterritorialization, vaguely understood as the dissolution of such stable orders. The idea current in the early 2000s that globalization would lead to the vanishing of borders and to a fluid world of flows and connectivities has proven illusory. As recent work has shown, it is more useful to speak of regimes of territoriality—changing relationships between the nation and the state, between population and infrastructure, between territory and global order. Changes in these regimes result from the dissolution of some ties, while other structures and forms of embeddedness come to the fore. Elements of deterritorialization have always gone hand-in-hand with processes of reterritorialization.[20]

Networks

A particularly popular approach that promises a way out of the methodological fallacies of bounded space has made use of the concept of the "network." Since the 1990s, the term has become an almost ubiquitous buzzword in globalization research in the social sciences, and it has achieved wide currency in historical scholarship as well. A large part of its cachet is due to the widespread impression that the ongoing globalization process is characterized by a fundamental reconfiguration of power and space that in its outlines resembles a network. According to this view, the era of nation-states bent on controlling territories—conceived as contiguous geographical areas—has been replaced by an age of interconnection in which the transfer of commodities, information, and people increasingly takes place between points, or nodes, within networks. "The critical matter is that these different positions do not coincide with countries," writes sociologist Manuel Castells, one of the pioneers of this approach. "They are organized in networks and flows, using the technological infrastructure of the informational economy."[21]

Castells sees the network society as a product of the late twentieth century. In his view, the development of computer-based information technologies, and the Internet in particular, helped to maintain and perpetuate modes of communication and interaction that replaced older forms of community-building.

Castells sees this as the threshold to a new era, one ultimately determined by technology. "This new economy emerged in the last quarter of the twentieth century because the information technology revolution provided the indispensable, material basis for its creation." Social relations and networks have of course been around for a long time, but Castells believes it is only now that it has become possible to organize complexity in a sustainable manner and beyond narrow boundaries.[22]

Even if one is not as unreservedly enthusiastic as Castells about network society as a radically new form of social order, the network concept does offer important points of reference for global historical studies. For example, historians who have traced the historical roots of the world's infrastructural interconnectedness have pointed to parallel ways in which earlier technological advances profoundly changed society. Media revolutions—such as the invention of writing in ancient Sumer and Mesoamerica, or the introduction of moveable type printing in Korea, China, and by Gutenberg—expanded spheres of communication. The laying of submarine communications cables and the telegraphic system in the nineteenth century—the "Victorian Internet"—both contributed to a communications revolution similar in some respects to the changes observed by Castells.[23]

The concept of the network can prove helpful in other ways as well, quite independent of its relevance to infrastructure and technological development. After all, for centuries networks shaped the world's connectivity. Even large empires, such as the Mongol Khanate, were built on the interpersonal bonds between rulers, governors, and vassals. Consider also networks of trading posts—the Portuguese *Estado da India*, for example, which was, for all its economic power, no more than a fragile system of Asian port cities, often isolated from their environs and exposed to constant danger. We must, in fact, imagine large parts of the history of cross-border interactions as a network structure. This applies to commodity flows, where for centuries good relations between suppliers and vendors were crucial; it applies also to the movements of people, as they often took the form of chain migrations; and it applies just as readily to trans-border capital investments that brought bankers into contact with debtors they could trust.

It is no wonder then that the notion of a network has caught on among historians. Whether it be networks of Hadhramaut merchants, Jesuit missionaries, Sufi saints, or anticolonial activists, historians have been quick to appropriate the fashionable term when inquiring into the human webs that shaped past interactions.[24] The large literature on the go-betweens of globalization—the interpreters and translators, the travelers and experts, the brokers and intermediaries—owes part of its effectiveness to the way in which it portrays the world as "networked," and global power as dispersed and discontinuous, rather than as a hermetic totality. The network analogy also serves to link real people to global processes, and to rehabilitate individual agency vis-à-vis larger structures.[25]

While many historians find the notion of the network intuitively useful, its theoretical status is much less clear. Usually, there is little systematic reflection on what actually constitutes a network and distinguishes it from a loose sequence of contacts. How dense need the web of interactions be in order to qualify as a network? What level of consolidation and stability can be observed? What is the frequency and duration of interactions? Which media make it possible for networks to be maintained and perpetuated? The analytical value of the network concept frequently remains indeterminate and vague as well.

Heuristically productive though it may be, the literature on global networks shares some of the shortcomings that attend an un-reflected emphasis on connections and entanglement. Such studies do not always pay sufficient attention to the fact that networks are parts of broader power structures. The remote outpost of an empire still draws its authority from contexts that cannot be satisfactorily characterized as simple network effects: differences in military power, market-induced dependencies, or discursive structures that legitimize and shore up the hegemony. Conversely, networks have a direct impact even on those who are not a part of them; exclusion and marginalization by no means grants immunity from the networks' effects. We must keep in mind that the network is embedded in structural inequalities, lest the impression arise that it operates in a vacuum.

Much the same can be said about the internal workings of a network. At first glance it might seem to consist in those who are "in" as opposed to those who are "out." Membership is assumed to grant access to resources and power, while marginalization is the fate of those who are excluded. There is certainly a grain of truth in this. However, we must bear in mind that hierarchies play a key role *within* networks, too. And the overarching transition that Castells describes, from an age of hierarchies to an age of networks, is not an adequate description of historical change.[26]

It is important, therefore, that the discussion of networks and flows does not create the impression that we are looking at self-generated processes—just as it is not helpful to see connectedness, and globalization more generally, as devoid of agency. Networks, after all, are made. In some cases, state institutions drive their creation—entities hardly considered in network studies. More often, they are created and upheld by the people who operate them. This is explicitly recognized by Bruno Latour, another inspirational figure for network theory. His mantra has it that historians should "just follow the actors."[27] Best known for his controversial suggestion that non-humans such as animals and objects be included in networks, Latour sees networks as operating from the bottom up, constantly reproducing connections whose stability cannot be simply assumed. He holds that, empirically, we can only observe small-scale forms of interaction and for that reason we should focus on their dynamics, and not on large structures. A society, for example, should be understood not as "a place, a thing, a domain or a kind of stuff," but as a "provisional movement of new associations."[28]

Latour's is a useful reminder of the importance of looking closely, and of the dangers of prematurely positing causalities that are abstract and not traceable. "If connections are established between sites," he postulates, "it should be done through more descriptions, not by suddenly taking a free ride through all-terrain entities like Society, Capitalism, Empire, Norms, Individualism, Fields and so on."[29] Both his call for more manageable scales and his attention to concrete links and interactions have been particularly influential in recent global histories of science. In particular, his advice that the historian focus on what he calls "immutable mobiles," that is the standardized forms of measurement and representation—including their corresponding instruments and charts, graphs and texts—has proven heuristically useful. It has facilitated the analysis of how networks are established and held together across space and time. If Latour is perhaps not the best guide for the historian aspiring to write a global account, this is not so much due to how closely his approach comes to that of micro studies. For as the next section will show, going micro can be entirely in keeping with exploring different scales, from the local to the global.[30] Rather, Latour's strong opposition to concepts of structure would make it difficult to reconcile his approach with the notion of integration on which global history ultimately rests.

Micro-histories of the global

Most people intuitively associate global history with macro-perspectives, with planetary narratives of change as seen on the greatest possible scale. Frequently, the debate on the "Great Divergence" and studies of economic globalization are understood as synonymous with global history. And indeed, many works written with a large general audience in mind do span the entire world. But the equation of global history with a macro-historical orientation is misleading. Far more common, and in many cases also more rewarding, are studies that analyze one concrete subject in its spatial and social specificity, and at the same time position it in global contexts. The most fascinating questions are often those that arise at the intersection between global processes and their local manifestations.

The global and the local are thus not necessarily opposites. In *The World and a Very Small Place in Africa,* Donald R. Wright traces the ways in which the tiny Niumi region in present-day Gambia has been integrated into the world economy since the fifteenth century. Wright describes the large and overarching processes that affected the community through the centuries: the spread of Islam, the trans-Saharan slave trade, the arrival of the Portuguese, the European demand for groundnuts from the region beginning in the 1830s, colonization by the British, and independence during the Cold War. At the same time, he follows the currents of local reactions, forms of appropriation, and spaces for agency that made the inhabitants of Niumi into world-historical actors in their own right. In every chapter the book focuses on individual Africans and their responses to major developments, and on how they coped with, managed, and in their own ways influenced change on the global level.[31]

While Wright, owing to his theoretical investment in World Systems Theory, tackles the question of individual agency through his understanding of large structures, other historians have more wholeheartedly embraced an individualized approach. They identify the micro-level with single historical actors whose cross-border itineraries become the stuff of global biographies. In some cases these life stories trace familiar terrain and are based on conventional methodology; in others they are more explicitly linked to a strategy designed to enable the reading of history "from below." An example of the latter strategy is Natalie Zemon Davis's study on Leo Africanus (c. 1486–1554), in which she draws a portrait "of a man with a double vision, sustaining two cultural worlds, sometimes imagining two audiences, and using techniques taken from the Arabic and Islamic repertoire while folding in European elements in his own fashion."[32]

Born al-Hasan ibn Muhammad ibn Ahmad al-Wazzan in Muslim Granada (now Spain), Leo Africanus grew up in Fez in Morocco and travelled all the way across the Sahara to Cairo and Istanbul, before being captured by pirates and presented as a gift to Pope Leo X. He was baptized in Rome in 1520 and rose to become the confidant of a number of scholars and even of the Pope himself. Leo received far greater attention in Rome than his social status would have afforded him in his home country, and he was in the fortunate position of being able to make use of the opportunities afforded by his mobility across cultural boundaries. His was an exceptional case, and his was an unlikely fate for a captive of pirates.

Davis, one of the pioneers of micro-history, presents her protagonist as representative of a transitional period. During his time, the Muslim and Christian worlds came into closer contact with each other, and although the tensions between religious, ethnic, cultural, and national identities that were subsequently to intensify were already quite noticeable, the possibility existed that some level of mutual understanding might be reached. Davis's text is pervaded by a desire for dialogue across cultures, and in this respect it is a typical product of its time—she wrote in reaction to the predictions of a "clash of civilizations" and the return of religious conflicts that were widespread at the beginning of the twenty-first century. And indeed, there is a tendency in many—though not all—global biographies to romanticize individual experiences of border-crossing, and of globalization.[33] Frequently, this is the result of a perspective that sees the world through the eyes of the protagonists and tends to slight larger structures unless the historical actors themselves are cognizant of them.

In the best of cases, however, a focus on individuals or small groups can lead us to fascinating insights into processes of global change and how they frame the space for individual agency. Not least, micro-perspectives are able to reveal the heterogeneity of the past and the stubbornness of historical actors. "Local history can point us to the ways in which local particularities challenge the homogeneity of global narratives and where local practices point to divergence from the path to ever increasing connectedness. The place of the local is to remind us of the local diversity that flourished both because and in spite of the connections that shaped the early modern world."[34]

A good example is a study by Sho Konishi, in which he traces the travels of Lev Mechnikov, a Russian member of the early anarchist movement, to Japan in the immediate wake of the 1868 Meiji Restoration. Ignoring the perspectives prevalent in the Europe of his day, Mechnikov saw Japan not as backward and a potential object of colonization. He was convinced instead of its revolutionary potential, and of the possibilities of a non-Eurocentric, non-Social Darwinist anarchism "from below." His enthusiasm for the mutual aid associations he found in the Japanese countryside was later taken up by other anarchists, such as Kropotkin—with such enthusiasm that when in the early twentieth century aspiring Japanese anarchists borrowed from their Russian mentors, they were confronted with traditions that had originated in their own society in the Tokugawa period.[35]

Generally speaking, a global history agenda and an interest in concrete and individual cases are by no means mutually exclusive. As the catchword of "glocalization" suggests, global processes were experienced in, and constituted by, local constellations. An exclusive focus on macro-perspectives is therefore not sufficient—and neither is a language of specificity and contingency alone. To better understand the "translation," appropriation, and modification of global structures, institutions, and ideas within the frameworks of local idioms and institutional settings—and the way in which these settings were in turn reconfigured as the result of such global connections—are among the most essential and the most fruitful tasks that global historians set for themselves.

The units of global history

Oceans, networks, the local—or the planet in its totality? What are the units of inquiry most appropriate to global history? These questions might well come to mind, but they are in fact the wrong questions. For there is no unit that is by definition better suited to global approaches than another. In the end, the entities studied will vary depending on the questions asked. Some issues—take for example: How did the introduction of the printing press affect sociability in Calcutta's rural hinterland?—require the close-up; others, such as an inquiry into the effects of the transition to agriculture on demographic growth, are best tackled through a macro-perspective. To answer some questions, we need to understand the motives of specific individuals, while other questions can only be answered on an aggregate level.

No unit is inherently superior. Some simply enable us to generalize, while others encourage us to be more specific. This also means that our selectivity—what to include, what to leave out—will depend on the units chosen. Adam McKeown makes this abundantly clear: "Just as the historian of Potosí need not know the history of every mine, church, and individual in the city in order to write a convincing narrative, so the historian of Bolivia need not know the history of every city in Bolivia, and a historian of the world need not know the histories of every nation, empire, and trade diaspora. Similarly, nobody expects a generalization about industrialization in the United States to apply equally to Chicago, Georgia, and the Hopi Indian reservation." No unit is the one and only true unit of inquiry. What is more, different units direct our attention to different processes. Different units, in other words, are not only different windows on the same object, but each window allows us to

see processes that might not have come into view through another window. "The common criticism that grand narratives
get the details wrong is beside the point—they aim at larger
processes and trends."[36]

If different units are thus complementary, we are led to three
further conclusions. First, global perspectives cannot take any
unit for granted as a convenient building block in an increasingly integrated world. Instead, they need to be attentive to
the processes that generated cohesion and propelled particular sites or regions into existence in the first place. This in turn
compels us to be attentive to the constructed character of any
territorial entity. It also implies that the forces that made these
spaces cannot be found entirely within the units themselves.
The conventional conception of territorial units—be they regional, national, or even local—is based on images of self-
sufficiency and autarchy. But the historical emergence of such
spatial entities defies the fiction of autonomy. Forces external
to the spaces in question have been as instrumental for their
formation as were internal factors. The constitution and fixa-
tion of special units must be read as part of the transformation
of territoriality on a global scale.[37]

Second, in the sequence local-national-regional-global, the
national is simply one level among others. In programmatic
statements, the nation-state may be the abhorred specter of
global historians who aim to transcend the juxtaposition of
national narratives as a series of pearls on a string. However,
this does not mean that nations and the nation-state are now
obsolete. Since the nineteenth century, a single global political
system based on nation-states has emerged. Nation-states have
shaped many societies, and in many respects their institutional
reality—the political order, the welfare state, the knowledge
systems, and much more—is still nationally determined. Some

topics may even suffer a distortion when forced into transnational frameworks. For many questions, then, the national will remain one important level of analysis.

Third, if fear of methodological nationalism should not lead us to abandon the nation altogether, neither should it lure us into its twin predicament: methodological globalism. For some topics, and some questions, the global is the appropriate level of analysis; for others, it may be less useful. The Italian port city of Genoa was deeply enmeshed in transnational circuits for centuries; some mountain villages in Switzerland, today only a few hours away, were not. Not every place is entangled in the same way, and it would be wrong to privilege world-spanning processes over more local dynamics in every case. We should not, in other words, take the causal priority of global structures for granted.[38]

Shifting scales

The quest for alternative units and sites, however, has frequently only shifted the problematic of how best to spatialize the global past without resolving it. In many cases, historians have opted for novel geographies, but in the end have tended to then treat these new spaces as given. Take the history of oceans: The focus on maritime encounters posed an important challenge to conventional landlocked notions of national space. But while it cannot be disputed that the critical impulse of this shift was to undermine conventional units, the oceans soon emerged as the new privileged entities, as guarantors of commonality and cohesion. Instead of serving as heuristic spaces, oceans soon jelled into fixed territorial entities in their own right. Historians had simply replaced one space—the nation—with another. In this way, many works in the field remain tied to forms of container-thinking that the new approach had claimed to discard. They presuppose fixed spatial entities instead of exploring them. The geography of a research project—its spatial units—cannot be the point of departure, it needs to be seen as part of the puzzle. This is a fundamental challenge facing the practice of global history, which more often than not "simply respatializes the past, not through a radical reconsideration of the spaces of history, but simply by rearranging existing spaces from a perspective that supposedly transcends them all."[39]

The crucial distinction to be made here is between units and scale. We can study a particular location—such as Potosí—and still relate this unit of analysis to a variety of scales: national, regional, trans-Pacific, global. On every such level, different dimensions of the topic come into view. We can remain in Potosí and ask questions concerning ethnic and class differences, gender relationships, and local cultural expressions; we can also, however, reference the global level and ask big questions, even though we are looking at a small place. This does not mean that we need to study all of the potential different levels at the same time. Just as scientists may opt to study a forest, a tree, or the cells in a tree without claiming a principled priority for any of them, historians will privilege a particular scale depending on the question that they are asking. The issue of scale is certainly not an exclusive preserve of global history; but it is one of the assets of the approach that it very explicitly raises the issue of interlocking scales on the one hand, and of appropriate spatial perspectives on the other, and forces historians to be reflective about their choices.[40]

It is important to recognize that the scales in question are not given. They are instead constituted through social activity and everyday practices. The "local," for example, has emerged as a category of identification, and of analysis, in response to processes of nation-building and of globalization. "What is often referred to as the local," writes social scientist Roland Robertson, "is essentially included within the global."[41] The "global," too, should not be supposed as a given formation, but rather as constituted and instantiated through the activities of social actors.

It is through the interplay of different measures of reality—what Jacques Revel has called "scale shifts" (*jeux d'échelles*)—that different dimensions of the past become visible. History must be understood as a multilayered process, in which the different layers follow, to some extent, each its own respective logic; they cannot be simply conflated, or added up to compose one smooth and coherent whole. Conclusions reached at one level do not simply transfer to the next. Their effects, however, are palpable and have an impact on other levels. In the historical process, different scales of inquiry are mutually constitutive: huge macro-processes impact societies down to the level of the individual, while changes on the ground may in turn affect larger structures.[42]

Overly abstract as this scaling of the past with its overlapping and interrelated levels of human activity and entanglements may seem, it is particularly attractive to global historians. Let us conclude this section with the example of Andrew Zimmerman's *Alabama in Africa*, a book that begins with individual lives but eventually brings larger configurations into view.

Zimmerman's story begins on a rainy November day in the year 1900, when four graduates of the Tuskegee Normal and Industrial Institute in Alabama boarded the "Graf Waldersee" for a voyage that would take them from New York, via Hamburg, to the German colony of Togo. They had been recruited by the German Colonial-Economic Committee (*Kolonial-wirtschaftliches Komitee*) for the explicit mission of teaching "the negroes there how to plant and harvest cotton in a rational and scientific way."[43] Togo had been a German colony since 1884, and after an initial phase of private initiatives and exploitation, reform-minded colonial bureaucrats at around the turn of the century began to aim at more systematic and sustained interventions with the goal of modernizing the colony and turning it into a profitable enterprise. In taking this new, scientific tack, they recognized that the native population would have to play a central role. Schooling, health provisions, and the ubiquitous "education of the negro to work," therefore, were among the reformers' central concerns.

The Germans' interest in the Tuskegee graduates was rooted in the conviction that race relations in the American South might offer a model for Germany's African colonies. German bureaucrats and social scientists were particularly taken with Booker T. Washington, the director of the institute, who had imparted to the institute's African American students his conception of natural hierarchies of race. Washington assumed that there would be a need—after the abolition of slavery— first to "educate" the African Americans in a Christian life, manual labor, and small-scale farming, so that gradually over time they might acquire the status of full citizens. His conservative views on social and racial relations were well aligned with the European imperialist understanding of control and segregation. The Tuskegee graduates thus appeared to be ideal facilitators for a modernization project that would not threaten political and racial order in the colonies. Washington, for his part, supported imperialism, for he regarded Africa as backward and in need of a civilizing mission—and he was convinced that the Germans were particularly well suited for that task. In the end, however, the Togo project—a school to train students to grow cotton for the European market—was a political and economic failure.

This experiment can be analyzed on different levels of social experience. On a micro-level, both the inner workings of the Tuskegee complex in Alabama and of the social make-up of colonial Togo are crucial for an understanding of the fate of the project. For example, without a close analysis of social relations in the territory of the Ewe—the dominant ethnic group in the south of Togo—it would not be possible to understand what caused the conflict between imported and local farming methods, the specific role played in the story by Togolese women who had previously been engaged primarily in agriculture, or the fierce resistance of the population to recruitment, instruction, imposed labor conditions, and social intervention.

Beyond the local, the episode also sheds light on other scales that had impact on this story. Among them was the German Empire, as the supply of raw cotton—around 1900, the German cotton industry was the third-largest in the world—was a primary objective of German colonial policy. A further level was the inter-imperial space, the larger formation of Western colonialism that supplied the hegemonic discourse and overall rationale of colonial intervention, and which was epitomized by a civilizing mission and a rhetoric of "improvement" and development. Third, the Togo experiment was set in what has been called the "Black Atlantic," amidst the ties established by the trans-oceanic mobility of African Americans and debates on Pan-Africanism. On a fourth level, Togo was linked to the expectation of German social scientists that the social order in the American South might provide a model on which to structure ethnically segregated labor relations in agriculture—not only in the colonies, but in the medium term also in the Polish-speaking regions of East Prussia; on this level, Togo was incorporated into a system that exploited agricultural hinterlands under (quasi)colonial conditions. And last but not least, there is one crucial scale of analysis in this example that is explicitly global, connected to the integration of markets and of the world economy. On this level, the Togo project can be understood as an effect of the global restructuring of the production of raw materials after the end of the slave trade, and as part of on-going efforts to replace slave plantations with nominally free—but in reality often not free—labor.

It is clear that much of the dynamic of the case was driven by the overlap of a variety of forces and by the interaction of different scales. Through such an interplay, global historians are able to negotiate various levels of social practice, and to address global interactions without having to treat the whole world as their unit of analysis. The global, in other words, is not a distinct sphere, exterior to national/local cases; it is, rather, a scale that can be referenced even when we look at individual lives and small spaces.

CHAPTER 7

Time in global history

On its surface, global history does not speak the language of time. Its immediate association is instead with space. The privileged vocabulary of global historians—mapping, circulation, flows, networks, deterritorialization—is almost exclusively concerned with a new understanding of the role of space in history. The flip side of this fascination is the challenge it poses to the hegemony of time, a hegemony that was long characteristic within historical narratives. All variants of modernization theory, for example, assumed time as their central category. A whole rhetorical arsenal of temporal terms—revolution and progress, advanced and backward nations, stagnation and catching up, the *longue durée*, and the synchronicity, of the non-synchronous—was mustered to locate people, societies, and civilizations within a larger temporal matrix. History, indeed, was largely chronometry. Global history as an approach poses a fundamental critique to this paradigm. It challenges the privileging of temporal metaphors and the established view of history as genealogy and (internal) development.

This does not mean, however, that the issue of time has been entirely sidelined so that it is no longer of conceptual importance. Partly as an effect of the prerogative of space in its perspectives, global history has also led to a reconfiguration of time in historical accounts. Two propositions, in particular, merit discussion here. They are situated at opposite ends of the time scale, focusing on the longest and shortest possible extensions of time. At one end of the spectrum, historians have begun to cover all of human history (and even more) in one coherent framework. At the other end, the notion of synchronicity has emerged as a characteristic trope that challenges notions of developmental time.

As a discussion of these extremes on the broad spectrum of temporal scales ultimately illustrates, different time frames are appropriate for different questions and shape the answers they yield. There is thus no inherently superior frame; rather, different temporal scales are complementary. Every study will privilege the particular scale most conducive to addressing the issues at stake. This chapter will argue, however, that most case studies will benefit from considering different time scales together and attending to their respective analytical purchase.

Big and deep history

Global historians have begun not only to move across the planet, but also to expand the temporal frame of their studies. The "telescope rather than the microscope" is their privileged optic.[1] Many works cover huge swaths of time, and their authors seem to have no qualms about traversing an entire millennium, or more. Large time frames are, of course, the stock in trade of any work of synthesis. But the desire to go global seems to have unleashed a special eagerness to cover everything, everywhere, and always. Some historians who propagate radically long-term perspectives have gone so far as to suggest that only huge time frames will reveal the truth about the human past.

"Deep history" and "big history" are the names of the game. Their proponents present them as analogous to the critique of Eurocentrism that is often identified with global history. As Daniel Lord Smail and Andrew Shryock put it, "We can follow the lead of postcolonial theorists who have pursued a similar agenda in the medium of space, though they have done so rarely, if ever, in the medium of time." After "provincializing Europe," then, the call is now to provincialize modernity: to extend the time frame back into the remotest past, and to liberate historical time from the teleology of the modern.[2]

Smail's concept of a "deep history" proposes a study of all of the human past, and further suggests the need to overcome the conceptual barrier between historians, archaeologists, and biologists. As he has perceptively argued, the discipline of history operates with a fundamental boundary that is equated with the invention of writing. There is no convincing reason, however, to differentiate between the deep human past, and societies with script.[3] The field of "big history," made popular by the Australian historian David Christian, goes even further back in time and starts with natural history before the advent of humans, and for that matter before the advent of life on the planet. Beginning with the Big Bang and the formation of the solar system, big history reduces conventional world history almost to the level of a micro-study, and the history of the human species to a few pages. Both deep and big history devote a lot of attention to the millennia occupied by hunting and gathering societies, intimating that they shaped humans in ways still crucial to our understanding of families, religions, and the obsessions of the present day.[4]

These approaches promise to generate new perspectives not otherwise accessible to historians. Just as some issues require the close-up, others can only be tackled within such an extended time frame. A good example is Jared Diamond's *Guns, Germs, and Steel,* one of the most popular works in this emerging field. Among the issues the book pursues is an inquiry into the causes of the European conquest of the American continent. How did it come about that the Spaniards landed in America—and not the Incas in Europe? And how was it possible, in 1532, for a small group of 168 Spaniards to defeat an army of 80,000 Incas and conquer the most powerful state on the American continent? Was it their superior weapons, the swords and guns? The greater courage of Spaniards? Their Catholic faith? Was it Spanish inventiveness or some other cultural factor? Was it indeed any of the stuff that historians usually deal with? Diamond thinks not. For him, the crucial difference was geological. The North-South axis of the American continent slowed the spread of usable plants and animals—a precondition for complex sedentary societies— across the continent's climatic zones. In Eurasia, with its East-West orientation, this process took much less time, an advantage that enabled Eurasian societies to grow more rapidly in size and complexity. And as a side effect of the spread of draft animals, their populations were accustomed to fatal diseases. When the Europeans arrived in America, they brought with them pathogens against which the indigenous population was entirely unprotected; an estimated 95 percent of the continent's population fell victim to newly introduced diseases. Different geological conditions, in other words, allowed societies to develop in the core regions of Eurasia that were better equipped to cross oceans, to withstand diseases, and to subjugate other groups than the natives of the Americas. In

Diamond's reading, the "Collision at Cajamarca"—the first meeting of Pizarro and Atahualpa in the highlands of Peru in November 1532—was decided long before it took place.[5]

As the example above shows, long-term perspectives are able to bring into view important dimensions easily lost sight of in more traditional historical time frames. Students of deep and big history may thus offer insights not afforded by their colleagues with a less galactic vision. This is why some have applauded the new approach so enthusiastically. "This is a great achievement," exclaimed William McNeill upon reading David Christian's book, "analogous to the way in which Isaac Newton in the seventeenth century united the heavens and the Earth under uniform laws of motion."[6] More palpably, Christian has received the support of Bill Gates and his foundation, and together they have initiated the Big History Project dedicated to bring big history into the school curriculum.

Most historians are, however, somewhat reluctant to embrace the call to go big, or deep. Methodologically, two premises of the genre are essentially at odds with the usual historical approach. First, the search for ultimate causes and primal driving forces in history has led many big historians to develop a determinist view of the past. In some ways, this is a direct corollary of the time frame applied. "There are," David Christian asserts, "aspects of human history that cannot be adequately handled using the familiar mantras of agency and contingency."[7] In many big histories, the power of geography and the environment is so absolute as to render human interventions almost meaningless.

This first hazard, the determinist fallacy, is closely tied to a second: the perils of attempting to fuse the natural sciences and the humanities into one overarching paradigm. The debate between nomothetic sciences and their quest for general laws on the one hand, and idiographic sciences such as history on the other, has a long history. Proponents of deep and big history very consciously aim to bridge the divide—but they too often do so in a way that turns the past into a province of the natural sciences. As Jared Diamond openly acknowledges, the "subject matter is history, but the approach is that of science."[8] For Ian Morris, "history is a subset of biology is a subset of chemistry is a subset of physics."[9] The effect of such a fusion is to subordinate history to the same quest for universal laws that characterizes the natural sciences.[10] Given their predilection for laws, it is no wonder that big historians regularly venture inferences about the future—as when Ian Morris confidently declares that "2103 is probably the *latest* point at which the Western age will end."[11] While most global historians have set out to challenge the teleologies that have long stained historical accounts, big history is poised to restore notions of progress and directionality to the historical process.

Scales of time and Zeitschichten

In the end, the difference between big historians and the rest of the discipline boils down to the issue of scale. As in the case of space, the appropriate time frame depends on the issues covered and on the scope of questions asked. Conversely, our understanding of any event or process will vary depending on the temporal order of analysis. In principle, any occurrence can be interpreted within different and multiple time frames. Historians have long known about multi-layered time regimes that overlap in different ways. Fernand Braudel has famously emphasized the plurality of historical times, being himself particularly interested in the extended time frame of the *longue durée* and thus in temporal rhythms so slow that they otherwise do not come into view. More recently, Reinhart Koselleck has introduced the geological metaphor of *Zeitschichten*, layers of time that pile up and interact. They alert us to different levels in the temporal scaffolding, to different sequences of acceleration and duration, and to intervals characterized by their own tempo of change. Needless to say, these different temporalities each require different spatial frameworks; scales of time and scales of space are thus always immediately linked.[12]

In such a scheme, there is room for a variety of time frames, ranging from moments and singular events all the way up to the very longest spans of big history. These scales coexist, and complement each other, even if approach and findings may be different or even incompatible. Their relevance, too, will vary considerably. The very short term—a moment, a day— will not be a rewarding time frame for most issues; neither will the very long term. For most topics—and this includes events long past, such as the invention of writing—the origins of the planet, and the succession of protohumans and their spread across the earth, do not much matter.[13] The majority of issues that historians set out to resolve cannot be sensibly addressed through big history (which looks back several millions of years), or deep history (40,000 years). Even a view that begins with the Anthropocene Epoch (the past 200 years) will be too broad to cover meaningfully what is at stake in many questions. That said, it is very likely that, compared to recent decades, the relevance of larger scales will increase, and that to some extent we will witness a return of the *longue durée*. After decades in which micro-history and cultural history dominated parts of the discipline, recently time frames have once again expanded, due both to the global history agenda and to the huge data sets made available to the discipline by the digital humanities.[14]

Whatever the topic, different layers of time will offer different perspectives. And depending on what we want to explain, and on what scale, these layers may overlap. Take the example of China's rise to economic superpower status in the early twenty-first century. If we looked only at the two most recent decades, since the death of Deng Xiaoping in 1997, we would be less surprised at China's enormous growth rates than at the ability of a Communist Party to manage capitalist change. If we were to extend our time frame back to 1978, when Deng's reform program began, the subsequent rise to national wealth becomes virtually incomprehensible. Post-Maoist China was among the poorest of countries worldwide, run by one of the most authoritarian governments on the planet. Viewed from that time frame, it would seem a highly unlikely setting for a groundswell of entrepreneurial energy. The historian's explanatory focus would necessarily turn to the decisions taken by the political oligarchy.

If we adjust our lenses to take in broad swaths of time, say the past one thousand years, the picture again changes. For a very long time, and well into the eighteenth century, the prosperous regions of China belonged to the economically most productive centers of settlement in the world. Seen from such a vantage point, China's current rise looks less like a new beginning than a homecoming: a structurally determined return to the "normality" of China's power status. The picture would be incomplete, however, if we did not pay attention to the middle-range time frame of the past one hundred and fifty years. Starting in the 1860s, under the pressure of imperialist penetration, the Qing government experimented with strategies of economic modernization, based on state control of private enterprise. This form of embedded capitalism gave birth to an important pattern of path-dependency that persists in China today. And finally, the 1930s—a golden age of unfettered Chinese capitalism in an age of weak state institutions—saw the rise of private capital, which subsequently survived in Hong Kong and among the overseas Chinese, and which continues to have an effect on the Chinese economy.[15]

China's present rise was not predicated on any one of these factors alone. It was not determined in the long run, but it was conditioned by a range of historical circumstances. Each different time frame adds an explanatory dimension not visible otherwise. As with space, such a scaling of the past, or *jeux d'échelles*, is the best methodological tool to accommodate different temporalities.

The global dimension is not intrinsically connected to any one of these time frames. Global perspectives can be integrated on every level, from macro-accounts spanning several centuries and more, to the analyses of the short-term and even of crucial moments. The general public most often associates global history with long-term studies, with the portrayal of whole centuries if not millennia of the planet's past. Methodologically more challenging, however, and therefore deserving our attention, are approaches with a temporal framework of much shorter duration: that focus on particular moments and short-term events, and indeed on situations of synchronicity.

Synchronicity

The concern with synchronicity, with the contemporaneous even if geographically distant, has become a hallmark of global approaches. Historians pay attention to events across borders and their simultaneous effects, and more generally to the synchronic conditions that empower and limit historical actors. Such a focus contrasts strikingly with the conventional preoccupations of the discipline, for it abandons the traditional quest for long continuities and for the earliest roots of phenomena; and it makes no assumptions about the staying power of traditions, the effects of "remnants" of the past, and the path-dependency of development.

What does a shift from a genealogical to a synchronic model imply? Let us look, by way of example, at the virtual explosion of controversy about the memory of World War II in East Asia after 1990. At that time, throughout the whole region, war memories turned into memory wars, both within countries and internationally. The publication of a Japanese history schoolbook could lead to heated debates among the Japanese public and trigger violent clashes on the streets of Seoul and Beijing. This outbreak of fiercely contested memory is usually described as a "return of the repressed," an almost natural eruption of memorial activity after many decades of suppression and amnesia, a resurgence of a traumatic past that continued to haunt the present. The genealogical model, in other words, put the emphasis on the relationship between the past and the present, on delayed responses to something that happened fifty years ago.

It is much more productive, however, to understand the memory wars in Japan, China, and Korea as an effect of contemporary, and synchronous, transformations: as responses to something that happened in the 1990s, in other words, and not as distant reverberations from1937 or 1945. Such a reading situates the memory boom at the end of the Cold War and within the transformation of the political and economic order of the region that took place at that time. The end of a regime formatted largely on the East-West dichotomy sparked a shift that enabled political groups and civil society initiatives, as well as corporate interests, to focus on East Asia. This regionalization had important repercussions for the field of memory. It shifted the parameters of public debate. Voices of Korean and Chinese victims could now be heard in Japan, and new discursive and political coalitions emerged across borders. Politically, interpretations of the past turned into a favorite arena within which possibilities of Asian exchange and cooperation were negotiated. This was, then, not primarily a return of war memories, but the advent of a new Asian public sphere, conditioned by global geopolitical transformations and new structures of economic exchange.[16]

Paying attention to synchronic factors and to relations in space does not of course mean ignoring the diachronical dimension of history. The question of how to negotiate the impact of synchronous structures on the one hand, and continuity on the other, remains a crucial concern of all explorations in global history. In a key study, Christopher Hill has pushed the discussion further by looking at the specific moment when national history writing and its claims to continuity were established. His *National History and the World of Nations* is ostensibly a comparative analysis of the emergence of the genre of national histories in late nineteenth-century France, Japan, and the United States. But it is not a comparison in the conventional sense, juxtaposing separate countries and societies that seem to exist as timeless entities. In fact, it is precisely the ideology of the nation-state as the independent and self-evident container of history that Hill seeks to challenge. In all three countries, beginning in the 1870s, publicists and state officials began to rethink the history of their nations. And in all three this happened after moments of social upheaval and crisis: the Meiji Restoration in Japan, the Civil War in the United States, and the fall of the Second Empire and the Paris Commune in France. Japan, the U.S., and France occupied very different positions in the world, and their versions of a national past were thus by no means identical. But they partook in the general currents of the late nineteenth century: the development of interstate relations, growing international trade and capital accumulation, and the revolution in communications. As Hill argues, it is precisely within such global structures that the appeal of national history as a genre and of the nation-state as a form needs to be grasped. In this positioning, Hill's analysis differs markedly from other accounts that either emphasize a history of diffusion or of imperialist suppression, or that find a nation's roots primarily in indigenous and parallel traditions of community.

Hill is himself by no means oblivious to the diachronic dimensions of his study. He charts the political and social changes that prompted the formulation of very specific ideas about each nation. A focus on simultaneity alone would have been misleading. But continuity alone—and this is where most historians have tended to place their bets—would have been equally problematic. Such fictions of national diachrony, for Hill, are an ideological inversion of the real mechanisms at play. Instead, he argues, the "national-historical space" of modern nations was constructed within a developing modern world-system of nations—and their prehistories can appear as genealogy only in retrospect. "The synchronic conditions that create consciousness and value," as Hill phrases it, "are inverted into diachronic narratives of their emergence. As a consequence of the inversion, the structural conditions that constitute nation-states as terms in the world market and the international system of nation-states appear to be the results of nationally bounded historical processes."[17]

A blinkered attention to synchronous constellations has prompted many historians to look at narrow "moments" and slices of time. Popular versions of this approach are studies of a particular year—where all kinds of events are juxtaposed, with no larger argument and without considerations of causality: global histories of 1688, 1800, 1979, for example. "The historian seeking to sketch a world," as one of the practitioners of this approach observes, "tries not to be confined to any style, any set of questions but to follow hunches, to let one thing lead to another. [. . .] He hopes to avoid system, reflecting the unconfinable variety, splendor, and strangeness of the human condition."[18]

For less traditional tastes, and for historians with a stronger analytical bent, the notion of "global moments" has proved more attractive. Landmark events—such as September 11, 2001, the upheavals of 1989 or the protests of 1968, the 1929 Wall Street Crash, the Japanese victory over Russia in 1905, or even the eruption of the Indonesian volcano Krakatoa in 1883 (which historians have called the first-ever global media event)—have been understood as global moments, events that were perceived in quite different and in some cases contradictory ways, but which were nevertheless appropriated and served as reference points globally.

An emblematic and much discussed study in this field, Erez Manela's *The Wilsonian Moment*, may help us to get a clearer idea of the benefits and also the potential costs of such an approach, and of the consequences of a focus on synchronic-ity more generally. Manela's account begins in the spring of 1919, when nationalist uprisings against the imperial order broke out in a number of different places almost simulta-neously and yet seemingly entirely independently of one an-other. On March 1, Korea experienced its largest revolt against the Japanese colonial power that had ruled the country since 1910. In Egypt that same March, people from all sections of the population took to the streets to demonstrate against British rule; the fierce conflicts that ensued became known as the "Revolution of 1919." In India, increasing protests by the nationalist movement provoked a violent response from the British, culminating on April 13 in the Amritsar massa-cre, which claimed the lives of almost four hundred unarmed civilians. And in China, the great uprising of May 4th marked the climax of the New Culture Movement, which had dedi-cated itself to a cultural renewal modeled on Western moder-nity and to a rejection of the imperial order in Asia.[19]

These four events are not only well known, they are also iconic moments in their respective historiographies and key events in national memory cultures. All four cases have al-ready inspired substantial and indeed extensive history writ-ing. If Manela can nevertheless contribute something new to these topics, it is because he approaches the subject matter from a new perspective. His aim is to explain the simultaneity of the events with reference to the broader international con-text, and to relate it to the transformation of the international order that followed the end of the First World War.

Accordingly, the four cases are not simply juxtaposed; Manela goes beyond a classic comparison. He also does not focus on direct relationships between Korea and India, China and Egypt. And his work differs from conventional transfer history approaches as well. Instead, he poses his case studies in relation to a common point of reference, Woodrow Wilson and his proclamation of the right of nations to self-determination. The rapid adoption of Wilson's catchphrase was promoted by a press campaign and a propaganda machine that transformed Wilson into an icon of liberation from the colonial yoke. When it became clear, however, that the Versailles settlement would not meet these high hopes, euphoria turned into deep disappointment, which then became a catalyst for the violent eruption of nationalist protest movements.

While the emphasis on synchronicity is thus revealing, it also has its analytical costs. At issue is the relationship between synchronicity and continuity, between the global moment and its diverse pre-histories. And indeed, in its enthusiasm over Wilson's worldwide impact, the book pays little regard to the long-separate traditions of nationalist movements in all four cases. Clearly, the author recognizes that these movements were not doomed to remain in limbo until Wilson came along and energized them. But the book's subtitle, which identifies the Wilsonian moment with the *International Origins of Anticolonial Nationalism*, suggests too strong a causal relationship.

Attention to the synchronic context is a potential eye-opener. It connects events to others across borders, and it opens the view to entanglements in space. The focus on global contexts can help explain the simultaneity of events that fail to come into view within conventional national frameworks. Moreover, it sensitizes historians to causal factors operating beyond, and across, the society or locality under study. But for a full picture, a deeper historical perspective is also indispensable—even if later conjunctures may shape the way in which such pre-histories become relevant. To steer between the fictions of continuity and the promises of the "moment" and to negotiate genealogy with synchronous contexts are among the most demanding tasks for any global history.

Scales, agency, and responsibility

At the end of this chapter, let us briefly return to the issue of scale. From what has been said, it is apparent that there is not a privileged time frame for every historical question—just as no spatial entity is ideally suited for every topic. Every issue requires its own temporal and spatial order, and this is more than a technical and methodological issue. Opting for a particular scale in global history requires that critical decisions be made about what will count as the primary forces and actors in the narrative. The choice of scale, in other words, always has normative implications.

Consider the case of Nazi Germany. When we zoom in on specific moments and short time frames, personal decisions and individual agency move center stage. A study on the final weeks of the Weimar Republic, or an inquiry into the Wannsee Conference and the decision to murder the European Jews, will emphasize the range of individual options and the many different directions that development might yet take. As soon as the time frame is extended, more anonymous factors will gain analytical weight at the expense of personal accountability. When the decision is to take a very long-term perspective—to include, for example, the role of anti-Semitism in Germany since the nineteenth century or even earlier, or to take account of the authoritarian tendencies some historians have traced back to Luther, what appeared as contingency in the close-up may dissolve into large and seemingly unstoppable processes.[20]

The same is true when we scale spatially. A micro-study of a family, or of a small town, allows us to focus on individuals, on their interests and choices: How did the local school teacher deal with the presence of Jewish children? What were her motives for asking students about their parents? And so forth. Then, if we shift the scale to the national level, other actors come into view, and larger forces begin to dominate as the focus shifts to the party elite, to competition between groups in the bureaucracy, and to the institutional logic that many historians now hold responsible for important, and often fateful, developments. If we continue on to a global context, the relevant issues again are of a different order: the impact of the great depression, the transformation of the international order after the Versailles treaties, the global search for a third way between communism and liberal capitalism, the quest for regional blocs and economic autarchy, and the hegemony of racial discourse. On such an aggregate level, individual agency recedes to the background, and the question of responsibility gives way to an analysis of structural factors and of collective causality. If individuals were found blameworthy (or praiseworthy) in a micro-study, they now may appear as victims of the political elite in a national history and at the mercy of large structural transformations in a global perspective.

This has earned global history the criticism that it ignores individuals and eschews issues of accountability by hiding behind anonymous flows, impersonal structures, and metaphors of circulation. In their effort to explain broader developments and to forge interpretations that bridge historical experiences in different regions, global historians do sometimes opt for analytical categories that tend to exclude human agency. Is global history, then, a history with the people left out? On one level, this depends on the historian's narrative style. There is no reason why global overviews should be any less engaging than national histories. Just as macro-accounts of the history of a nation can be colorful and mindful of the decisive role of individual agency, so can global histories.

However, by locating causality at least partly on a global level, global historians may appear to treat issues of responsibility that arise closer to home as secondary. This is to some extent the effect of a methodological choice characteristic of the global approach, namely of the decision to emphasize synchronous factors in space over long-term genealogies and internal temporal continuity. The motive of an escape from internalist narratives is a laudable one, but what if it comes at the price of slighting agency on the ground? If the Holocaust can be explained partly by synchronous global forces, would this not relativize the guilt of Nazi perpetrators? Such over-contextualization—the privileging of global factors over local actors—might externalize issues of accountability, and of guilt. To go global, then, may impart an air of inevitability to what looks much more haphazard when viewed close up. The greater the scale, the less contingency and individual agency—and all the more so when time frames are huge. "My explanatory scheme", admits big historian Fred Spier, "is about necessity."[21]

To counter this trend, many historians have made it a point to stress the reverse and to replace the vocabulary of necessity with a rhetoric of the accidental. They praise the advantages of going local and insist that historical reality on the ground is much more messy and fragmented than macro-perspectives can show. They question, moreover, the teleological assumptions of existing narratives. A good example of the promotion of "contingency" to highest analytical status is the debate about the rise of the West, which was treated as a given and almost as a natural development by an earlier generation of

historians. This metanarrative is now questioned and relativ-
ized in key texts of the field that stress the idiosyncrasies and
the unforeseeable character of historical development. "There
was no *inherent historical necessity*," insists Janet Abu Lughod
in her musings on the thirteenth century, "that shifted the
system to favor the West rather than the East."[22] Other historians portray the "great divergence" between England and
China since the late eighteenth century and the gap caused by
industrial development as results of good luck, of a "windfall"
and "geographic good luck." Europe, in this reading, was but
a "fortunate freak."[23]

Necessity versus contingency: each scale comes with its
own ideology. A good example of this is the tension that has
marked recent debate about the Anthropocene—the period
since the Industrial Revolution and the advent of mankind as
a geological agent. For the first time in the history of the earth,
one species is able to alter the fundamental conditions of life
on the planet. As a consequence, scientists and like-minded
historians have made a case for taking a very long view. They
make the point that only by placing the Anthropocene within
the much longer natural history of the planet can we realize
the impact of the human species as the central agent of climate
change. Such a paleo-biological perspective is plausible given
the immense time scale of hundreds of thousands of years,
and it is instructive heuristically, pointing to the urgency of
ecological protection. But while a huge time frame has its undeniable advantages, it also produces its own myopias. In this
case, the focus on the species as such makes it impossible to
distinguish between groups and individuals who have caused
environmental damage and those who have not, between people who have benefited from climate change and those who
are its victims. While providing important and indispensable

insights, the category of "species," and of large time frames alone, does not enable us to address questions of responsibility, either historically or in the present. It hides from view the group interests and power relationships that have driven capitalist-industrial change in modern societies and have pushed through a developmentalist agenda over alternative visions of society and alternative conceptions of man's relation to nature. Operating on a large scale runs the risk of glossing over the social tensions within what is presented as undifferentiated "humanity." It may blind us also to the forces—such as capitalism and imperialism—that have impacted the world around us, and which can be addressed critically in a quest for environmental change.[24]

While proponents of big history aim to create a form of history that resembles science even to the point of positing "historical laws" analogous to the laws of chemistry or physics, many historians instead emphasize heterogeneity, contingency, and the fragmentary. But the challenge is not to decide in favor of one or the other, but to balance the multiple scales and their explanatory claims. In addressing different temporal and spatial levels of analysis, we can attempt to go beyond such dichotomies of structure and agency, of necessity and the contingent. In their own ways, both aggregate causality on a macro-level and individual agency on a micro-level are legitimate angles, and both are necessary for a full picture.

In the 1930s, to return to our example, it was highly unlikely that any society in the middle of Europe could have remained immune to the effects of global transformations and to the ensuing allures of fascism. But this was not the end of the story. Notwithstanding heavy pressures exerted by structural transformations, whole societies (such as the Swiss) and individuals within Germany (such as our school teacher, potentially) had it in their power to make dissenting choices. It is therefore important to remember that global structures are as much shaped by human activity as they shape it; they are the result of processes of structuration. As such, they provided the conditions under which people acted, but they did not in the last instance determine what groups and individuals chose to do.[25]

Positionality and centered approaches

What is the location of the world? Where do historians stand when they write its history? Can global historians rise above the parochialism of national perspectives to arrive at some form of disinterested objectivity? Some programmatic statements indeed ascribe to the global approach the promise of achieving such an Archimedean vantage point. They foresee arriving at "a transcultural version of history that may become acceptable all around the globe."[1]

These stands are, however, illusory. Global histories are not written in a vacuum. Historians may cover the history of the whole world, but they do so from a specific location, and they write at a particular time, embedded in their own life-worlds. It is misleading to suggest that simply shifting our attention from national history to world history would remove us from the conflicts of the present. Today, national and institutional contexts remain crucial in shaping both the theoretical interpretations and the narratives of historical development.[2] Most accounts of the history of the world are framed by axiomatic assumptions and are based on value judgments and a hierarchy of meaning. They are thus in some fundamental way locally "centered," even when they purport to speak on behalf of the world or of "humanity." This chapter will explore what such inherent positionality implies for the practice of global history.

Among the various centrisms that shape historical interpretation, Eurocentrism has been dominant over the past two centuries. And as global history is generally associated with the ambition to move beyond a Eurocentric vision of the world, this will be our point of departure. Global history, then, promises to transcend the narrative typical of the older genre of world history, which narrowly focuses on the "rise of the West." But what exactly does that imply? Is it Eurocentric to emphasize Euro-American hegemony in the nineteenth and twentieth centuries? Conversely, is it automatically Sinocentric to underline the sophistication of Song China? Do we need to discard the terminology of the social sciences because it was originally coined in Europe?

At our present conjuncture, the challenge is this: How can we overcome Eurocentrism and take account of the multiple positions from which history can be written, without falling into the trap of nativism and without positing alternative forms of centrism? This chapter will tackle the inherent tension between positionality and centered approaches. On the one hand, it points to the undeniable positionality of any interpretation of the past—unless we want to reduce history to a single narrative, we need to take a multiplicity of perspectives into account. On the other hand, a strong emphasis on particularity and uniqueness can easily yield claims to incommensurability and to the assertion that the cultural resources that underlie different societies are so radically diverse as to render the societies mutually incomprehensible. Indeed, as we will see below, the desire to discard Eurocentrism has in recent years led to a proliferation of centrisms in various parts of the world. We will close the chapter with an appeal for a move beyond a culturalist understanding of positionality.

Eurocentrism

The debate on Eurocentrism is a dispute over basic methodological and epistemological questions in the field. In many instances, we encounter confusion between two dimensions of the problem. On the one hand, there is Eurocentrism as a point of view, a pattern of interpretation. On the other hand, there is the challenge of assessing the dominant role played by Europe in much recent history. The two dimensions are intimately related, but for heuristic purposes, it is helpful to differentiate between them. In what follows, therefore, I will distinguish between Eurocentrism (as a perspective) and the Europe-centeredness of some historical periods.

Eurocentrism (as perspective) comes in various guises and in a host of different incarnations.[3] To facilitate discussion, it is helpful to delineate clearly two main strands of Eurocentric thinking. The first consists of the idea that Europe was the prime originator of historical progress, that Europe essentially propelled the world into modernity (the Europe-as-prime-mover model). The second model, conceptual Eurocentrism, is concerned with the norms, concepts, and narratives that historians use to make sense of the past; these can be Eurocentric even in cases where Europe is not at issue. In what follows, I will proceed in three stages, discussing in turn the Europe-as-prime-mover model and attempts to overcome it; the relationship between Eurocentrism and Europe-centeredness; and conceptual Eurocentrism.

Let us begin with Eurocentric accounts of the history of the world. Robert Marks has summarized the basic assumptions of this manifestation of Eurocentrism as follows: "Eurocentric views of the world see Europe as the only active shaper of world history, its 'fountainhead' if you will. Europe acts, the rest of the world responds. Europe has 'agency'; the rest of the world is passive. Europe makes history; the rest of the world has none until it is brought into contact with Europe. Europe is the center; the rest of the world is its periphery. Europeans alone are capable of initiating change or modernization; the rest of the world is not."[4]

This Europe-as-prime-mover model was characteristic of many older world histories.[5] In recent years, it has been challenged on different counts. At its most basic, this challenge consists in a widespread effort to arrive at more inclusive and more geographically balanced narratives that do not simply move from Greek antiquity to the French Revolution on the assumption that such a narrowly European trajectory represents a full picture of the world's history. An early example of such a quest for geographical fairness is the twelve volumes of Arnold Toynbee's *Study of History* (1934–1961). When criticized that the space allotted to England amounted to only one-sixth of that of given to Egypt, he rebutted: "To give one-sixth as much space to England as to Egypt is fantastic, and nothing but my being an Englishman can account for my having gone to that length. It is fantastic because the proper proportion would be, not one-sixth, but something nearer to one-sixtieth."[6] Similarly, recent global histories have moved toward a more even distribution of coverage, more pages on Africa and Southeast Asia, and generally more inclusive narratives.

A related aim of anti-Eurocentric approaches is to liberate the history of a region from an obsession with demonstrating its links to the West. While older studies equated "global interconnectedness" with relationships with Europe, more recent accounts explore the full array of a region's contacts. Take the case of precolonial South Asia. It was shaped by close networks along the Coromandel and Malabar coasts, in Gujarat, and above all across the Indian Ocean. Economically as well as culturally, through the spread of Buddhism and Sanskrit, it maintained strong ties with other regions; with Africa, the Arab world, and Southeast Asia. To slight these earlier connections and highlight the way in which colonialism allegedly liberated India from stagnation and opened it to the world is to operate with a narrow and Eurocentric conception of "world." Vinay Lal has warned that such Eurocentric accounts will lead to a veritable "evacuation of the 'world' from world history."[7] In a similar vein, the rhetoric of "opening" as applied to places such as China, Korea, and Japan is typically employed to mark the beginnings of their relationships with Euro-America, regardless of the extent of their connections beyond the West.[8]

This critique has led historians to challenge the teleological trajectory of many older world histories. They argue that it is not possible to speak of global Euro-American hegemony much before the early nineteenth century. Europe, and the West, never went it alone. Recent literature has documented the extent to which many achievements counted as European were in fact results of a series of interactions, and of complex flows that coalesced in centers of European and American power but did not necessarily originate there.[9]

This leads us to our second issue: the relationship between Eurocentrism and Europe-centeredness. To do justice to the historical diversity of societies and to explore the multiplicity of connections between them, remains an urgent task for global historians. And a difficult one, for they immediately face the challenge of avoiding the opposite extreme and sweeping the role of power structures under a colorful patchwork of local histories. The goal is to overcome Eurocentrism without in turn marginalizing the historical role of Euro-America. When historians hail "world history [as it] represents a particularly appropriate means of recognizing the contributions of all peoples to the world's common history," then they do not only signal good ecumenical intentions, but also run the danger of ignoring underlying power structures.[10] Any alternative account of global dynamics, in other words, should not hide from view the episodes in which Western Europe and, later, the United States played a dominant role.

There is thus an important difference between emphasizing the Europe-centeredness of a particular phenomenon, and giving a Eurocentric account of it. To say that industrialization happened in England first is not Eurocentric; to assume that it could only have happened only there *is*. To refer to the ways in which many societies around the world began to look to Euro-America for models of schooling in the late nineteenth century simply attests to hierarchies skewed in favor of the West and to the power imbalance of the times. Such an observation would be Eurocentric only if we insinuated that modern institutions could have emerged only in the West and then diffused elsewhere.

To assess the role of Euro-America in the historical record is ultimately an empirical undertaking. Pointing to geopolitical hierarchies and to the dominant role of Euro-America in certain parts of the historical process is not in and of itself Eurocentric. At the same time, it is clear that both dimensions (process and perspective) cannot be disentangled entirely. It was precisely its geopolitical power that underwrote Europe's stories of its own rise and turned Eurocentric narratives into seemingly objective accounts.

Let us, therefore, move to the third aspect that we wish to explore, conceptual Eurocentrism. On this level, Eurocentrism means the projection of a particular set of concepts, values, and chronologies onto the past. Dipesh Chakrabarty has argued that "insofar as the academic discourse of history—that is, 'history' as a discourse produced at the institutional site of the university—is concerned, 'Europe' remains the sovereign, theoretical subject of all histories, including the ones we call 'Indian,' 'Chinese,' 'Kenyan,' and so on. There is a peculiar way in which all these other histories tend to become variations on a master narrative that could be called 'the history of Europe.'"[11]

Ironically, even accounts that try to bracket the historical influence of Europe and to emphasize in its place indigenous dynamics and trajectories, can be Eurocentric in their vocabulary, and in their general logic. For example, recent popular works that see a Chinese fleet under Admiral Zheng He reach California in 1421 and Florence in 1434 stake a claim to Chinese priority, but they identify as stepping-stones to modernity the same events as do traditional Eurocentric accounts—namely, the discovery of the Americas and the Renaissance, both of which they now attribute to China.[12] Among academic works, Andre Gunder Frank's invitation to *ReOrient* already in its title indicates a shift from Eurocentrism to an emphatic Sinocentrism. While Frank reduces the dominance of Europe to a brief interlude, his account is based on the same parameters—markets, trade, and economic growth—that also governed Eurocentric orthodoxy.[13] The result here is a simple reversal, minus any profound challenge to the underlying concepts and historical narratives.

In essence, the reason for this is that the modern disciplines that originated in Europe were soon adopted around the world. Over the course of the nineteenth century, under the pressures of global integration and Western hegemony, the parameters and concepts of European academic fields assumed hegemonic status beyond the societies for which they were originally devised. European history was treated as the model for universal development in places like Argentina and South Africa, India and Vietnam. This view was engrained in the conceptual tools of the modern social sciences and has thus been reiterated and reproduced constantly, and frequently unconsciously. Ostensibly analytical terms such as "nation," "revolution," "society," and "civilization" have transformed a parochial (European) experience into a (universalistic) theory that pre-structures the interpretation of all local pasts. "Only 'Europe'," as Chakrabarty has summarized this logic, "is theoretically [. . .] knowable; all other histories are matters of empirical research that fleshes out a theoretical skeleton which is substantially 'Europe.'"[14] In historiographical practice, the use of European terminology and the underlying philosophy of history developed in and for Europe have resulted in narratives of a long progression from feudal to civil society, from tradition to modernity. The historical differences and particular trajectories exhibited by non-Western societies are typically described in a language of lack and failure, in a rhetoric of "not yet," and treated as deficits.

To be sure, the "Europe" that is implied here was more a product of the imagination than a geographical reality; it was a reified category, charged with hopes and fears and shot through with the asymmetries of geopolitical power. The reality that Europe was never one homogeneous entity, but rather in fact very heterogeneous, did little to affect the attractiveness of the concept. Indeed, the hierarchies of Eurocentrism were applied within Europe as well, as exemplified by the image of a seemingly passive and backward Eastern Europe.[15] While thus excluding parts of Europe, Eurocentrism from the late nineteenth century onward expanded as it came to include the United States. Instead of Eurocentrism, therefore, "Euro-American historicist epistemologies" would be the more precise term.[16]

To liberate global history from the Eurocentric master narrative remains a complex epistemological and methodological challenge. It is also a political concern. The task is greater and more complex than merely reassessing the role of Europe (and the United States) in world history, for formerly European and now "universalized" concepts have a long history in many parts of the world; and narratives of modernization along Western lines are firmly entrenched in many institutional settings.

In the quest to leave behind Eurocentric perspectives, historians have pursued two main avenues. One is to stress the positionality of historical writing and, with this purpose in mind, to advocate for a multiplication of interpretations hailing from different locations. We will discuss positionality in the remainder of this chapter, together with its nemesis, the slide into forms of nativist thinking and alternative versions of centrism. We will take up the second avenue, the concern with concepts and terminology, in the next chapter.

Positionality

As a corrective to Eurocentrism, advocates of global history have emphasized the positionality of historical perspectives. They draw on critiques formulated in the field of postcolonial studies and on calls to move beyond the fiction of a neutral Archimedean point of observation: for such "hubris of the zero point," in the words of Columbian philosopher Santiago Castro Gómez, veils the power relationships that frame knowledge formation. Postcolonial scholars have thus proposed turning Descartes' dictum on its head: "Rather than assuming that thinking comes before being, one assumes instead that it is a racially marked body in a geo-historical marked space that feels the urge or gets the call to speak."[17]

Like every other form of historiography, global history is invariably influenced by the conditions under which it emerges and the specific social context in which it is written. Even if the object of study is the world, that does not mean that uniform interpretations are understood, let alone accepted, everywhere. Just as Serbian and French historians may hold competing views on the outbreak of World War I (and they do), so too do representations of world history sometimes differ in fundamental ways: in the subjects they focus on, in what they omit, and in the interpretation of the events they cover. The significance of individual issues (say, for instance, slavery), changes fundamentally depending on whether we look at them from the perspective of Angola or Nigeria, Brazil or Cuba, France or England. Nor is the notion of what constitutes the relevant "world" by any means the same across societies and nations.

As a result, some of its practitioners have equated global history with a call to multiply the perspectives and to augment the range of interpretations by adding voices to the historiographical chorus: the accents of Chinese, Zulu, and Aboriginal world histories. One of the appeals of global history with its diversity of historical narratives has been its promise to empower people from hitherto neglected locations and to enable them to stake their claims on the past.

To be sure, we should not exaggerate the differences and exoticize alternative perspectives. Historical scholarship is now a transnational phenomenon, with agendas, methodological schools, and interpretative modes rapidly spreading across borders. The transnational conversation of historians has leveled many of the idiosyncrasies that may have characterized an earlier age. What is more, the welcoming embrace extended to each and all—"How would the world's past change if it were written by all its people?"—is itself not entirely unproblematic.[18] Frequently, such calls for inclusiveness may be driven by a desire to make up for the one-sidedness of earlier world histories, or even by an urge to redeem past injustices and human suffering. The result, in the worst cases, may be a merely compensatory history. Moreover, as historians usually speak not for themselves but for larger groups, the question of representativeness needs addressing. And finally, on normative grounds, the consideration of more "indigenous" voices—think of Nazi perpetrators—is not by definition emancipatory.

Nevertheless, the recognition of a multiplicity of views on the world—both of historical actors, and by today's historians—is an important advance. On a practical level, it pushes historians to be aware of, and to include, both the agency and the perceptions of different actors so as not to limit colonial history to the story of the colonizers, missionary encounters to the views of the missionaries, and studies of border conflicts to only one of the two sides. For the field in its entirety, it requires recognition that many competing, and sometimes mutually exclusive, readings of the global past coexist.

History is still a far cry from the natural sciences as it has yet to morph into a global discipline. It remains heavily affected by local, national, and regional constellations. And given the proximity to state institutions and public memory, these local factors will continue to influence the study of the past. Competition between different interpretations may become even more intense in the future. Writing global history has thus remained an intrinsically diverse endeavor. In his instructive case study, Dominic Sachsenmaier has used the example of the United States, China, and Germany to demonstrate that all the transnational aspirations of its practitioners notwithstanding, global history has invariably been tied to national parameters, institutional settings, and cultural/political concerns. These contexts generate historiographies that differ not only normatively, but also conceptually. Even terms as general as "globalization," "modernity," and "history" are invested with different meanings in different locations.[19] The more such cases we include, the more apparent the heterogeneity of the world's perspectives on its past will become. Not all of these versions will carry the same weight or have the same traction and plausibility, but this still means that to some extent, global history "can be written ultimately only as historiography—as an account not just of different conceptualizations of the world, but also of different ways of conceiving the past."[20]

This has led to efforts to recuperate hitherto marginalized points of view, and to grant them historiographical citizenship. As one example among many, let us briefly look at the case of Africa. As elsewhere, the pedigree of such anti-Eurocentric interventions goes back to the nineteenth century. Its early exponents include thinkers like Frederick Douglass and Edward Wilmot Blyden, and later W.E.B. DuBois, whose *The World and Africa: An Inquiry into the Part Which Africa Has Played in World History* (1946) is an early classic.[21] In the decolonization era, laments about the fringe-status of Africa in the world historical arena have increased in vehemence. Historians have asked for affirmative action—more on the role of Africans, more on early African empires, more on the achievements of African civilizations. But their critique has also addressed more theoretical issues, as scholars like Martin Bernal, Valentin Mudimbe, Paul Gilroy, and others have made powerful claims for the inclusion of alternative ways of knowing as a way to substantially challenge the Eurocentrism that they see at the root of Africa's marginalization.[22]

How alternative, however, is "alternative"? Does difference translate into incommensurability? In their quest for "geographical fairness," some historians have embarked on the difficult "task of finding purely African narratives."[23] But against the background of many centuries of intense exchange across the Atlantic and Indian Ocean, one may be justified in doubting that there is anything that could be labeled "purely African". The same, of course, holds true for any claims to purity, be they French, Turkish, Russian, or Columbian. Put more generally, there is frequently only a thin line between the recognition of positionality and the affirmation of cultural incompatibility. To direct our attention to the cultural and social embeddedness of every historian will help us to take account of the standpoint that influences any interpretation of the past. Radically alternative views, however—the Aboriginal, the Native American, or the Chinese approach to history—can easily slide into new forms of centrism that make conversation beyond the boundaries of such native epistemologies difficult if not impossible.

The proliferation of centrisms and the return of civilization

Indeed such centrisms are now on the agenda, and this globally. Beginning in the 1990s in the aftermath of the Cold War, Eurocentrism has witnessed a gradual reversal of fortunes, increasingly coming under attack on its own turf. For a variety of reasons, a multiplicity of centrisms has begun to proliferate and clamor for recognition. These centrisms of the global South—frequently dressed up as liberation from Western dominance—are indications of the symbolic reconfiguration of spatiality triggered by the transformation of the contemporary world order. At the same time, they can be understood as part of the commodification of knowledge in an age of invigorated capitalist integration, in which cultural diversity has emerged as a marketable commodity. Not least, the global shock waves of September 11, 2001 have contributed to the intensified postulation of civilizational essences in various places—in Egypt and India, but also in the United States.

Many of these new centrisms have been couched in the language of civilization. The model of civilizational thinking harks back to a nineteenth-century pedigree, but it has enjoyed a remarkable comeback as a response to the disintegration of the bipolar postwar world order. What looks like a return of older interpretative schemes, in other words, must in fact be seen above all as a response to current experiences of globalization. In some ways, the paradigm of civilization can be understood as a specific variant of popular global history, drawing to some extent on local genealogies, but also on concepts as different as the "clash of civilizations" or the call for "alternative modernities." But in many other ways this approach runs counter to the concept of global history as proposed here. Rather than emphasizing entanglement and interaction, civilization discourse tends to focus on sharpening a sense of boundaries and on cultural specificity.[24]

The range of civilization models is wide; and, for all their structural and narrative similarities, their manifestations vary considerably from place to place. They often are inherently populist, with dynamics fueled by specific local and national conflicts. In the wake of the Cold War, the resurgence of the concept of civilization could be observed almost everywhere. Afrocentricity, for example, popular in the United States and parts of Africa, reverses old Eurocentric approaches to paint a picture of a homogeneous African civilization that is morally and culturally far superior to European civilization.[25] In the Middle East, in Turkey and Egypt for example, claims of an ontological difference for Islamic societies are popular with nationalist elites that seek to free themselves from intellectual dependence on the West. Malaysia is yet another of the many settings where an alternative to the dominant version of world history has arisen—in Malaysia's case in the form of growing popularity of religion-based history. At the International Islamic University Malaysia, the Department of History and Civilization has begun teaching an Islamic world history inspired by the Quran and guided by the idea of revelation, thus challenging the evolutionary metanarrative of a world history based on the notion of progress.[26]

In South Asia, authors such as Ashis Nandy have launched a fundamental critique against some of the tenets of modern history writing. For Nandy, the mode of history writing is itself an instrument of Western hegemony. Even today, he tells us, a large part of the Indian population does not think in categories of historicity. Thinking in the mode of history, Nandy holds, ignores other ways of accessing the past, leaving only one possible future.[27] East Asia was likewise gripped by civilization fever in the 1990s. In Japan, authors like Kawakatsu Heita used the concept to propose an alternative form of world history, which Heita explicitly pitted against narratives that were dominant in the West, such as world-systems theory. For instance, he interpreted the period between 1600 and 1853 when Japan maintained a strict seclusion policy as a phase in which indigenous Japanese culture was able to mature, insulated from Chinese and Western influences. He called for a return to self-sufficiency and the establishment of an "ecological niche" (*sumiwake*) in which the Japanese could live isolated from the globalized world.[28]

While we have seen the rise of cultural fundamentalisms in many societies, Sinocentrism remains to date the most powerful of these alternative centrisms. In part, this is due to China's prominent role on the world stage, and to the economic and, to some extent, political challenges that it has presented the international order. China's prominence has prompted scholars, both in China and beyond, to reimagine historical trajectories in such a way as to accord a privileged role to China, in the present and also in the past.[29] Sinocentrism draws on a perceived cultural core that is pitted against a material West. It is generally linked to Confucianism, which stands for timeless traditions that outlast the changes transforming modern society. The revival of the Confucian legacy was initially driven by academics in the United States, Hong Kong, Taiwan, and Singapore, many of them overseas Chinese, before it was taken up enthusiastically in China in the 1990s. In the political sphere, it is embodied in popular slogans such as "Asian values," an ethic championed by Dr. Mahathir Mohamad and Lee Kuan Yew, former prime ministers of Malaysia and Singapore, respectively.[30]

While the rise of China has propelled Sinocentrism, it has also, ironically, triggered a reinvigorated Eurocentrism. This may come somewhat as a surprise, given the longstanding critique of Western conceptual hegemony that has prevailed in Europe, the United States, and in many other places. But this strongly critical current notwithstanding, the Eurocentric master narrative has in fact experienced renewed popularity in the twenty-first century. Particularly after the events of September 11, 2001, which lent new plausibility to the old buzz phrase of an impending "clash of civilizations," historians have answered the public's hunger for a "Western" identity with narratives of the self-generated development of Europe. Due to its " 'restless' creativity and libertarian spirit," the story goes, "the West has always existed in a state of variance from the rest of the world's cultures."[31] The dynamics of global transformation, consequently, appeared as driven by a diffusion of the achievements of Western societies.[32] In the academy, such blatant Eurocentrism has on the whole remained marginal; in the broader public, and on the fringes of the educational system, it has fared much better.

In the United States, the new Eurocentrism must be situated in the context of the so-called "Culture Wars" that hit the academy in the 1990s, popular reactions against multiculturalism and the polarization of political culture in the wake of 9–11 and the rise of the Tea Party movement.[33] It also has links to the revival of religious fundamentalism and to the attempts to instill a Christian narrative in the broader public. The results are not only narratives of national and civilizational uniqueness, but also accounts of world history deeply imbued with a nativist logic, clear parallels to the Afrocentric and Islamocentric accounts that have emerged contemporaneously. This new Eurocentrism portrays Western history as a process of Christian self-realization that contrasts sharply with non-Christian societies, which it sees as trapped in the fetters of superstition, militancy, and fanaticism.[34] Though frequently written in a triumphant tone, many works in this camp nonetheless convey the feeling of a castle under siege and the fear "that we are living through the end of 500 years of Western ascendancy."[35] In a way, then, this is Eurocentrism reloaded—in substance it tells the same old story, but the tides have turned and it is not the power that it was before. Once the unquestioned bedrock of European hegemony, Eurocentrism in its present guise is just one ethnocentrism among many.

Beyond culture and the centrism debate

In the globalized decades after the Cold War, the simultaneous arrival of civilization-talk in diverse locations is no accident. While many historians are rather skeptical as to the civilization narrative's value, it is in general favorably received by the broader public. Often linked to nationalist and sometimes xenophobic agendas, the concept derives part of its global appeal from the fact that it suggests simple answers to problems raised by the transformation of the global order. It offers a vantage point from which it is possible to articulate criticism of impending global homogenization and to express reservations about global migration and unease over the hegemony of the United States. As a counter-discourse to globalization, the civilization approach postulates autonomous cultural areas, repositories of supposedly pure traditions that will forge unique paths of development specific to each region.

In their broad outlines, different versions of the civilization approach show similarities. They operate with a dichotomous worldview, pitting their respective civilizations against the "West." A typical notion is that of the inherently peaceable nature of one's own civilization, which has now changed as a result of contact with the modern West. Many approaches share a hope for the future vitality of their civilization—whether it be Islamic, African, Chinese, or Guaraní—which will realize its potential if only it can restore indigenous forms of rationality, faith, and social order. While the various forms of centrism emphasize particularity and uniqueness, they wear essentially the same clothes and feed on the same assumptions. This has facilitated exchanges between them, even if these similarities may blur real disagreements over questions of ideology and political influence.[36]

The proliferation of centrisms, facilitated by the changing momentum of the global order, has frequently been the work of what we could call "nativist entrepreneurs." Their calls for an alternative modernity are part of a complex field of struggles. In part these are internal conflicts about possible futures within their own societies; the insistence on indigenous ways of knowing can then serve to discredit rival political and social claims. In part they result from competition with other elites internationally. Visions of alternatives then serve to stake out claims to a modernity that is no longer seen as derivative of Euro-American culture, but as the product of indigenous traditions. Such claims, interestingly, rarely culminate in a critique of the concept of modernity itself. In this respect, the concept of civilization in its current guise differs from some of its historical precursors. During the Second World War, for example, Japanese intellectuals at a famous conference in Tokyo sought strategies to "overcome modernity." We rarely encounter such rhetoric today. Instead, the respective traditions are mobilized as resources for uniquely Chinese, Islamic, Japanese, and Euro-American paths to a capitalist future. In most cases, the concept of civilization serves as a cultural justification for alternative paths toward modernization, not for alternatives to modernity itself.

Their obsession with particularity notwithstanding, the proponents of claims to alternative modernities thus operate in an international arena. This means that their protagonists, the nativist entrepreneurs, respond to exigencies in the global intellectual marketplace—and not just to the call of tradition or to long-past ways of living. Arif Dirlik has asked the poignant question, "Is it possible that those who presently claim 'alternative modernities' are closer to those to whom they are alternatives than they are to their national or civilizational forebears with whom they assume a cultural identity?"[37] It is no accident that many advocates of centrist ideologies have developed their penchant for indigenous epistemologies in diaspora situations. The critique of Eurocentrism and the call for alternative perspectives thus frequently deteriorate into forms of cultural essentialism and identity politics.

This should not however discourage attempts to acknowledge positionality or render critical reflection on the structures of contemporary knowledge production any less urgent. Different perspectives on the world and a decentering of our interpretations of the past remain crucial. The challenge will be to navigate between Eurocentric categories, engrained as they are in the institutional structures of knowledge production, and the non-conversation between indigenous paradigms. The question, in other words, is: How can we best draw the line between positionality and the nativism of the new centrisms?

The most promising responses will be those that do not foreground different perspectives as inherently cultural. Instead, scholars should focus on the confluence of political, economic, institutional, and cultural constellations that have affected and shaped the way in which dominant power relationships impact ways of knowing. Put more simply, competing views are not simply expressions of different cultures; rather, what is now championed as a "culture" has itself been worked over by powerful forces, among them imperialism, capitalist integration, and the Cold War. Any attempt to recover these traditions must start not with allegedly pristine cultural essences, but with a reconstruction of the processes by which older forms of regional belonging and "civilization" have been reworked. Positionality, then, is never the product of culture and/or discourse alone. Instead, it is deeply embedded in the power relationships of the past and present through the agency of institutional factors and the unequal integration of different societies into the structures of the global political economy. One should therefore not regard national differences as givens, or as direct expressions of the incommensurability of cultures.[38]

This is all the more true as a clear differentiation according to national and civilizational positions is in many cases highly problematic. Whom can intellectuals in the globalized academy purport to speak for? Historical scholarship is so internationally interconnected that even explanations and interpretations that insist on their national point of view rarely give expression to fundamental cultural differences unmediated by other factors. Where would we place someone like Dipesh Chakrabarty, born in Bengal, trained in Australia, working with European texts, teaching in Chicago, and lecturing just about everywhere in the world? As a result of translations and conferences, publications in other languages, the international careers of the historians themselves, and their international audience of students and readers, certain positions can often no longer be readily ascribed to a particular location.

Finally, and importantly, writing from a particular cultural context is only one of the reasons why interpretations can differ. Conversations between "Western" and "African," "Russian" and "Chinese" perspectives are important, but we should not organize global history like the Olympic Games. In fact, while nation and culture garner the most attention in our globalized world, a great many other factors are at least as powerful in their impact on historical narratives. Social and political differences, in particular, can heavily influence the view of the past. Opposing political viewpoints often produce contrasting interpretations, both within individual societies and beyond. The call for "history from below" or subaltern studies, promises to yield alternative, previously marginalized readings of historical development. Culture talk and the quest for alternative epistemologies may thus obfuscate internal differences, and might, for example, erroneously assign to a range of conflicting interpretations the label "African."[39]

To counter such cultural essentialism, scholars have proposed alternative paradigms that do not hinge on the premise of cultural alterity. For example, Jean and John Comaroff have claimed that their project of "theory from the South" is not "about theories of people who may be wholly or partially of the south [. . .] it is about the effect of the south *itself* on theory." In other words, alternative positions take into account alternative historical experiences but do not presuppose that scholars have lived through these experiences themselves.

Writing from the global "South," consequently, is not primarily a geographical or ethnic designation, but an epistemological position.[40]

This is all the more important as world and global history—as indeed all academic scholarship—are written primarily by members of the intellectual and urban middle classes, and also most frequently by men. In view of these inequalities and exclusion mechanisms, it would be misleading if not outright ideological to elevate national/civilizational perspectives to the most important distinguishing criterion. Powerful culture discourse suggests that inequalities and competing positions in today's globalized world were primarily attributable to national, perhaps even cultural essences, and thus veils the material and structural factors that govern the political economy of the globe. The idea that culture makes all the difference is itself an effect of contemporary globalization and the commodification of these very differences.

CHAPTER 9

World-making and the concepts of global history

Global history, understood as a distinct approach, refers to a particular perspective, a form of world-making. Neither "world" nor "global" are self-evident, naturally existing categories. They come into view as the result of specific questions and concerns. This is particularly salient in the current conjuncture, in which a rhetoric of globalization has come to pervade the public sphere. In this context, politicians and scholars, artists and social movements have each in their own ways evoked the "global" as a practical and cognitive category. Historians are part of this larger trend as well.

When referencing the "world" as a constitutive frame, historians are not only making descriptive statements, for global history is in part a constructivist endeavor. To some extent it creates its own object. In this, it is much like other approaches, such as social history or gender history, which format past reality according to their particular take on their subject. The more global historians scan the documents for links and exchanges, the more connections they find, and the more they are ready to grant those connections privileged status and causal force: "Global perspectives yield global histories."[1]

To be sure, the dialectics of process and perspective are not unique to global history. It is a concern of all historians, no matter where they work, and regardless of their personal background or regional and period specialization. Historians have long debated the relationship between specificity and generalization, and the use of indigenous (emic) versus analytical terminology. Any account that moves beyond individual cases has to rely on abstractions of some sort.[2] In the field of global history, however, this general problematic presents itself with particular urgency. Given the vast stretches of time and space that some studies cover, the creation of aggregate categories runs the risk of obfuscating historical particularity to a much greater degree. For the sake of a general framework, hugely diverse historical experiences are translated into equivalents. While this may sacrifice plurality, such a disappearance of the "foreign," as it were, is both the price paid for, and the very condition of, a conversation among different if related pasts.

In this chapter, we will explore what it means when we say that historians are engaging in a form of world-making of their own. This is not to say that writing about the history of the globe is *only* an abstraction, an invention, or a construction. Global history as a perspective and the processes of global integration are both interrelated and mutually constitutive; we cannot separate one from the other. While keeping the dialectic of process and perspective in mind, the emphasis in the following sections will be on questions of approach.

Historians and their world-making

As a philosophical concept, world-making looks back to a long pedigree that includes Nietzsche, Heidegger, Gadamer, and Jean-Luc Nancy, but also speech act theory. In his influential *Ways of Worldmaking*, Nelson Goodman introduced a radically constructivist and relativist understanding of the processes through which humans construct their "worlds" symbolically. People continuously create worlds around them that are not simply found, but generated through various meaning-making activities. For Goodman, there is "no such thing as the real world, no unique, ready-made, absolute reality apart from and independent of all versions and visions. Rather, there are many right world-versions, some of them irreconcilable with others; and thus there are many worlds, if any." In other words, local sign-systems are generated and constantly reproduced, and historians can chart the processes through which one such cosmology supersedes—and in some cases annihilates—another. The postcolonial concern with the destruction of local life-worlds in the age of imperialism, and with the "colonization of the imagination," is a prime example of such an interest in the forced replacement of meaning systems.[3]

Such world-making, in Goodman's reading, potentially includes all forms and varieties of the social production of meaning. For our purposes, it is helpful to replace such an all-encompassing agenda with a more specific focus, and to substitute for multiple life-worlds an attention to the emergence of "the world" as a social category. Departing from Goodman, our attention thus focuses on the ways in which historians express their views on connections and exchange, and their visions of the totality (their ecumene, the world, the planet, the universe) of which they feel a part. Seen in this way, "worlds" are plural, and each version reflects the position from which it was conceived. As we saw in chapter 2, such constructions of the world changed over time and differed across space. While reflecting their conditions of emergence, forms of world-making were also active interventions into social reality. More than merely disinterested and detached activities, they corresponded to particular interests and agendas.

Consequently, critics have inquired into the effects of present-day efforts in global history and have questioned its politics. Particularly relevant are forms of postcolonial critique that have drawn attention to the linguistic and narrative mechanisms by means of which the world is posited, and produced, as a coherent, interdependent totality. "In recent discussions of globalization, the adjective 'global' is tacitly assumed to refer to an empirical process that takes place 'out there' in the world," remarks literary scholar Sanjay Krishnan. "In contrast, I argue that the global describes a mode of thematization or a way of bringing the world into view." The language of the global, Krishnan asserts, creates an impression of transparency, of direct access to a process that can be empirically observed. In actuality, however, it is a mode of seeing that brings together very different phenomena in a common discourse, and it thus reduces heterogeneity. "It does not point to the world as such but at the conditions and effects attendant upon institutionally validated modes of making legible within a single frame the diverse terrains and peoples of the world."[4]

The proposition of globality is thus invariably and directly linked to interests, standpoints, and relations of power; it is subject to the hierarchies of knowledge production. From his postcolonial perspective, Krishnan sees global history as an instrument of potent ideologies, a tool for rule and domination. "The global stands as the dominant perspective from which the world was produced for representation and control. As importantly, this perspective set the terms within which subjectivity and history came to be imagined."[5] This is an important and productive critique, given the often careless and un-reflected ways in which the "global" is taken for granted. Reappraising the various strategies of world-making that historians employ can help us to avoid falling into the trap of a simplistic teleology of globalization.

But one need not side with the conspiracy-theory take on global history expressed by those who, like Krishnan, see it as a ruse of the mighty and powerful. Global history is not exclusively a top-down structure; and global perspectives are not instruments of control or of (Western) imperialism.

On the one hand, our global perspectives are not mere abstractions. They derive, at least in part, from the ways in which historical actors themselves saw the world. Historians are not alone in world-making. A multiplicity of actors has preceded them, including socialists and anarchists, feminists and religious minorities, diaspora communities and anticolonial activists. All these groups have constructed their notions of the world, for very different purposes, and not exclusively in the interest of gaining or sustaining power. When historians reconstruct the history of the world, they take such alternative cosmologies into account.

On the other hand, global historians today also operate within a broad spectrum of postulations of the global. For heuristic purposes, we can understand contemporary "globe-making"—with its emphasis on planetary scope, and on globe-spanning systems of circulation—as a particular, twenty-first century version in the long history of world-making. Some of these conceptions of the globe indeed treat the world as flat, and equate globalization with convergence.[6] Others see the

globe as much more rugged terrain, fragmented into civilizations, dissolving into outright anarchy, governed by local frictions and "awkward engagements."[7] Yet others propose radical
alternatives to neoliberal ideas of globalization, such as Antonio Negri and Michael Hardt's concepts of "empire," "multitude," and "commonwealth."[8] We should not, therefore, equate
global perspectives *a priori* with a particular—in Krishnan's
case neoliberal—form of globe-making.[9]

How to make worlds with words

The process of world-making carried out by historians is not
limited to the large and sweeping narratives that indicate the
direction of social development or define the significance of
events within the historical continuum. Beneath the level of
such metanarratives, lies one of the most powerful ways in
which historians construct the world: through the concepts
they use in describing it. Terms such as "trade," "migration,"
"empire," "nation-state," "religion," "demography," and so on, are
not simply references to a non-mediated, extra-linguistic reality. While describing historical processes, they have also become part of our conceptual apparatus, and that apparatus
functions to reduce conceptual and linguistic complexity so as
to make the global past legible. They thus create equivalence
between various forms of social practice, and in doing so to
some extent reconfigure—and in a way iron out the complexities of—historical reality.

To illustrate this point, let us look at two of these concepts
in more detail: migration and empire. Mobility on a mass scale
has profoundly altered the shape of the world. Its deep impact
is not limited to the modern period, but reaches back many

millennia, as far back, in fact, as the spread of early humans across the earth before 15000 B.C.E., a process that helped disseminate languages, genetic information, and material traditions. In the centuries that followed, processes of mass migration frequently spawned changes in technology and modes of cultivation. Gradually, networks of information and technologies of transportation improved, rendering cross-border mobility less hazardous. Particular patterns of travel along routes, such as the Silk Road or the maritime routes connecting the Mediterranean to the South China Sea, persisted for centuries. Mobility across large distances, and on a mass scale, has thus been one of the signature drivers of global interaction throughout the ages.[10]

Migration would, then, seem to be uncontestable as a historical process, something self-evident that historians need only observe. But the term is less transparent than at first appears, for the notion of mobility/migration comes with a lot of historiographical baggage. This is most conspicuous when we consider the case of nomadic people, for their movements are typically not recognized as migration of the kind that interests transnational historians. The exclusion of nomadism from the purview of "migration" suggests that the concept typically applies to sedentary populations living under some form of statehood. Even then, it remains unclear how far one need move in order for the movement to qualify as "mobility." When characterizing forms of displacement as mobility, most historians tacitly assume that some kind of boundary has been crossed. In the modern period, the concept of mobility/migration tends to presuppose the nation-state, thus rendering a short move from Tijuana to San Diego "migration," while the much longer journey to Guadalajara earns no such terminological dignity. Any focus on migration thus implicitly rests on assumptions about the difference between everyday forms of movement that can remain unmarked, and other forms of mobility that involve the crossing of boundaries and state borders and that historians therefore recognize as migration.[11]

In addition, the notion of migration lumps together under one conceptual roof a large variety of forms of mobility. It is an umbrella term that disregards such factors as the multiplicity of motivations that go into such movements and the various experiences that accompany it. Under this rubric fall small peddlers in border areas, as well as long-distance merchants; temporary workers as well as itinerant Sufi saints; slaves deported on the middle passage as well as tourists flocking to spas and beach resorts. The term does not differentiate between conquerors and refugees, between shipowners and those who are confined below deck as indentured laborers.

The notion of migration is thus part of our conceptual toolkit. It is a perspective. It helps to make different historical realities both compatible and translatable. Does this constructive dimension make it less universally applicable? On one level, it does indeed challenge the inherent universality of the concept. It certainly requires historians to reflect carefully on the categories they use, and global historians particularly so. On the other hand, it does not compel us to discard the category altogether. I will return to this issue, but let me indicate already here that this has to do with the dialectic between perspective and process that characterizes the use of modern concepts more generally. The concept of migration was not developed solely by historians; the term as we use it today is the product of a particular historical conjuncture. Born out of the classifying needs of the nation-state and of the modern social sciences, "migration" as we know it is not merely a descriptive term. Rather, it emerged in the modern period as a social science term linked to the overlapping projects of nation-building, imperialism, and labor recruitment. These projects have led to a wide range of strategies—such as the surveillance of borders, the control of unwanted forms of mobility, the legal and ideological creation of migrants as free individuals—that have impacted the flow of people itself. They have, in other words, not only produced the terminology we work with, but in some ways have generated the phenomenon itself. The term "migration" is thus the product of a complex history that has not only shaped how we think about the world, but has also shaped the very social processes themselves.[12]

Before taking up this theoretical issue in more detail, let us move to the second example, empire. Indeed, empire is something like the darling of global historians—not necessarily because they like it, but because it is so ubiquitous. Empires—understood as states that rule over ethnically and/or culturally different groups, often building on a hierarchy that exists between those groups—have had a trans-historical career. They appear early in human history and extend into the present. "Empire," writes John Darwin, "has been the default mode of political organization throughout most of history. Imperial power has usually been the rule of the road."[13]

As empires are political formations that are composite and extend beyond single, ethnically defined units, they epitomize the trans-local aspirations of global historians. The shift to transnational and global perspectives has led many historians to the study of empire, and has prompted them to relativize the role of the nation as the principal container of the past. "Empire was a remarkably durable form of state," write Burbank and Cooper. "By comparison, the nation-state appears as a blip on the historical horizon."[14] The result of such expansive (not to say imperialist) use of the term is a tension inherent in other concepts as well. On the one hand, by translating disparate historical experiences into the omnibus term "empire," one risks bracketing real differences between them; on the other hand, a shared term makes it possible to compare different cases in the first place, and to engage in a conversation about them.

The example of the "Comanche Empire" may illustrate this point. In a thought-provoking and award-winning study, Pekka Hämäläinen has challenged the standard narrative of Native Americans as victims of European expansion by focusing on the polity created by one group in the late eighteenth and early nineteenth centuries. Through extensive raids on the Great Plains and deep into Mexico, the Comanche were for many decades able to control a large territory, subdue and incorporate neighboring tribes, and ward off rivaling imperial claims. Hämäläinen's intentions are both revisionist and political, as most Americans today would find it difficult to believe that indigenous Americans could have created something that merited the designation "empire." This move allows him to discuss the Comanche on a par with the rivaling empire of Spain and the westward expansion of the United States. To be sure, there are huge differences between the Comanche polity and contemporary bureaucratic empires such as the Qing, or the French in Algeria. Hämäläinen speaks of a nomadic or "kinetic empire" to acknowledge the gap, which creates a conceptual space for comparisons with other non-sedentary imperial formations.[15]

Is it helpful to speak of a Comanche empire? Or does it force the Comanche economy, based on bison hunting and on occasional raids, into a conceptual Procrustean bed, and thus distort historical reality? Certainly, it does subsume the Comanche experience under a terminology alien to it. For, as far as we know, the Comanche would not have spoken of their realm as an empire. So why call their captives "slaves" and their winter camps "cities"? Why speak of them as a "superpower" with its own "foreign policy"? Instead of using Western concepts, why not adopt indigenous categories and thus truly globalize our perspectives on the past? Does the attempt to emphasize native agency hinge, "ironically, on downplaying Native epistemology"?[16]

To be sure, the Comanche never lived in isolation. On the contrary, their polity was deeply affected by, and reacted to, competing imperial formations. The adoption of horses as well as firearms was indispensable to Comanche way of life in this period, and the strategies they employed were partly responses to the imperial projects of Spain and the early United States. More generally, the Comanche struggle was part of a larger conjuncture, relying on global trade circuits and culminating in the 1846–48 war for hegemony in North America. Comanche practices can thus be linked to larger processes of globalization in the nineteenth century. Restricting ourselves to native terminology might not capture these broader entanglements.[17] But the question remains: Are the categories of the modern social sciences appropriate and adequate to uncover the heterogeneity of global realities, or should they be complemented with indigenous terminology to give full recognition to the multiple ways of experiencing the past?

Native epistemologies?

In recent years, attempts to move beyond the Eurocentric bias of academic vocabularies have surfaced in many places. They have initiated a broad quest for radical alternatives, as well as for concepts and value judgments originating in the indigenous cultures. A sophisticated example of the search for native categories is found in the early publications of the Subaltern Studies Group, which aimed to write a history of South Asia from the perspective of the oppressed, independent of the discourse of the elites. The goal was recuperating fundamentally different and long-inaccessible interpretations of the world. This archeology of alternative cosmologies and authenticities proved methodologically difficult, however, and was strongly criticized as nostalgic back-projection and essentialism. Influenced by poststructuralist approaches, the studies collective abandoned the project and concentrated instead on analyzing subaltern positions as effects of hegemonic discourses.[18]

More recently, proposals for native categories have proliferated, encouraged by the decision of the World Bank in 1997 to foster research into indigenous knowledge systems. In Latin America, indigenous movements have called for recognition of Aymaran, Mayan, and other epistemologies and alternative ways of knowing.[19] In South Africa, the government adopted a national policy on indigenous knowledge in 2004 in the name of an "African Renaissance."[20] In China, "Chinese studies" (*guoxue*)—harking back to a discipline of the same name, created in the early twentieth century as a response to the rise of the modern social sciences and the proliferation of Western terminology—has had a powerful comeback. Colleges and research centers at prestigious universities dedicated to the discipline have mushroomed, while the educated public has been flooded with books and newspaper supplements, television lectures and summer camps related to the movement. On the surface, this bespeaks nostalgia for prerevolutionary Chinese history and its cultural traditions. Behind a fascination for the exploits of past dynasties, however, lies a more fundamental quest to recover Chinese ways of knowing long sidelined by the Enlightenment sciences.[21]

The attempt to recover older epistemologies and ways of thinking that do not line up neatly with political thought in the West certainly has its merits. It can foster a better understanding of the inner logics of past life-worlds, and it can lead to a new appreciation of their legacies. "Chinese studies" may open up a space in which to think through questions such as: Was Confucianism a form of philosophy or of religion? Are Song period ink paintings adequately labeled as Chinese "art"? The methodology gives promise of a better understanding of China's history obtained by navigating Chinese traditions "on their own terms."[22] In addition, the probing of earlier traditions may serve as a point of departure for a critical engagement with the present, when such resources are mined for perspectives that facilitate a reassessment of specific features of capitalist modernity.[23]

However, the search for alternatives is fraught with problems of its own. There is only a thin line between such critical reappraisals, and sweeping claims about endogenous paradigms and new centrisms. Too often, the unearthing of autochthonous traditions looks more like a symptom of the current global conjuncture—with its demand for cultural diversity as marketable goods—and less like a response to the theoretical challenges facing us. What is disguised as an epistemological position can easily fall prey to agendas linked to national identity and to holistic views of human communities.[24] This runs counter to the ecumenical and dialogic inclinations of global history as a field. Even as we recognize the legitimacy of different life worlds and cosmologies, there are clear advantages in remaining able to speak to one another, and to hold on to the idea of a general compatibility of human experiences.

Beyond discourse alone

It may well be, then, that the concepts of the modern social sciences will not be all that easy to replace. The two obvious alternatives—rejecting them altogether or indulging in a cultural relativism that sees all terminological systems as equally applicable—are neither convincing nor satisfactory. If we decide to forego radical counter-models we do so because we understand that, to put it somewhat simplistically, we cannot turn back the historical clock—even if we might like to do so. This is so because the development of our conceptual language cannot be severed from the dynamics of the historical process.

The concepts of the modern social sciences now have a long global history, and they have deeply affected societies around the world. Our conceptual apparatus, in other words, is not a set of rhetorical devices that can easily be replaced. It has long influenced the way people have engaged with, and cognitively grasped, the world. Not least, it has defined the ways in which traditions and native categories themselves are apprehended and understood. Social science concepts thus may be "inadequate," in Dipesh Chakrabarty's apt formulation, but they are also "indispensable" in helping us come to terms with the dynamics of the modern world.[25]

A good example of this dialectic of process and terminology is the modern concept of religion. In most societies, some form of cultic and ritual practice can be traced back many centuries. The concept we know as "religion," however, surfaced only in the early decades of the nineteenth century. As a separate sphere of social activity, the term presupposes the institution of the state and the recognition of a secular realm to which religion is counterpoised. This invention of "religion" happened in Euro-America first, and the worldwide career of the notion was facilitated by European imperialism. At the same time, local elites and newly emerging middling classes outside of the West embraced the term and used it for their projects to reform social practices at home. As a result, they refashioned cultural traditions—such as Buddhism and Hinduism, but also Islam and Confucianism—into "religions" and created new ones, such as Sikhism and the Baha'i religion.

The term "religion"—as opposed to "superstition" on the one hand, and to philosophy and science on the other— bequeathed to social practices a form of legitimacy and rec- ognition in an age when the lack of a religious tradition was easily interpreted as the absence of a high culture. On the surface, then, the term resembles a particular (i.e., European) perspective that due to European power and hegemony was grafted onto other social realities. To call all of these prac- tices "religion" thus tended to level the differences between them in a way that might tend to mislead. However, the new term—most notably in its incarnation as "world religions"— was more than a descriptive tool; it had the effect of radically changing social practices, and of railroading them into the "re- ligions" of the modern age. Accordingly, many of the practices now qualified as "religions" began to share certain features, such as a centralized bureaucracy and a systematized form of dogma, but also the idea that belief was accessible to individ- uals without the mediation of a professional class of clerics. This process, to be sure, was never complete, and important differences in the meaning of the term "religion" and in the practices associated with it remain to this day.

On the one hand, then, the concept of religion is a tool that historians use to translate between historical cases and to render a range of experiences comparable with one another. Such an operation has its obvious advantages—without it, we would not be able to gauge the similarities and differences between societies, and each religious practice could only be analyzed in isolation. It also has its costs, for it risks leveling difference so as to diminish the richness and fecundity of the past. But on the other hand, the concept cannot simply be written off as a scam that distorts reality in the interest of a homogenizing point of view. The term itself emerged as a response to thorough transformations of the social sphere; and it has not only re-labeled social practices, but has also helped to change them, sometimes radically. The term and what it purports to describe have thus mutually influenced each other. In the modern age, one would be hard pressed to find a community of belief that did not develop in response to the notion of "religion."[26]

If concepts cannot be disentangled from historical processes—where does this leave us? It certainly does not excuse historians from the task of reconstructing the moments in which the modern terms emerged and found acceptance around the world, or from analyzing the power asymmetries that went into their making. Concepts do not owe their global prevalence to an inherent universalism; frequently, their hegemony is brought about by compulsion and repression, and through the displacement of alternatives. As the example of religion has underlined, an attention to the history of concepts, and to their leveling effects, thus remains crucial. Given the heterogeneity of social practices and the diversity of the phenomena associated with them, the attempt to sort them into universal concepts can never be fully successful.[27] We therefore need to be open to conceptual innovation, and to the introduction of new terminology that draws on non-Western historical experiences.

At the same time, we should be wary of calls to jettison the tools of the social sciences and their universalizing claims altogether. There are good reasons to believe that the conceptual arsenal of the modern disciplines will continue to do useful analytical work for us. Such a spirit of reflective, self-critical universalism remains a worthy and achievable goal for at least four reasons.

First, and not least, this is a normative choice. Global history as practiced today rests on the assumption that unifying frameworks and dialogue across societies and cultures is both possible and desirable. Universally applicable terms may have their shortcomings; but on the whole, their ability to facilitate conversation across borders may still outweigh the advantages of a more fragmented vocabulary. A place-specific terminology, after all, would make it difficult to speak of states, family, knowledge, and so forth across borders.

We see such normative considerations at work in many conceptual choices that global historians make. A good example is the widespread use of the term "early modernity" as a period marker. When John F. Richards introduced this formulation in the 1990s, his explicit intention was to make India seem less "exceptional, unique, exotic," and less "detached from world history."[28] Such a gesture, as Dipesh Chakrabarty has reminded us, may be "expressive of our collective preference for treating different histories equally, for not allowing the West to be the center of the world, and so on." It may look like "we have 'equal' histories of the past because we would like histories to be equal," as a result of the multi-cultural and cosmopolitan Zeitgeist of our times.[29]

This is a useful reminder of the value judgments that go into our seemingly abstract terminology—and, particularly, of the egalitarian promises frequently associated with global histories. However, a terminology applied to different cases does not necessarily render pasts equal. Rather, it provides a common frame within which to understand different histories, including their points of deviation. Partaking in early modernity, after all, does not make India and England the same; it only underlines the large worldwide processes of change in which both societies shared. In fact, some of the ways in which both societies differed—their complementary roles in the textile trade, their roles in empire—were precisely the result of the ways in which they interacted. A vocabulary that facilitates the commensurability of different pasts, then, does not automatically imply homogeneity, or equality. In fact, differences may be articulated in very pronounced ways, even as they are expressed in an increasingly similar terminology and through a common conceptual language.

Second, many actors around the world have appropriated the language of the social sciences for their own purposes, and thus "indigenized" it. From the mid-nineteenth century (at the latest) on, Euro-America and the "West" was a central (though never the only) point of orientation referenced in modernizing strategies of cultural and political elites almost worldwide. It is indeed difficult to imagine a position entirely exterior to this discourse and not caught up in its premises and claims. The universalization of these concepts—understood as their increasingly ubiquitous application—has thus been the work of many actors in diverse locations.[30]

Third, the formatting of the world through conceptual language has had a very real and fundamental effect on the social order itself. Concepts are not merely discursive entities that have emanated from various traditions; rather, they emerged as responses to structural conditions—while at the same time representing, and transforming, these structures in particular ways. The introduction of the concept of the nation-state, for example, was not only a discursive and legal imposition. It also changed the way in which societies organized themselves. It is thus no longer possible to simply exchange one set of vocabularies for another, and a simple recovery of lost meanings and the recuperation of vanished alternatives is a futile endeavor.

In any event, fourth, just replacing terminology will ultimately prove insufficient. Frequently, efforts to move beyond Eurocentrism, to generate alternative concepts, and to rehabilitate indigenous forms of knowledge remain limited to a critique on the level of discourse and representation. However, the production of knowledge cannot be separated from the geopolitical conditions that engulf it. After all, modern concepts developed in tandem with larger structural transformations and forms of global integration. These processes have not only left their indelible marks on social science concepts, but have also invested them with authority and power. The universalization of "Europe" arose not only from an admiration of European culture and political systems, but was inseparable from the economic and imperial power balance of the time. "Without the power of capitalism and all the structural innovations that accompanied it in political, social, and cultural organization," writes Arif Dirlik, "Eurocentrism might have been just another ethnocentrism."[31]

There is no doubt that the world-making of historians and the rhetorical power of the terminology they employ produce a form of convergence and, to some extent, render invisible the diversity of past experience. In this, moreover, historians—and the humanities more generally—are not alone. In our present, the sequencing of genetic information, market logic in economics, the colonizing of local meaning through big data and "digital humanities" projects, the language of environmental threats, and so much else, are all engaged in a crowding out of peculiarities and specificities.

But whatever the discipline, and whatever the language employed, the "flattening" of the world that we now ascribe to the operations of discourse cannot be separated from the historical process itself. Increasing integration—whether initiated by Olmec civilizational hegemony in ancient Mexico, Russia's early-modern thrust into Siberia, or the rules and regulations of the International Monetary Fund—has always imposed shared vocabularies and mediated between social practices across different spaces. In the modern era, state building, imperialism, capitalism, and a range of developmental projects, to name only a few enterprises, have formatted—and in a sense "flattened"—social realities more powerfully than historians will ever manage to do.

CHAPTER 10

Global history for whom?

The politics of global history

———— ◦ ————

When history emerged as an academic discipline in the nineteenth century, it developed in close relation to the institutions of the nation-state. Many historians had a national readership in mind. While some deliberately pursued the agenda of creating and shaping the nation, others did so inadvertently, merely by granting the travails and achievements of their own nation center-stage. Most historians wrote in the local language and addressed an audience with whom they had much in common, both politically and culturally. There was a sense that most, in one way or another, were contributing to producing the nation. Similarly, global history, in a very basic sense, is about coming to terms with the global past, and thus about *creating the world* for the purposes of the present. These purposes are manifold, and they may be conflicting and contested. Historians may have in mind a borderless world of liberal capitalism, but their reconstructions of the world may also be linked to the agendas of environmental movements, indigenous communities, and social pressure groups. While historians are engaged in their different forms of world-making, it is important to reflect on the implications of making a world. If the "world" is the subject, who, then, is the "we" that global historians write for? And what are the politics of such an approach?

Global history for whom?

The most common answer to this question is: Global history is an inherently cosmopolitan endeavor. At its core, it is an inclusive project, both geographically and normatively. To begin with, it provides a broad account of humanity's past. At a time when news is no longer confined to one's own society; when tourists roam the planet, and migration links labor markets in different parts of the world; when we eat food grown in faraway locations and buy goods produced elsewhere: in our globalized present, in other words, global history is a contribution to making sense of the world in which we live.

To be a historian in the twenty-first century, then, in some fundamental sense means to be a global historian. Gone are the days when history departments could be content with a focus on one nation alone. "Such narrowness is the equivalent of a chemistry department committing itself to teaching and researching the workings of only one element [. . .] while ignoring all others."[1] What is imperative today is an awareness of different pasts in many regions of the globe, and of the interactions and exchanges between them. Our present invites historians to design their questions and answers within this broader framework, and to engage with other narratives, perspectives, and voices. This has long been the aspiration of broad-minded historians. "The boundaries which states and nations set up in their hostility and egoism have been pierced,"

Friedrich Schiller declared back in 1789. "All reflective men today are joined as citizens of the world."[2]

Herein lies the utopian promise of global history: to turn us into citizens of the world. The plausibility of such a promise is based on the extent to which the planet has been integrated on various levels so that many larger processes can no longer be studied, or understood, in isolation. Global ideologies and political movements, financial and economic crises, and the expansion of web-based communication—it is no longer possible to make sense of these things if a study is strictly confined to one place alone. Many of the problems that societies face today—from environmental and climate issues, working conditions and the functioning of markets, to cultural exchange—require an awareness that we all inhabit the same earth and share its resources.[3] In practice, however, the notion that one is a global citizen has remained only a weak factor in the identities of most people, an idea only tenuously rooted in their life-worlds.

The terms "cosmopolitanism" and "citizen" both look back to a longer European genealogy. However, the debate about cosmopolitanism has now emancipated itself from its exclusive concern with Western philosophy, abstract universal reason, and normative claims to universality. In recent years, scholars have unearthed a multitude of cosmopolitan approaches from a variety of locations beyond the West that defy easy classification as either all-inclusive or narrow, either assimilationist-universal or parochial. Instead, they have explored the many ways in which social groups practiced ways of coming to terms with one another, and very pragmatically engaged in conversations and forms of cooperation, beyond the idealist conceptions of philosophers. Such "cosmopolitan thought zones" have emerged where dissimilar groups sought to solve problems together, thus bridging (cultural and other) divides even when not subscribing to a common universal outlook.[4]

However, cosmopolitan outlooks are not a vision subscribed to by all. Global history as an approach lends itself to a variety of competing and contradicting purposes. Some groups employ world and global history explicitly as a means to highlight and aggrandize their nation. In China, for example, historians have recently revived the memory of the transoceanic voyages of Zheng He and other feats of past trans-regional engagement in order to stimulate Chinese initiative and encourage China's accession to a leadership position in the world. Indeed, the popularity of world history in China is quite clearly connected to the country's status as a global economic and political power. In public discourse, globalization is sometimes seen almost as a political instrument of the Chinese state. Global history is therefore not generally regarded as a methodological alternative, but as a context in which the growth of the nation can be explained and promoted.[5]

The link between global history and more circumscribed identities can be observed elsewhere, too. "World-history-as-context is not in and of itself inconsistent with claims to national or civilizational supremacy, as it may provide an occasion for rendering either nation or civilization into the central moment of world history."[6] This link does not have to be blatantly ideological, either. Strictly speaking, whenever global history is conceived as a context that helps to better explain a nation or civilization, it tends to reproduce the spatialities it purports to challenge. This is true even for accounts that are highly critical of the national past.

The tension between cosmopolitan and national/civilizational perspectives, however, should not be exaggerated. For many historians, the nation has long ceased to be the privileged point of reference, even when they are not thinking about humanity as a whole. Frequently, the imagined community is not the nation, but fragments of it, or transnational groups: the working class, women, Buddhists, environmental movements. But when historians write with such audiences in mind, their readers are often a much narrower constituency: essentially their own colleagues. If we exempt the few popular works of synthesis and focus on the specialist works that use a global perspective, this tendency is even more pronounced. In the institutional framework of academic research, writing global history is part of a professional conversation, and the "we" in question are our fellow historians.

That said, historians today are nevertheless accountable to a larger public, and in most places, this public is now implicated in broader global trends more than ever before. Potential readers, ranging from students to the educated public, experience their quotidian lives as increasingly globalized. For this group, the international middle classes that control high concentrations of financial, but also social and intellectual capital, transnational and global perspectives make a lot of sense. While catering to these markets, historians also feel the need to legitimize their use of public funds and institutional power. This may lead some to emphasize the global dimensions of their work, as it addresses pressing issues on a planetary scale. At the same time, it remains important to demonstrate that studies on other pasts—e.g., U.S. historians who study the trans-Saharan trade or rubber plantations in Malaysia—are not exotic and peripheral, but produce work crucial to an understanding of the place our societies hold in the larger world in which we live.

Global history as the ideology of globalization?

Global and other spatial questions are often also normative questions. Apart from the tension between nationalism and cosmopolitanism, the most pressing concern is to clarify the relationship between global history and globalization. There is no doubt that the broad appeal of global perspectives corresponds with, and is triggered by, the current globalization process. But how exactly are the two related? Or, to put it more provocatively: If national history emerged in collusion with the nation-building project in the nineteenth century, and area studies as a product of the Cold War—is twenty-first century global history not essentially a handmaiden of twenty-first century globalization?

As critics have pointed out, it is clear that global history at times comes close to constructing a genealogy of the current globalization process. The enthusiasm for movement, mobility, and circulation can make the ever-closer integration of the world appear a more or less natural development, so that globalization begins to look like a process taking place behind the backs of and independently of historical actors. Rhetorically, the celebration of different forms of "flows" is not far removed from the invocation of versatility and flexibility in management circles and the market-liberal language of globalization. Anthropologist Karen Ho has argued that "the language of flows, decenteredness, and immateriality" in social science literature has its roots in the elevation of capitalism's self-image to the level of theory.[7] Fernando Coronil sees a legitimizing discourse at work in the notions of "one world" and the peaceful "global village." For him, such "globalcentrism" is but an ideological veil that misrepresents globalization and obscures the fact that it is driven by financial capital.[8] Training in global history or global studies, then, would nurture expertise in all things global and produce students attractive to global corporations.

Paradoxically, the very rejection of Eurocentric narratives can create the impression that there is no alternative to the rise of global capitalism, thus in fact taking Eurocentrism to its extreme. Indeed, in recent decades, historians in various places have argued against a diffusion model, and have instead embarked on a quest for the indigenous origins of capitalism in places such as Egypt, Japan, and China. They have emphasized culturally specific resources and a variety of paths into the modern world, making the case that global modernity has a plurality of roots, which are no longer to be sought only in Europe, but outside the West as well. From such a perspective, Chinese traditions, for instance, become ingredients for a Chinese capitalism. This kind of construction, however, suggests a universality that was home-grown and developed naturally. It is part of what Immanuel Wallerstein once termed "anti-Eurocentric Eurocentrism," for even as it takes an anti-Eurocentric stance, it may cause us to neglect the dominant and oppressive role that imperialism and European capitalism played in the forging of a global world order in the nineteenth century.[9]

Some recent readings of the global process that emphasize cultural diversity thus can easily morph into an ideological prop of globalization. They understand difference above all as cultural, as a conflict between "Western," "Chinese," and "Indian" traditions, while largely ignoring socioeconomic inequalities.

The concept of multiple modernities, for example, is open to appropriation by non-Western elites who are competing with other elites for global influence, but are less inclined to face up to the demands of their own workers for economic inclusion. Such back-projections of indigenous modernities frequently present their nations as homogenous cultural units and ignore the internal controversies that surround issues of modernity within the nation.[10]

This fundamental objection to discourses of globality and globalization cannot be simply dismissed—not even if one is skeptical about the clear-cut dichotomies of labor and capital and the rhetoric of veiling in which they are frequently formulated. Global historians therefore must be attentive to the ways in which their findings can be used, and to the logics that sneak into their own projects inadvertently. They need to be aware of the power structures of which they are part, even when they analyze these same structures. Essentially, this means that one of the crucial tasks of global history is to offer a critical commentary on the ongoing globalization process. Global history can offer a reflexive awareness and problematize the narratives that interested parties employ to legitimize their political agendas, be it the curtailing of the welfare state or the abolition of border controls. There are at least four ways in which this can be done.

First, global history can be used as a methodology that challenges the teleology of globalization rhetoric. By situating events and processes in concrete (global) contexts, the approach offers an important corrective to assumptions of long-term continuity and secular change, and to the metaphysics of globalization frequently encountered in the economic and social science literature.[11] Second, historians can remind us that global structures are always partly the result of global-izing projects, and thus of historical actors pursuing their own interests and agendas. In this way, a global history perspective is an antidote to assumptions of a naturally evolving process.

Third, historians will be in a position to assess both the costs and benefits of global integration. Connections are not in themselves either a good or a bad thing, neither inherently beneficial nor detrimental. Slavery, war, empire, epidemic dis-eases are potential high and exacting costs of connectivity. But at the same time, cross-border interactions make objects and ideas available and create new spaces where individuals and groups can form alliances, demand reforms, and think through the complexities of global reality. Much will depend on how historians assess the globalization process. A variety of actors have associated globalization with expanding worldwide in-equalities, new modes of exploitation and domination, dis-placement, marginalization, and ecological holocaust. Others have praised the process as creating unprecedented forms of prosperity, freedom, emancipation, and democracy. Was the Mongol empire an engine of trans-border commerce, of cul-tural interaction, and of a general widening of horizons—or did it bring destruction and facilitate the spread of the Black Death? To some extent, both are true. Certainly there were ca-sualties and victims who suffered from new forms of exchange, while others benefited and flourished. Conversely, although some have paid a high price for parochialism, there are also benefits to salvaging the local and the unconnected, in not being subsumed under global structures. We may be critical of the specific ways in which markets were made to converge, cultural hegemony was established, and transnational politi-cal institutions formed or were hampered. But on the whole, it will be difficult to argue that connectivity, any more than history itself, bears responsibility for the shortcomings.

Finally, global history as an approach moves us beyond internalist explanations. This point may seem rather technical and inconsequential. However, it makes it possible to question genealogical explanations, which ascribe historical developments—such as rise and decline, prosperity and deprivation, openness and isolation—directly to the inherent qualities of individual persons, societies, and "cultures." Global history thus challenges the ideology that individuals and larger groups are entirely responsible for their own happiness or misery. Given the strong tradition of methodological individualism in the social sciences, this is an important corrective. Global history can shift our attention to the hierarchies of power and the geopolitical structures that conditioned the way in which the world became integrated, with important effects on individuals, groups, and whole societies.

Who writes the world? Hierarchies of knowledge

At the turn of the millennium, Dipesh Chakrabarty alerted his fellow historians to the "inequality of ignorance" as a pervasive structure of global knowledge production. "Third-world historians," as he put it at the time, "feel a need to refer to works in European history; historians of Europe do not feel any need to reciprocate." Historians in India, Kenya, or Argentina can only ignore the works of their prominent Western colleagues at their peril. Conversely, when scholars like Edward Thompson, George Duby, Carlo Ginzburg, and Natalie Davis crafted their studies, they were hardly expected to be conversant with historiographies outside Euro-America.[12] In our globalized present, to what extent has this changed? Has global history as a paradigm enabled a broader range of voices to participate in the scholarly conversation? Where does global history writing actually take place?

We must first admit that well into the twenty-first century, global history remains primarily a domain of the industrialized and economically privileged parts of the world. As a perspective, as an additional dimension, it is beginning to have some influence elsewhere; but it is primarily in the United States and in other Anglophone countries, in parts of Western Europe, and in East Asia that global history has found anything like a permanent home in the university system. Institutional structures are important. The different perspectives on global history do not depend solely on theoretical debates and on discursive traditions; to a large extent they are the outcome of diverging sociologies of knowledge.

The reasons for this unequal development are manifold. In any single country, the appeal of global history depends on a variety of internal conditions. In the United States, for example, the rise of area studies, controversies over curriculum reform, and the demands of a society shaped by immigration all played an important role. As a result, the World History Association was founded in 1982, and the *Journal of World History* began publication in 1990. In Britain, the tradition of imperial history enabled a broader representation of the histories of Asia and Africa than in many other countries. Whatever the domestic specificities, however, it is hard to ignore that the rise of global history as a paradigm occurred primarily in countries that actively participated in, and benefited from, the globalization process. In some places—notably the

United States and China—the resonance of global history is keyed to a broader public awareness of the country's leading role in the world.[13]

Why is global history less prominent elsewhere, and what does its lack of popularity imply? To a large degree, different institutional conditions help explain the lack of enthusiasm in some quarters. One crucial factor is the extent to which academic communities are in touch with Anglophone discussions and affected by them. In many Arab countries, and to some degree also in countries such as France and Italy, contact with English-language debates is often minimal, and publication in the national language remains standard. Traditionally, many historians in Latin America tend to be influenced more by French or Spanish scholarship than by research from Britain or North America—a situation vastly different from that in places such as Denmark and the Netherlands where global history caught on much earlier.

Global history is also less attractive in countries where nation-building ranks high on the public and intellectual agenda. This is the case in many parts of Africa, but also in Eastern Europe in the wake of the Cold War. Under such conditions, funding—when at all available—tends to be allocated primarily to projects relating to the national past.[14] And more generally, of course, the issue of funding is crucial—and not only for global history agendas. In Africa in particular, many universities and academic institutions are in deep crisis, so much so that instruction in history itself may be called into question. Global history can be a particularly expensive undertaking. Journals and research centers, language training, international conferences, and the like can flourish only where foundations and government organizations are willing to promote, and take a risk on, the new approach, and where publishers can count on a return on their investments. Their willingness depends not least on the extent to which societies can benefit politically and economically from the globalization process. As a result, the affluent nations in the West and in East Asia are still overrepresented in this field—and many of the internationally minded historians from other regions now teach at universities in the United States, Great Britain, or Singapore. Moreover, in a world of widely accessible online instruction (Moocs), the hierarchies created by Google Scholar, and the Shanghai Ranking of universities, there are massive incentives for an internationalization and globalization of research. The global political economy of the academy is a crucial factor in understanding the dynamics of agenda setting and the uneven landscape of knowledge production.

The institutional geography of global history is thus highly uneven. This does not mean, however, that we do not find trans-border perspectives elsewhere. While the history of one's own nation does remain the privileged form almost everywhere, the relevance of transnational research agendas has increased markedly in many countries since the 1990s, and the demand for alternative narratives and spatial visions has also grown. Usually the aim is not to abandon national history entirely, but to "transnationalize" it.[15] The absence of an explicitly global approach should not, therefore, be equated with parochialism.

In this context, transnational perspectives—studies of oceans and regional spaces, such as the Indian Ocean, the South Atlantic, East Asia, etc.—have played a crucial role for many historians outside the West. Working with such geographies may challenge the priority of the nation-state; and it can also be understood politically, as a response to the globalization process. It then often serves as a point of departure for an alternative narrative that transcends the gradual incorporation of the "rest" into the Euro-American world system. This is why some historians pay particular attention to entanglements outside the West—to contacts between Angola and Brazil, migration from Korea to Manchuria, Islamic networks from Indonesia to Mauretania. This is also the reason why the focus of such studies is often on the time before the nineteenth century, before the ascendancy of Western imperial hegemony.

While a transnational historiography is thus well established, outside the Anglophone literature, the term "global" appears much less frequently; in some countries, historians explicitly avoid using it. This reluctance is linked to a general skepticism about an approach that, for all the anti-Eurocentric rhetoric, is perceived by some essentially as an imperialist discourse, as a Western imposition. According to the discipline's critics, global historians speak of interactions and entanglements, but in fact narrowly focus on relations between the West and the "rest." "Indian intellectuals have habituated themselves to the idea of a bi-polar world of India and the West," notes Vinay Lal. "This is the condition of colonized people everywhere. The frame is self-evidently furnished by European colonialism."[16]

In some cases, global history comes up against a historiography that has very consciously liberated itself from the pattern of "indigenous responses to the Western challenge," a pattern that includes studies of, for example, Latin America and the West, Africa and imperialism, India and the Raj, China after the Opium Wars. Instead, the focus shifts to endogenous dynamics, to an inductive history "from below," in which external influences are present as a general context but do not dominate developments. Against the background of such scholarship, the call for global narratives can appear as a regression to interpretations that were thought to have been left behind.

The avoidance of the global, then, cannot always be easily discredited as mere recidivism. Rather, it is linked to conditions of knowledge production both within countries and beyond. To be sure, local concerns and historiographic traditions continue to shape the way the world is appropriated, or excluded, from national narratives. At the same time, "openness" and "resistance" to global frameworks only partly explain the appeal of global approaches. Their varying attractiveness also needs to be understood as an effect of larger geopolitical structures and of the ways in which different countries are implicated in the globalization process.

Geopolitics and language

Objections to the global history paradigm are particularly powerful when they are tied to a critique of the dominance of Anglophone scholarship. The issue of language is indeed crucial. The hegemony of English as an academic idiom is a fact, even if it has not affected the humanities quite as strongly as it has the natural and social sciences. In the field of global history it is particularly marked—so much so that the field is frequently seen as an American-British endeavor. Most global historians today continue to ignore scholarship written in other languages and produced outside the institutional frame of Western universities—particularly those in the United States and Great Britain. As Dominic Sachsenmaier has pointed out, such a marginalization of other historiographical traditions, even where works are available in translation, stands in stark contradiction to the inclusive and post-Eurocentric rhetoric of the global history approach. "Until now, hierarchies of knowledge, which have emerged over the past one or two centuries, obviously remain intact and still channel the range of awareness and academic interest in the world." Sachsenmaier also alerts us to the after-effects that the global hegemony of the English language has produced outside of the West. "For instance, in China scholars in world and global history are usually quite familiar with the recent literature in the West but they are typically oblivious to developments in their field in societies such as India, let alone in Latin America, the Middle East or sub-Saharan Africa." [17]

The hegemony of English has the power to marginalize other languages and historiographical traditions. Of that there can be no doubt. And yet, the emergence of a global *lingua franca* is not only a tool of domination; it also harbors the potential to enable conversations across boundaries to an extent not seen in the multilingual universe of earlier, more Babylonian centuries. Unlike Latin, Persian, Chinese, and other regional idioms, it is no longer confined to a particular ecumene but is accessible globally. In principle, it facilitates access to scholarship hitherto arcane and impenetrable, allows broad participation in debates, and creates resonance for voices previously heard only locally.

The authority vested in English-language scholarship has also allowed historians elsewhere to use it strategically, and to criticize peculiarities and forms of parochialism in different national traditions. For example, historians in Germany, Italy, Korea, and China have explicitly distanced themselves from earlier (national) traditions of writing about the world, and have instead introduced global history by means of translation and methodological borrowing—with the explicit aim of transcending earlier traditions, such as universal and overseas history. Referring to Anglophone debates could thus serve to open up a space for a new intellectual agenda and for liberation from older and more parochial (e.g., Eurocentric) readings of the world's past.[18]

What is more, the hegemony of English in this field will never be absolute. After all, for global historians, proficiency in many languages is a crucial advantage. All technological homogenization notwithstanding, there is an indissoluble linguistic heterogeneity to the past, and this is true even in periods that now appear increasingly global. As Benedict Anderson remarked, nineteenth century Filipinos "wrote to Austrians in German, to Japanese in English, to each other in French, or Spanish, or Tagalog [. . .]. Some of them knew a bit of Russian, Greek, Italian, Japanese, and Chinese. A wire might be sent around the world in minutes, but real communication required the true, hard internationalism of the polyglot."[19] Whatever the future fortunes of global English, the documents of the past are written in Malay and Persian, in Russian and in Telugu. In the long run, the vogue of global history may even disadvantage scholars who are not freely conversant with such languages, who have not left the comfort zone of their native English out of a misplaced trust in its universal power and reach.

That said, English has emerged as a hegemonic language to an extent that no other language has before; frequently, the meaning of the term "international" is essentially narrowed to "Anglophone." This of course privileges native English speakers. Those scholars who do not speak English as their mother tongue may not be able to express themselves as well, write as fluently, or stand their ground as effectively as Anglophones in academic conferences. More important, the dominance of English language scholarship turns the specific customs of

Anglo-American universities into broadly accepted scholarly norms, with effects on the preferred length of a book (which is certainly not the length of a French *these d'État*), on how empirical or thesis-driven a dissertation should be, and on the kinds of questions and research agendas that are deemed "cutting edge." The asymmetry of linguistic reach thus also profoundly impacts the forms and contents of scholarship, and the digital circulation of information and research will not alter the situation. Online courses may be accessed around the world, but the source material that can be used, both for reasons of accessibility and out of legal considerations, tends to be English translations. We likely face a digital age that will be more Anglophone than any before it.

The dominance of the English language, and more fundamentally, the powerful role of American (and some British) institutions are fairly obvious; they are essentially an effect of the geopolitical power of the United States. But the terrain of global history is also tilted in a way that has received much less attention. In this emerging field, there is a clear Asian bias. On one level, this bias is institutional: scholars in Japan, Korea, China, and Singapore have begun to work on global problematics, and institutional support in these countries continues to grow. The Asian Association of World Historians, founded in 2008, is a flourishing enterprise. But on another level, and more unexpected, Asia is also a privileged subject of global history writing. Many current studies focus on events in Asia and on the history of the links that connected Asia to Europe and to the New World. In most syntheses and overviews, Asia features prominently, frequently at the expense of Latin America, Russia, and sub-Saharan Africa. A striking example is John Darwin's impressive *Global History of Empire*, which mentions not a single imperial formation outside of Eurasia.[20] Discovering Asia is really what much of global history seems to be about.

This Asia, to be sure, is neither the continent, nor a purely geographical designation. The focus is less on Afghanistan and Iran than it is on Japan and the four Asian "tigers" (Hong Kong, Korea, Singapore, and Taiwan); it is less on Malaysia and the Philippines than it is on China. In a fundamental sense, global history has been triggered by the rise of China, and in particular by the need to come to terms with a changing geopolitical situation. In this respect, Kenneth Pomeranz's comparative study of economic development and industrialization in England and China is the paradigmatic work of the new approach.[21] More than all of the methodological debates and other intellectual currents in the academy, the rise of Chinese capitalism has provoked a rethinking of global hierarchies, both politically and epistemologically. For an understanding of the trajectories of global history debates, the China challenge is as important as the dominance of American institutions and the hegemony of the English language.

Limitations of the "global"

After having devoted some time to the sociology of global history, let us shift gears and conclude this chapter, and this book, by briefly looking into the potential drawbacks and intellectual costs of global history as an approach. The concept of the global helps us move beyond isolated stories and beyond the bilateral structure of narratives of influence and transfer, diffusion and borrowing. It is part of a methodological revolution that challenges internalism in historical analysis. At the same time, the concept of the "global" also has its limitations, and its inherent dangers.

Some of the potential pitfalls of the approach have been touched upon in preceding sections. Especially sensitive is the issue of scales as discussed in chapters 6 and 7. Opting for large spatial and temporal frameworks may bring to light broader contexts and the structural constraints impacting a particular event or situation. At the same time, it may occlude the role of actors and their motives and choices, thus potentially obfuscating individual responsibility in history. The dichotomy of local actors versus global factors is certainly misleading, as neither can be neatly disentangled from the other. Nevertheless, the privileging of large scales may come at the price of downplaying local agency.

Apart from this problematic, let us consider four additional challenges that global historians face. Briefly put, the concept of the "global" may lead historians to erase the specific logic of the past, to fetishize connectedness, to neglect the issue of power, and to flatten historical reality in a quest for unifying frames. All four hazards caution us not to overstate global claims. Let us take up these four issues in turn.

First, the concern with globality and globalization has led many historians to privilege interactions and transfers, and to treat them as ends in themselves. Connectedness then becomes the only language that the sources seem to speak, as if this was their deep and true meaning; all other possible stories—be they about faith, war, political intrigue, intimacy, environmental protection, or working habits—are treated as superficial and ephemeral. Sometimes, global historians claim an ability to see through the veil of all such surface events, so that they can mine the sources for what they have to tell us about the state, quality, and logic of connectivity.

If that is what we are after, then such an approach is of course appropriate. But a quest of this nature can also be limiting, as it effaces the richness and the complex texture of the past. The biography of a German migrant to the American Midwest in the 1840s can tell us something about the political history of 1848, about economic conditions in rural Germany, about German diaspora communities in Michigan, about relations between immigrants and Native Americans, about masculinity and gender relations in the family, and much else. To use these stories primarily as a means of access to the state of connectedness can end in an impoverishment of historical analysis. "Indeed," John-Paul A. Ghobrial has cautioned us, "we risk finding ourselves in a world populated by faceless globe-trotters, colourless chameleons and invisible boundary crossers, individuals stretched so far out of any local, confessional or personal context as to make them little more than panes of glass through which to view [. . .] the connected world in which [they] lived."[22] If we reduce all historical biographies, stories, and events to metaphors of globality, we end up with a one-dimensional and shallow image of the past.

This also means, secondly, that global history needs to move beyond the fetishization of mobility, which is so characteristic of much recent work in the field. Indeed, in many discussions, mobility has become the hallmark, if not the equivalent, of global history. The movement of people across borders—as travelers and immigrants, as slaves and laborers, as traders and as prisoners of war—is one of the key mechanisms that created internationality and globality—and also the key means by which they were experienced first-hand. This is why much of the relevant literature has concentrated on migrants and mobile groups. Such a perspective has opened up important new windows on the past; but at the same time, the preoccupation with mobility tends to render the past into a simple prehistory of globalization. As a result, everyone and everything appears to be on the move, everywhere. In reality, such an image tells us more about the desires of the present than it does about the past.

The obsession with mobility and movement thus leads to exaggerations and distortions. Take the numerous examples of global historical surveys in which sections on social change are replaced by chapters on migration. Millions of peasants gradually disappear from the radar, while the crews of ships receive scholarly attention well in excess of their actual numbers. The majority of people traveled rarely or not at all, and certainly not for long distances or to foreign cultures; existing social, political, and economic conditions and the lack of infrastructure in many parts of the world made such pervasive mobility quite impossible. Global historians would be ill-advised, therefore, to turn non-movers into the casualties of their current preoccupation with circulation and fluidity. It is an irony of sorts: Itinerant and nomadic peoples were among the victims of the globalization process—and now it is the sedentary, those who stay put, who are neglected by historians and thus pay the historiographical price.

One of the unacknowledged effects of this phenomenon is the privileged role allotted to elites in some global history texts. Of course, there was slavery, coolie labor, and mass migration. But in many accounts, key roles are reserved for educated travelers to faraway lands, for the sages who were able to report from distant realms, for the few who put their global consciousness into words and onto paper. In the long run, therefore, global history will benefit from a social turn—after all, even those who hardly ever moved were affected by larger processes. It is not difficult to foresee that historians will eventually begin to turn their attention back, more and more, to those who were settled, autochthonous, and less privileged; and to those who have remained largely unconnected and outside the fold of globalization. Think of the more than 100 million people belonging to marginalized groups in the mountainous regions of Southeast Asia that historians have termed "Zomia." For centuries these groups have avoided integration, steering clear of institutions and exploitative relationships controlled by the state. Groups such as these—the "refugees of modernity"—are currently almost entirely absent from narratives of globalization.[23]

Put more generally, the social science of globalization has prioritized mobility and celebrated the flows of goods, people, and ideas. Flows, understood as persistent patterns of circulation, have emerged as a key metaphor in the literature. They promise to undermine fixity, place, and territory, as they proclaim globalization's mantra of "everything solid melts into air." Flows are equated with "de-territorialization," and in particular with overcoming the framework of the nation-state. But while we need to study the flows, we also need to be aware of the slumps and obstacles. Some of the abhorred processes of territorialization, in fact, are not the result of stubbornness or of tears in the tightly knit webs of globalization. Instead, they should be seen as responses to global integration; the rise of the nation-state, most prominently, was a reaction to global pressures in the nineteenth century.[24] Usually, both processes went hand in hand. When the Suez Canal opened in 1869 and drastically shortened travel time between Britain and India, the new waterway also forced camel caravans and dhows to stop and to wait, thus disrupting longstanding routes of trade and mobility. Acceleration and forms of deceleration thus conditioned each other.[25]

This also means that not everything moves and not everyone travels—and that, consequently, we will have to supplement the rhetoric of flows with a language of frictions, of non-transfers, and of inertia. Why did certain forms of knowledge never travel? Why were some ideas not passed on—even when the political and infrastructural conditions not only allowed, but actually encouraged such transfer? Take just one example, the story of the peacock flower. Peacock flowers were used as a contraceptive and abortifacient in Latin America and the Caribbean. In the eighteenth century, slave women acquired knowledge of the medicinal effect of the flower and employed it to abort offspring who would otherwise be born into slavery. Yet this knowledge remained local, even after the close integration of the Caribbean into the capitalist structures of the Atlantic economy. Historian of science Londa Schiebinger has introduced the concept of "agnotology"—the study of the culturally induced forms of non-knowledge—to describe factors, ranging from cultural and institutional priorities to individual likes and dislikes, that stood in the way of knowledge becoming more broadly disseminated.[26]

Third, global history as an approach is not immune to the criticism that it neglects issues of power. The concept of the "global," so the claim goes, can conceal the social hierarchies and the asymmetries of power that have shaped the modern world. And indeed, in some works there is a tendency to see global connections not as a project, driven by individuals and groups pursuing interests of their own, but as a quasi-natural process. In their celebration of connectedness, such accounts use the "global" to conceal, usually inadvertently, underlying inequalities of power.

The results are—or rather can be—stories of self-generated flows, of an effortless expansion of commerce, and of free-floating movement. In his nostalgic musings about the *World of Yesterday*, novelist Stefan Zweig gave vivid expression to such a utopia of borderless mobility: In the nineteenth century, he writes, "the earth belonged to all people. Everyone went wherever he wanted and stayed as long as he wished." To Zweig, there existed no borders that were more than "symbolical lines that were transgressed as easily as one stepped across the meridian at Greenwich."[27] But his experience was hardly representative. The lived experience of millions of indentured laborers and Asian coolies working the mines and plantations in Southern Africa, in Cuba, and in Hawaii was vastly different from that enjoyed by a handful of Austrian novelists and English tourists. Zweig's borderless mobility—"we embarked and disembarked without ever asking or being asked"—is a far cry from the experience of the masses of people who faced immigration procedures, hygienic controls, quarantine stations, nationality acts, fingerprinting and document examinations, citizenship laws and exclusion acts.

We can observe similar myopias in other fields. In some recent writing, empires appear as the self-evident forms of political rule over heterogeneous populations and no longer as based on infringements upon individual and group rights. Markets seem to converge naturally—even though many of them were opened to outside trade only at gunpoint. The spread of religions is portrayed as the result of translations and conversations, and less of prosecutions and crusades. There is a tendency, in some accounts, to de-politicize our understanding of history and to frame the past according to a liberal market imaginary.[28]

On the level of theory and method, such an expulsion of politics corresponds with the way in which "global history" is sometimes touted as an antidote for the perceived exaggerations of postcolonial studies on the one hand, and world systems scholarship on the other. While both of these approaches are built on a critique of power, some of their more recent strains, identifiable in global economic history and in the natural-science inclinations of big history, have largely eliminated issues of social and political hierarchies. It is therefore essential to remind ourselves that cross-border interactions and processes of global integration were deeply shaped by asymmetries of power and by violence. While transnational and global connections are frequently hailed as inherently progressive and benevolent, many of them were the work of more sinister forces. We may be accustomed to read Jules Verne's journey *Around the World in 80 Days* as symbolic of an emerging global consciousness, but it was World War I that displaced millions of people to faraway shores, battlefields, and graveyards, and thus created global experiences that left indelible wounds.

What does "the global" conceal?

The fourth point of contention explicitly addresses issues of normativity and, more specifically, the question of responsibility. In overviews in particular, and in studies spanning long periods of time, there is a tendency to describe the unfolding of large and anonymous processes as if individual humans had no role in them. In an effort to explain broader developments, and to arrive at interpretations that bridge historical experiences in different regions, historians opt for analytical categories that virtually exclude human agency. This tendency is particularly apparent in the extreme case of big history, but it also extends to accounts of less sweeping temporal reach. Is global history a form of history with the people left out?

On one level, this is a matter of narrative style. But is there any reason why global overviews should differ from national histories in the vividness of their presentation? Just as macro-accounts of the history of a nation can be colorful and mindful of the decisive role of individual agency, so can global histories, at least in principle. Some genres of global history writing indeed privilege individual activities to an extent that distracts from the larger conditions under which they acted.[29] On the whole, however, many overviews of the history of the world seem to struggle with questions of agency. As a result of the need to range across vast spaces and long swaths of time, we frequently encounter a vocabulary of necessity and inevitability.

More fundamentally, by locating causality at least partly on a global level, global historians may appear to relativize issues of responsibility that lie closer to home. This may be the effect of a methodological choice characteristic of the global approach, namely the choice to emphasize synchronous factors in space over long-term genealogies and internal temporal continuity. A wholesome escape from internalist narratives would then be purchased at the cost of slighting agency on the ground. If the Holocaust, to take one example, can be explained partly by synchronous global forces, then this could relativize the guilt of Nazi perpetrators. Such over-contextualization—the privileging of global factors over local actors—might externalize issues of accountability, and of guilt. It is therefore important to remember that global structures are as much shaped by human activity as they are responsible for shaping it; they are the result of processes of structuration. As such, they help define the conditions under which people act, but they do not dictate their behavior. Structures frame specific situations and render certain developments unlikely. They do not determine human agency.[30]

The fifth challenge is in many ways the most fundamental. Simply put, it is this: If the term "global" is used to describe both the travels of Marco Polo and the workings of the financial crisis in 2008, is it then not too general? How effective is a term that is universally applicable? If we subsume all sorts of trans-border exchanges under "global," how useful is the term as an analytical category?

To be sure, through the ages different parts of the world were connected to one another, and zooming in on these connections yields valuable insights. However, not all of these links were of the same kind. They were enabled, moreover, by very different structures—some of them coalescing, and others competing. To lose sight of the particular logics of the conditions under which interactions took place would result in a loss of historical specificity. To render all of them "global" may be accurate on one level, but it is as unspecific as replacing individual names with the word "person." We want to know more precisely who initiated the Crusades or the storming of the Bastille, and who suffered in the Taiping Rebellion; the term "person" would abolish all personalities. Equally, it is crucial to understand whether the durability of faraway links is guaranteed by an Islamic ecumene, by the Persian language, by the routes of transatlantic steamships, by the chain migration of Chinese clans, by the power of the British Empire, or by the silent mechanisms of supply and demand. "Global" as a stand-in for everything may blind us to these crucial distinctions.

The notion of the "global" suggests a continuity that is frequently fallacious. Spatially, it translates different forms of entanglement into sameness. Temporally, it suggests that earlier links were the pre-history of later connections. Was the great Moroccan traveler Ibn Battuta (1304–1377) simply the precursor of today's tourists on low-cost airlines? Did British colonialism pave the way for globalization—for "Anglobalization," as some historians now hold?[31] The British Empire certainly established new connections—but at the same time, it destroyed old ones, time-honored links that no longer served the interest of the London City. Colonialism also imposed new borders that inhibited mobility and trade. Sri Lanka, for example, was downright "islanded" in the early nineteenth century, as the British sought to sever its links to the mainland and to Indian Ocean networks by making it into a separate territorial unit.[32] Whatever the links between earlier and later forms of connectivity, then, they are more complicated than the term "global" suggests.

What is at issue is not so much whether large-scale structures were literally "global," that is planetary and reaching into every corner of the earth.[33] Rather, the problem is terminological: to translate a variety of empires (as diverse as the Mongol and the British), trade networks (ranging from trans-Saharan caravans to current multi-national corporations), discursive hegemonies, and so forth into "global structures" can only be achieved by an act of conceptual violence. Such an abstraction might help to answer a few large-scale questions, but it will prove less appropriate for addressing the concerns that most historians, and a reading public, have today. Employed in this way, the notion of the "global" threatens to level historical reality and, in some ways, to take the history out of global history.

Does this mean we need to abandon the vocabulary of the "global" altogether? Certainly not. On the most general level, we need it as a catchword that allows us to discuss seemingly different pasts in one frame, and to look into connections that earlier paradigms rendered invisible. On a very specific level, it helps us address the emergence of truly global structures. And politically, we need it as a rallying cry. Global history is not only an approach; it is also a slogan that is necessary for reshaping the landscapes of knowledge and for revamping institutions of knowledge production. It signals that the past was global—and not limited to American, Italian, or Chinese history alone. For the purposes of a revolution in our paradigms of knowing, and to rescue history from container thinking, the concept "global history" will remain indispensable.

As an analytical device, however, it competes with more specific and frequently more accurate terms. In the long run, therefore, the heuristic surplus of the notion of "global" is bound to decrease. It is safe to predict that the better we understand to what degree various regions of the world were interlinked, and the more we recognize the ways in which larger structures impact local events, the more we will, gradually, liberate ourselves from the rhetoric of the global. There is, to be sure, still a long way to go. Historians virtually everywhere predominantly focus on their own nation. In many countries, institutional settings and public expectations collude to keep the national framework firmly in place. Given the close ties of the discipline of history to questions of national identity, this is not likely to change any time soon. By contrast, the institutionalization of global history is a slow business, and to this day remains largely stalled in the Anglophone world and in parts of Western Europe and East Asia. And even in these regions its reach remains limited.[34]

But sometime in the future, once we can take a better understanding of global structures and world-wide dynamics for granted, the notion of the "global" may recede into the background and give way to a renewed emphasis on specificities. Historians will resort to new geographies, no longer *a priori* the nation-state, but also not necessarily the whole world. They will follow specific interactions and patterns of exchange, rather than taking any one scale as their point of departure. The gradual disappearance of the rhetoric of the "global" will then, paradoxically, signal the victory of global history as a paradigm.

Acknowledgments

———————◦———————

This book has been in the making for some time. And it could have been in the making for much longer for, given the speed with which the field of global history changes, such a taking stock can only ever be a snapshot. It started out as a translation of my book *Globalgeschichte*, published in German by C.H. Beck publishers in 2013, but I soon realized that it required not a translation but a new beginning—and I was gently encouraged in that direction by Brigitta van Rheinberg and Jeremy Adelman at Princeton University Press. Of the eight chapters of the German version, I revised two and discarded the rest in order to arrive at a more problem-oriented, and less strictly introductory text. The result is an entirely different book.

In this endeavor, I have been supported, inspired, and criticized by many colleagues around the world, too numerous to list here. I have presented and discussed ideas at conferences and workshops in Europe, the United States, and East Asia. Jeremy Adelman, Andreas Eckert, Catherine Davies, Michael Facius, Sheldon Garon, Masashi Haneda, Lasse Heerten, Christoph Kalter, Dörte Lerp, Kiran Patel, Margrit Pernau, Alessandro Stanziani, and Andrew Zimmerman have all read one or several chapters, and I benefited from their generous criticism. I was also pushed by an almost daily confrontation with questions and criticism in the seminars of the MA program in Global History in Berlin. Among the six anonymous reviews so-licited by Princeton University Press, the only one that was critical motivated me to rethink the entire organization and argument of the book. And finally, I am particularly indebted to Christopher L. Hill and Dominic Sachsenmaier for extensive and repeated discus-sions about some of the issues outlined here; without them, the book would not have taken the shape it has now, and it would be a much more provisional text.

Some parts of chapters 2 and 3, originally written in German, have been expertly translated by Shivaun Heath and Joy Titheridge. In preparing the text, I was fortunate to count on the help of my student assistants Stephanie Feser, Jannis Girgsdies, Matt Steffens, Matthias Thaden, and Barbara Uchdorf. This work was supported by the Laboratory Program for Korean Studies through the Minis-try of Education of the Republic of Korea and the Korean Studies Promotion Service of the Academy of Korean Studies (AKS-2010-DZZ-3103).

Notes

———————⊙———————

Chapter 1

1. C. A. Bayly, *The Birth of the Modern World, 1780–1914*, Oxford (Blackwell) 2004, 469.
2. Anthony G. Hopkins (ed.), *Globalization in World History*, London (Pimlico) 2002; Thomas Bender (ed.), *Rethinking American History in a Global Age*, Berkeley, CA (University of California Press) 2002.
3. Anthony D. Smith, *Nationalism in the Twentieth Century*, Oxford (Robertson) 1979, 191ff.; Ulrich Beck, *What is Globalization?* Cambridge (Polity Press) 2000, 23–24; Immanuel Wallerstein et al. (eds.), *Open the Social Sciences: Report of the Gulbenkian Commission on the Restructuring of the Social Sciences*, Stanford, CA (Stanford University Press) 1996.
4. For the notion of birth defects, see Jerry H. Bentley, Introduction: The Task of World History, in: Bentley (ed.), *The Oxford Handbook of World History*, Oxford (Oxford University Press) 2011, 1–16.
5. Dominic Sachsenmaier, Global History, Version: 1.0, *Docupedia-Zeitgeschichte*, 11. Feb. 2010, http://docupedia.de/zg/Global _History?oldid=84616.
6. For other ways of ordering the field, see Lynn Hunt, *Writing History in the Global Era*, New York (Norton) 2014; Diego

Olstein, *Thinking History Globally*, New York (Palgrave Macmillan) 2014.

7. Felipe Fernández-Armesto and Benjamin Sacks, Networks, Interactions, and Connective History, in: Douglas Northrop (ed.), *A Companion to World History*, Oxford (Wiley-Blackwell) 2012, 303–320, quote: 303.

8. Examples include: for the nineteenth century, Bayly, *The Birth of the Modern World*; Jürgen Osterhammel, *The Transformation of the World: A Global History of the Nineteenth Century*, Princeton (Princeton University Press) 2014; for years, Olivier Bernier, *The World in 1800*, New York (Wiley) 2000; John E. Wills, *1688: A Global History*, New York (W. W. Norton) 2002; for the last millennium, David S. Landes, *The Wealth and Poverty of Nations: Why Some Are So Rich and Some So Poor*, New York (Norton) 1998; for the world, Felipe Fernandez-Armesto, *The World: A Brief History*, New York (Pearson Prentice Hall) 2007; for big history, David Christian, *Maps of Time: An Introduction to Big History*, Berkeley (University of California Press) 2004.

9. John Darwin, *After Tamerlane: The Global History of Empire*, London (Penguin Books) 2007; Jane Burbank and Frederick Cooper, *Empires in World History: Power and the Politics of Difference*, Princeton (Princeton University Press) 2010.

10. Dipesh Chakrabarty, *Rethinking Working-Class History: Bengal, 1890–1940*, New Haven (Yale University Press) 1987; Frederick Cooper, *On the African Waterfront: Urban Disorder and the Transformation of Work in Colonial Mombasa*, New Haven (Yale University Press) 1987.

11. From this vast literature, see for example Wang Gungwu (ed.), *Global History and Migrations*, Boulder, CO (Westview Press) 1997; Natalie Zemon Davis, *Trickster Travels: A Sixteenth-Century Muslim between Worlds*, New York (Hill & Wang) 2006 ; Miles Ogborn (ed.), *Global Lives: Britain and the World 1550–1800*, Cambridge (Cambridge University Press) 2008;

Marilyn Lake and Henry Reynolds, *Drawing the Global Colour Line: White Men's Countries and the International Challenge of Racial Equality*, Cambridge (Cambridge University Press) 2008.

12. Christopher L. Hill, *National History and the World of Nations: Capital, State, and the Rhetoric of History in Japan, France, and the United States*, Durham, NC (Duke University Press) 2008. For more examples, see chapters 4 and 5 below.

13. Arif Dirlik, Performing the World: Reality and Representation in the Making of World Histor(ies), *Journal of World History* 16 (2005), 391–410, quote: 396.

14. Samuel Moyn and Andrew Sartori, Approaches to Global Intellectual History, in: Moyn and Sartori (eds.), *Global Intellectual History*, New York (Columbia University Press) 2013, 3–30.

15. See the very useful discussion in Jürgen Osterhammel, Globalizations, in: Jerry H. Bentley (ed.), *The Oxford Handbook of World History*, Oxford (Oxford University Press) 2011, 89–104.

16. This double reflexivity is the epistemological core of the notion of *histoire croisée*. See Michael Werner and Bénédicte Zimmermann, Beyond Comparison: Histoire Croisée and the Challenge of Reflexivity, *History & Theory* 45 (2006), 30–50.

17. Christopher Bayly, History and World History, in: Ulinka Rublack (ed.), *A Concise Companion to History*, Oxford (Oxford University Press) 2011, 13.

Chapter 2

1. Jan Assmann, *The Mind of Egypt: History and Meaning in the Time of the Pharaohs*, New York (Metropolitan Books) 2002, 151; Jan Assmann, Globalization, Universalism, and the Erosion of Cultural Memory, in: Aleida Assmann and Sebastian Conrad (eds.), *Memory in a Global Age: Discourses, Practices*

and Trajectories, New York (Palgrave Macmillan) 2010, 121–137.

2. J.A.S. Evans, *Herodotus, Explorer of the Past: Three Essays*, Princeton (Princeton University Press) 1991; Ernst Breisach, *Historiography: Ancient, Medieval and Modern*, Chicago (Chicago University Press) 1994.

3. See Tarif Khalidi, *Islamic Historiography: The Histories of Mas'udi*, Albany, NY (State University of New York Press) 1975.

4. See Siep Stuurman, Herodotus and Sima Qian: History and the Anthropological Turn in Ancient Greece and Han China, *Journal of World History* 19 (2008), 1–40; Grant Hardy, *Worlds of Bronze and Bamboo: Sima Qian's Conquest of History*, New York (Columbia University Press) 1999.

5. François Hartog, *Le Miroir d'Hérodote*, Paris (Gallimard) 2001; Q. Edward Wang, The Chinese World View, *Journal of World History* 10 (1999), 285–305; Q. Edward Wang, World History in Traditional China, *Storia della Storiografia* 35 (1999), 83–96.

6. Arif Dirlik, Performing the World: Reality and Representation in the Making of World Histor(ies), *Journal of World History* 16 (2005), 391–410, quote: 407.

7. See George Iggers and Q. Edward Wang, *A Global History of Modern Historiography*, New York (Pearson Longman) 2008; Daniel Woolf (ed.), *The Oxford History of Historical Writing*, 5 volumes, Oxford (Oxford University Press) 2011–12.

8. Sanjay Subrahmanyam, On World Historians in the Sixteenth Century, *Representations* 91 (2005), 26–57.

9. Quoted in Serge Gruzinski, *What Time Is It There? America and Islam at the Dawn of Modern Times*, Cambridge (Polity Press) 2010, 73.

10. Subrahmanyam, On World Historians, 37; Serge Gruzinski, *Les quatre parties du monde: Histoire d'une mondialisation*, Paris (Martinière) 2004.

11. Gruzinski, *What Time Is It There?*, 69.

12. Jürgen Osterhammel, *Die Entzauberung Asiens: Europa und die asiatischen Reiche im 18. Jahrhundert*, München (C. H. Beck) 1998, 271–348. See also Geoffrey C. Gunn, *First Globalization: The Eurasian Exchange 1500–1800*, Lanham, MD (Rowman & Littlefield) 2003, 145–168; John J. Clarke, *Oriental Enlightenment: The Encounter between Asian and Western Thought*, London (Routledge) 1997.

13. Quoted in Johan van der Zande, August Ludwig Schlözer and the English Universal History, in: Stefan Berger, Peter Lambert, and Peter Schumann (eds.), *Historikerdialoge: Geschichte, Mythos und Gedächtnis im deutsch-britischen kulturellen Austausch, 1750–2000*, Göttingen (Vandenhoeck & Ruprecht) 2003, 135–156, quote: 135.

14. Karen O'Brien, *Narratives of Enlightenment: Cosmopolitan History from Voltaire to Gibbon*, Cambridge (Cambridge University Press) 1997. For Gibbon, also see John G. A. Pocock, *Barbarism and Religion*, 5 volumes, Cambridge (Cambridge University Press) 1999–2011.

15. See, for example, Michael Harbsmeier, World Histories before Domestication: The Writing of Universal Histories, Histories of Mankind and World Histories in Late Eighteenth-Century Germany, *Culture and History* 5 (1989), 93–131. For the persistence of the biblical chronology, see Suzanne L. Marchand, *German Orientalism in the Age of Empire: Religion, Race, and Scholarship*, Cambridge (Cambridge University Press) 2009.

16. See, for example, Prasenjit Duara, *Rescuing History from the Nation: Questioning Narratives of Modern China*, Chicago (Chicago University Press) 1995.

17. John L. Robinson, *Bartolomé Mitre, Historian of the Americas*, Washington, DC (University Press of America) 1982; E. Bradford Burns, Ideology in Nineteenth-Century Latin American Historiography, *The Hispanic American Historical Review* 58 (1978), 409–431.

18. See, for example, Stefan Tanaka, *Japan's Orient: Rendering Pasts into History*, Berkeley, CA (University of California Press) 1993; Gabriele Lingelbach, *Klio macht Karriere: Die Institutionalisierung der Geschichtswissenschaft in Frankreich und den USA in der zweiten Hälfte des 19. Jahrhunderts*, Göttingen (Vandenhoeck & Ruprecht) 2003.

19. Reinhart Koselleck, *Futures Past: On the Semantics of Historical Time*, New York (Columbia University Press) 2004; Göran Blix, Charting the 'Transitional Period': The Emergence of Modern Time in the Nineteenth Century, *History and Theory* 45 (2006), 51–71. See also Stefan Berger, Introduction: Towards a Global History of National Historiographies, in: idem (ed.), *Writing the Nation: A Global Perspective*, Basingstoke (Palgrave Macmillan) 2007, 1–29.

20. Susan Burns, *Before the Nation: Kokugaku and the Imagining of Community in Early Modern Japan*, Durham, NC (Duke University Press) 2003.

21. Benjamin A. Elman, *From Philosophy to Philology: Intellectual Aspects of Change in Late Imperial China*, Cambridge, MA (Harvard University Press) 1984.

22. Dominic Sachsenmaier, Global History, Pluralism, and the Question of Traditions, *New Global Studies* 3, no. 3 (2009), article 3, quote: 3–4.

23. For global historical perspectives, see especially Dominic Sachsenmaier, *Global Perspectives on Global History: Theories and Approaches in a Connected World*, Cambridge (Cambridge University Press) 2011, 11–17. See also Daniel Woolf, *A Global History of History*, Cambridge (Cambridge University Press) 2011.

24. G.W.F. Hegel, *The Philosophy of History*, trans. J. Sibree, introduction C. J. Friedrich, New York (Dover Publications) 1956, 91; Duara, *Rescuing History from the Nation*.

25. For the traditional perspective, see Patrick O'Brien, Historiographical Traditions and Modern Imperatives for the Resto-

ration of Global History, *Journal of Global History* 1 (2006), 3–39.

26. Christopher L. Hill, *National History and the World of Nations: Capital, State, and the Rhetoric of History in Japan, France, and the United States*, Durham, NC (Duke University Press) 2008.

27. Rebecca E. Karl, *Creating Asia: China in the World at the Beginning of the Twentieth Century*, American Historical Review 103 (1998), 1096–1118, quote: 1109.

28. Karl Marx and Friedrich Engels, *The Communist Manifesto: A Modern Edition*, London (Verso) 1998, 39.

29. Cemil Aydin, *The Politics of Anti-Westernism in Asia: Visions of World Order in Pan-Islamic and Pan-Asian Thought*, New York (Columbia University Press) 2007; Stephen N. Hay, *Asian Ideas of East and West: Tagore and His Critics in Japan, China, and India*, Cambridge, MA (Harvard University Press) 1970; Rustom Bharucha, *Another Asia: Rabindranath Tagore and Okakura Tenshin*, New Delhi (Oxford University Press) 2006.

30. My interpretation is directed against Ian Buruma and Avishai Margalit, *Occidentalism: The West in the Eyes of Its Enemies*, New York (Penguin Books) 2004.

31. Prasenjit Duara, The Discourse of Civilization and Pan-Asianism, *Journal of World History* 12 (2001), 99–130; Andrew Sartori, *Bengal in Global Concept History: Culturalism in the Age of Capital*, Chicago (Chicago University Press) 2008.

32. Michael Adas, Contested Hegemony: The Great War and the Afro-Asian Assault on the Civilizing Mission Ideology, *Journal of World History* 15 (2004), 31–64; Dominic Sachsenmaier, Searching for Alternatives to Western Modernity, *Journal of Modern European History* 4 (2006), 241–259.

33. Paul Costello, *World Historians and Their Goals: Twentieth-Century Answers to Modernism*, DeKalb, IL (Northern Illinois University Press) 1993.

34. For the following, see the excellent outline of Sachsenmaier, *Global Perspectives*, 25–58.

35. William McNeill, *The Rise of the West: A History of the Human Community*, Chicago (University of Chicago Press) 1963. Later, McNeill repeatedly distanced himself from the Eurocentrism of his magnum opus, for instance in: idem, World History and the Rise and the Fall of the West, *Journal of World History* 9 (1988), 215–236. Further popular works of a similar thrust are: Eric Jones, *The European Miracle: Environments, Economies and Geopolitics in the History of Europe and Asia*, Cambridge (Cambridge University Press) 1981; David Landes, *The Wealth and Poverty of Nations: Why Some Are So Rich and Some So Poor,* New York (W. W. Norton) 1999; Michael Mitterauer, *Why Europe? The Medieval Origins of Its Special Path*, Chicago (University of Chicago Press) 2010.

36. Sachsenmaier, *Global Perspectives*, 184–191; Leif Littrup, World History with Chinese Characteristics, *Culture and History* 5 (1989), 39–64.

37. Immanuel Wallerstein, *The Modern World-System*, 4 volumes, Berkeley, CA (University of California Press) 1974–2011.

38. For the USA, see Peter Novick, *That Noble Dream: The 'Objectivity Question' and the American Historical Profession*, New York (Cambridge University Press) 1988.

39. Mark T. Berger, *Under Northern Eyes: Latin American Studies and US Hegemony in the Americas, 1898–1980*, Bloomington, IN (Indiana University Press) 1995; Masao Miyoshi and Harry D. Harootunian (eds.), *Learning Places: The Afterlives of Area Studies*, Durham, NC (Duke University Press) 2002.

40. Robert Young, *Postcolonialism: An Historical Introduction*, Oxford (Blackwell) 2001.

41. Cristobal Kay, *Latin American Theories of Development and Underdevelopment*, London (Routledge) 1989.

42. Gyan Prakash, Subaltern Studies as Postcolonial Criticism, *American Historical Review* 99 (1994), 1475–1490.

43. Sachsenmaier, *Global Perspectives*, 45.

Chapter 3

1. Heinz-Gerhard Haupt and Jürgen Kocka (eds.), *Comparative and Transnational History: Central European Approaches and New Perspectives*, New York (Berghahn Books) 2009; Deborah Cohen and Maura O'Connor (eds.), *Comparison and History*, New York (Routledge) 2004.

2. For a recent assessment of the comparative method, see George Steinmetz, Comparative History and Its Critics: A Genealogy and a Possible Solution, in: Prasenjit Duara, Viren Murthy, and Andrew Sartori (eds.), *A Companion to Global Historical Thought*, Malden, MA (Wiley Blackwell) 2014, 412–436.

3. Victor Lieberman, *Strange Parallels: Southeast Asia in Global Context c. 800–1830. Vol. 1, Integration on the Mainland*, Cambridge (Cambridge University Press) 2003.

4. Michael Werner and Bénédicte Zimmermann, Beyond Comparison: Histoire Croisée and the Challenge of Reflexivity, *History & Theory* 45 (2006), 30–50; Michel Espagne, Sur les limites du comparatisme en histoire culturelle, *Genèses: Sciences Sociales et Histoire* 17 (1994), 112–121; Sanjay Subrahmanyam, Connected Histories: Notes toward a Reconfiguration of Early Modern Eurasia, *Modern Asian Studies* 31 (1997), 735–762; Subrahmanyam, *Explorations in Connected History: From the Tagus to the Ganges*, Oxford (Oxford University Press) 2005.

5. Kenneth Pomeranz, *The Great Divergence: Europe, China, and the Making of the Modern World Economy*, Princeton (Princeton University Press) 2000, 9.

6. Pomeranz, *The Great Divergence*, 297.

7. For an exemplary case of such a global comparison, see Christopher L. Hill, *National History and the World of Nations: Capital, State, and the Rhetoric of History in Japan, France, and the United States*, Durham, NC (Duke University Press) 2008; see also my treatment of this book below in chapter 7.

8. Patricia Clavin, Defining Transnationalism, *Contemporary European History* 14 (2005), 421–439; Gunilla Budde, Sebastian Conrad, and Oliver Janz (eds.), *Transnationale Geschichte: Themen, Tendenzen und Theorien*, Göttingen (Vandenhoeck & Ruprecht) 2006; Pierre-Yves Saunier, *Transnational History*, Basingstoke (Palgrave Macmillan) 2013.

9. Thomas Bender, *A Nation among Nations: America's Place in World History*, New York (Hill and Wang) 2006, 3, ix.

10. Bender, *A Nation among Nations*, 4.

11. Bender, *A Nation among Nations*, ix, 5.

12. C. A. Bayly, in: AHR Conversation: On Transnational History, *American Historical Review* 111 (2006), 1441–1464, quote: 1442.

13. Ulrike Freitag and Achim v. Oppen (eds.), *Translocality—The Study of Globalising Phenomena from a Southern Perspective*, Leiden (Brill) 2010.

14. For a concise synthesis of the theoretical principles of world-systems theory, see Immanuel Wallerstein, *World-Systems Analysis: An Introduction*, Durham, NC (Duke University Press) 2004; see also Wallerstein, *The Essential Wallerstein*, New York (The New Press) 2000; Fernand Braudel, *The Perspective of the World (Civilization and Capitalism 15th–18th Century*, volume 3), New York (HarperCollins) 1984.

15. Immanuel Wallerstein, *The Modern World System*, 4 volumes, New York/Berkeley, CA (1974–2011).

16. Janet Abu-Lughod, *Before European Hegemony: The World System A.D. 1250–1350*, Oxford (Oxford University Press) 1989; Andre Gunder Frank and Barry K. Gills (eds.), *The World System: Five Hundred Years or Five Thousand?* London (Routledge) 1993.

17. Wallerstein, *World-Systems Analysis*, 24.

18. Göran Therborn, Time, Space, and Their Knowledge: The Times and Place of the World and Other Systems, *Journal of World-Systems Research* 6 (2000), 266–284.

19. Wolfgang Knöbl, *Die Kontingenz der Moderne: Wege in Europa, Asien und Amerika*, Frankfurt (Campus) 2007, chapter 4.

20. A particularly stimulating work in the world systems tradition is Giovanni Arrighi, *The Long Twentieth Century: Money, Power, and the Origins of Our Times*, London (Verso) 1994.

21. See, for example, Dale W. Tomich, *Through the Prism of Slavery: Labor, Capital, and World Economy*, Lanham, MD (Rowman & Littlefield) 2004.

22. See, for example, the extended space that some of the seminal studies in a cultural history of the global have dedicated to an engagement with Marxism, such as Dipesh Chakrabarty, *Provincializing Europe: Postcolonial Thought and Historical Difference*, Princeton (Princeton University Press) 2000; Rebecca E. Karl, *Staging the World: Chinese Nationalism at the Turn of the Twentieth Century*, Durham, NC (Duke University Press) 2002; Andrew Sartori, *Bengal in Global Concept History: Culturalism in the Age of Capital*, Chicago (Chicago University Press) 2008; Andrew Zimmerman, *Alabama in Africa: Booker T. Washington, the German Empire, and the Globalization of the New South*, Princeton (Princeton University Press) 2010.

23. Leela Gandhi, *Postcolonial Theory. A Critical Introduction*, New York (Columbia University Press) 1998; Robert Young, *Postcolonialism: An Historical Introduction*, Oxford (Blackwell) 2001.

24. Nicholas Dirks, *Castes of Mind: Colonialism and the Making of Modern India*, Princeton (Princeton University Press) 2001; Bernard Cohn, *Colonialism and Its Forms of Knowledge*, Princeton (Princeton University Press) 1996; Ann Laura Stoler, *Carnal Knowledge and Imperial Power: Race and the Intimate in Colonial Rule*, Berkeley, CA (University of California Press) 2002.

25. Ashis Nandy, *The Intimate Enemy: Loss and Recovery of Self Under Colonialism*, Delhi (Oxford University Press) 1983, 63.

26. Arif Dirlik, The Postcolonial Aura: Third World Criticism in the Age of Global Capitalism, in: Padmini Mongia (ed.),

Contemporary Postcolonial Theory: A Reader, London (Hodder Arnold) 1996, 294–321; Sumit Sarkar, The Decline of the Subaltern in Subaltern Studies, in: *Writing Social History*, Delhi (Oxford University Press) 1997, 82–108.

27. Johann P. Arnason, *Civilizations in Dispute: Historical Questions and Theoretical Traditions*, Leiden (Brill) 2004; Said Amir Arjomand and Edward A. Tiryakian (eds.), *Rethinking Civilizational Analysis*, London (Sage) 2004.

28. S. N. Eisenstadt, Multiple Modernities, *Daedalus* 129 (2000), 1–29, quote: 2–3. See also Dominic Sachsenmaier, Jens Riedel, and Shmuel N. Eisenstadt (eds.), *Reflections on Multiple Modernities: European, Chinese and Other Interpretations*, Leiden (Brill) 2002; Wolfgang Knöbl, *Spielräume der Modernisierung: Das Ende der Eindeutigkeit*, Weilerswist (Velbrück) 2001; Eliezer Ben-Rafael and Yitzak Sternberg (eds.), *Identity, Culture and Globalization*, Leiden (Brill) 2001.

29. Tu Wei-Ming (ed.), *Confucian Traditions in East Asian Modernity: Moral Education and Economic Culture in Japan and the Four Mini-Dragons*, Cambridge, MA (Harvard University Press) 1996.

30. On alternative modernities, see Dilip Parameshwar Gaonkar, On Alternative Modernities, in: Gaonkar (ed.), *Alternative Modernities*, Durham, NC (Duke University Press) 2001, 1–23; Charles Taylor, Two Theories of Modernity, in: Gaonkar, *Alternative Modernities*, 172–96.

31. For critical perspectives, see Volker H. Schmidt, Multiple Modernities or Varieties of Modernity? *Current Sociology* 54 (2006), 77–97; Arif Dirlik, *Global Modernity: Modernity in the Age of Global Capitalism*, Boulder, CO (Paradigm Press) 2007; Timothy Mitchell, Introduction, in: *Questions of Modernity*, Minneapolis, MN (University of Minnesota Press) 2000, xi-xvii; Frederick Cooper, *Colonialism in Question*, Berkeley, CA (University of California Press) 2005, 113–49. From a world systems perspective: Stephen K. Sanderson (ed.), *Civili-*

zations and World Systems: Studying World-Historical Change, Walnut Creek, CA (AltaMira Press) 1995.

Chapter 4

1. Examples include Raymond Grew (Hg), *Food in Global History*, Boulder, CO (Westview Press) 2000; Robert Finlay, *The Pilgrim Art: The Culture of Porcelain in World History*, Berkeley, CA (University of California Press) 2010; Alan Macfarlane and Gerry Martin, *Glass: A World History*, Chicago (Chicago University Press) 2002; Giorgio Riello, *Cotton: The Fabric that Made the Modern World*, Cambridge (Cambridge University Press) 2013.

2. William McNeill, *The Rise of the West: A History of the Human Community*, Chicago (University of Chicago Press) 1963. For a similar argument, see Eric Jones, *The European Miracle: Environments, Economies and Geopolitics in the History of Europe and Asia*, Cambridge (Cambridge University Press) 1981; John M. Roberts, *The Triumph of the West*, Boston (Phoenix Press) 1985; David Landes, *The Wealth and Poverty of Nations: Why Some Are So Rich and Some So Poor*, New York (W. W. Norton) 1999.

3. David Washbrook, Problems in Global History, in: Maxine Berg (ed.), *Writing the History of the Global: Challenges for the 21st Century*, Oxford (Oxford University Press) 2013, 21–31, quote: 23.

4. Reference here is to Andrew Sartori, *Bengal in Global Concept History: Culturalism in the Age of Capital*, Chicago (Chicago University Press) 2008.

5. Martin Bernal, *Black Athena: The Afroasiatic Roots of Classical Civilization: The Fabrication of Ancient Greece, 1785–1985*, vol. 1, New Brunswick, NJ (Rutgers University Press) 1987; Robert Bartlett, *The Making of Europe*, Princeton (Princeton University Press) 1994; Jack Goody, *The East in the West*, Cambridge (Cambridge University Press) 1996.

6. C. A. Bayly, "Archaic" and "modern" Globalization in the Eurasian and African Arena 1750–1850, in: A. G. Hopkins (ed.), *Globalization in World History,* New York (W. W. Norton) 2002, 47–68; see also C. A. Bayly, *The Birth of the Modern World, 1780–1914,* Oxford (Blackwell) 2004.

7. For the development of synchronicity, see David Harvey, *The Condition of Postmodernity: An Enquiry into the Origins of Cultural Change,* Oxford (Blackwell) 1989.

8. Serge Gruzinski, *What Time Is It There? America and Islam at the Dawn of Modern Times,* Cambridge (Polity Press) 2010.

9. John Darwin, Globe and Empire, in: Berg (ed.), *Writing the History of the Global,* 197–200, quote: 198.

10. Jerry H. Bentley, Globalization History and Historicizing Globalization, in: Barry K. Gills and William R. Thompson (eds.), *Globalization and Global History,* London (Routledge) 2006, 18–32, quote: 29.

11. William H. McNeill and John Robert McNeill, *The Human Web: A Bird's-Eye View of World History,* New York (W. W. Norton) 2003.

12. Stefan S. Tanaka, *New Times in Meiji Japan,* Princeton (Princeton University Press) 2004.

13. Washbrook, Problems in Global History, 28.

14. Samuel Moyn and Andrew Sartori, Approaches to Global Intellectual History, in: Moyn and Sartori (eds.), *Global Intellectual History,* New York (Columbia University Press) 2013, 3–30, quote: 21.

15. Landes, *The Wealth and Poverty of Nations,* xxi.

16. For such a view, see e.g., John M. Headley, *The Europeanization of the World: On the Origins of Human Rights and Democracy,* Princeton (Princeton University Press) 2008; Anthony Pagden, *Worlds at War: The 2,500-Year Struggle Between East and West,* Oxford (Oxford University Press) 2008; Toby E. Huff, *Intellectual Curiosity and the Scientific Revolution: A Global Perspective,* Cambridge (Cambridge University Press) 2010; Niall

Ferguson, *Civilisation: The West and the Rest,* London (Allen Lane) 2011.

17. Robert Young, *White Mythologies: Writing History and the West,* London (Routledge) 1990; Edward Said, *Culture and Imperialism,* New York (Alfred A. Knopf) 1993.

18. Sanjay Subrahmanyam, Hearing Voices: Vignettes of Early Modernity in South Asia, 1400–1750, *Daedalus* 127, no. 3 (1998), 75–104, quote: 99–100.

19. Lynn Hunt, *Inventing Human Rights: A History,* New York (W. W. Norton) 2007.

20. Laurent Dubois, *Avengers of the New World: The Story of the Haitian Revolution,* Cambridge, MA (Harvard University Press) 2004.

21. Samuel Moyn, *The Last Utopia: Human Rights in History,* Cambridge, MA (Harvard University Press) 2010; Roland Burke, *Decolonization and the Evolution of International Human Rights,* Philadelphia, PA (University of Pennsylvania Press) 2010.

22. Martti Koskenniemi, *The Gentle Civilizer of Nations: The Rise and Fall of International Law, 1870–1960,* Cambridge (Cambridge University Press) 2001; Anthony Anghie, *Imperialism, Sovereignty and the Making of International Law,* Cambridge (Cambridge University Press) 2005; Turan Kayaoglu, *Legal Imperialism: Sovereignty and Extraterritoriality in Japan, the Ottoman Empire, and China,* Cambridge (Cambridge University Press) 2010.

23. All four approaches, to different degrees, are present in the contributions to Bardo Fassbender, Anne Peters, Simone Peter, and Daniel Högger (eds.): *The Oxford Handbook of the History of International Law,* Oxford (Oxford University Press) 2013.

24. Sebastian Conrad, Enlightenment in Global History: A Historiographical Critique, *American Historical Review* 117 (2012), 999–1027.

25. First, albeit very provisional forays into the problematic can be found in Stein U. Larsen (ed.), *Fascism outside Europe: The*

European Impulse against Domestic Conditions in the Diffusion of Global Fascism, Boulder, CO (Social Science Monographs) 2001.

26. Ernest Gellner, *Nations and Nationalism*, Oxford (Blackwell) 1983, 57. For an overview on the theory of nationalism, see Geoff Eley and Ronald Grigor Suny (eds.), *Becoming National: A Reader*, Oxford (Oxford University Press) 1996; Umut Özkirimth, *Contemporary Debates on Nationalism: A Critical Engagement*, Basingstoke (Palgrave Macmillan) 2005.

27. Benedict Anderson, *Imagined Communities: Reflections on the Origins and Spread of Nationalism*. Revised edition, London (Verso) 1991, 81.

28. For a perceptive critique of Anderson's concept, see Manu Goswami, Rethinking the Modular Nation Form: Toward a Sociohistorical Conception of Nationalism, *Comparative Studies in Society and History* 44 (2002), 776–783.

29. Partha Chatterjee, *Nationalist Thought and the Colonial World: A Derivative Discourse*, Minneapolis, MN (University of Minnesota Press) 1993.

30. Partha Chatterjee, *The Nation and Its Fragments: Colonial and Post-Colonial Histories*, Princeton (Princeton University Press) 1993, 6. See also Etienne Balibar, The Nation Form: History and Ideology, in: Balibar and Immanuel Wallerstein, *Race, Nation, Class: Ambiguous Identities*, London (Verso) 1991, 86–106.

31. Sumit Sarkar, The Decline of the Subaltern in Subaltern Studies, in: *Writing Social History*, New Delhi (Oxford University Press) 1997, 82–108.

32. This line of critique is inspired by Christopher L. Hill, *National History and the World of Nations: Capital, State, and the Rhetoric of History in Japan, France, and the United States*, Durham, NC (Duke University Press) 2008.

33. Sartori, *Bengal in Global Concept History*, 5.

34. Rebecca E. Karl, *Staging the World: Chinese Nationalism at the Turn of the Twentieth Century*, Durham, NC (Duke University Press) 2002.

35. Rebecca E. Karl, Creating Asia: China in the World at the Beginning of the Twentieth Century, *American Historical Review* 103 (1998), 1096–1118, quote: 1099.

36. For further examples, see Manu Goswami, *Producing India: From Colonial Economy to National Space*, Chicago (University of Chicago Press) 2004; Sebastian Conrad, *Globalisation and Nation in Imperial Germany*, Cambridge (Cambridge University Press) 2010; Hill, *National History and the World of Nations*.

Chapter 5

1. See the very helpful discussion in Jürgen Osterhammel, Globalizations, in: Jerry H. Bentley (ed.), *The Oxford Handbook of World History*, Oxford (Oxford University Press) 2011, 89–104.

2. On the history of the concept, see Olaf Bach, *Die Erfindung der Globalisierung: Untersuchungen zu Entstehung und Wandel eines zeitgeschichtlichen Grundbegriffs*, Frankfurt am Main (Campus) 2013.

3. Michael D. Bordo, Alan M. Taylor, and Jeffrey G. Williamson (eds.), *Globalization in Historical Perspective*, Chicago (University of Chicago Press) 2003; Anthony G. Hopkins, *Globalization in World History*, London (Pimlico) 2002; Michael Lang, Globalization and its History, *Journal of Modern History* 78 (2006), 899–931; Jürgen Osterhammel and Niels P. Petersson, *Globalization: A Short History*, Princeton (Princeton University Press) 2009.

4. Adam McKeown, Periodizing Globalization, *History Workshop Journal* 63 (2007), 218–30, quote: 219. I have also borrowed

the four preceding quotes from McKeown, Periodizing Globalization, 218–219.

5. Frederick Cooper, What Is the Concept of Globalization Good for? An African Historian's Perspective, *African Affairs* 100 (2001), 189–213, quote: 190.

6. Andre Gunder Frank and Barry K. Gills (eds.), *The World System: Five Hundred Years or Five Thousand?* London (Routledge) 1993.

7. Jerry H. Bentley, Cross-Cultural Interaction and Periodization in World History, *American Historical Review* 101 (1996), 749–70, quote: 749. See also Jerry H. Bentley, *Old World Encounters: Cross Cultural Contacts and Exchanges in Pre-Modern Times*, New York (Oxford University Press) 1993.

8. William H. McNeill and John Robert McNeill, *The Human Web: A Bird's-Eye View of World History*, New York (Norton) 2003.

9. For the typology of always, never, and sometimes, see Samuel Moyn and Andrew Sartori, Approaches to Global Intellectual History, in: Moyn and Sartori (eds.), *Global Intellectual History*, New York (Columbia University Press) 2013, 3–30.

10. Michael Lang, Globalization and Its History, *Journal of Modern History* 78 (2006), 899–931; David Held and Anthony McGrew, The Great Globalization Debate: An Introduction, in: Held and McGrew (eds.), *The Global Transformations Reader*, Cambridge (Polity Press) 2006.

11. David Held et al., *Global Transformations: Politics, Economics and Culture*, Oxford (Blackwell) 1999.

12. On issues of periodization, see Anthony G. Hopkins, The History of Globalization—and the Globalization of History? in: Hopkins (ed.), *Globalization in World History*, London (Pimlico) 2002, 21–46; Robbie Robertson, *The Three Waves of Globalization: A History of a Developing Global Consciousness*, London (Zed Books) 2002.

13. Kevin H. O'Rourke and Jeffrey G. Williamson, *Globalization and History: The Evolution of a Nineteenth-Century Atlantic Economy*, Cambridge, MA (MIT Press) 1999.

14. Sandford Fleming, *International Meridian Conference: Recommendations Suggested*, Washington, DC (sine nomine) 1884, 6.

15. Charles S. Maier, Consigning the Twentieth Century to History: Alternative Narratives for the Modern Era, *American Historical Review* 105 (2000), 807–831.

16. Serge Gruzinski, *Les quatre parties du monde: Histoire d'une mondialisation*, Paris (La Martinière) 2004; Dennis O. Flynn and Arturo Giráldez, Born with a "Silver Spoon": The Origin of World Trade in 1571, *Journal of World History* 6 (1995), 201–221; Geoffrey Gann, *First Globalization: The Eurasian Exchange, 1500–1800*, Lanham, MD (Rowman & Littlefield) 2003.

17. Raymond Grew, On the Prospect of Global History, in: Bruce Mazlish and Ralph Buultjens (eds.), *Conceptualizing Global History*, Boulder, CO (Westview Press) 1993, 227–249.

18. Osterhammel, Globalizations, 91.

19. For a discussion of the concept of structure, see Anthony Giddens, *The Constitution of Society: Outline of the Theory of Structuration*, Cambridge (Polity) 1984; William H. Sewell Jr., *Logics of History: Social Theory and Social Transformation*, Chicago (University of Chicago Press) 2005. The concept of circulation is discussed by Engseng Ho, *The Graves of Tarim: Genealogy and Mobility across the Indian Ocean*, Berkeley, CA (University of California Press) 2006.

20. Daniel R. Headrick, *Power over Peoples: Technology, Environments, and Western Imperialism, 1400 to the Present*, Princeton (Princeton University Press) 2009; Manuel Castells, *The Information Age: Economy, Society, and Culture*, 3 volumes, Oxford (Blackwell) 1996–1998.

21. John Darwin, *After Tamerlane: The Global History of Empire*, London (Penguin) 2007; Jane Burbank and Frederick Cooper,

Empires in World History: Power and the Politics of Difference, Princeton (Princeton University Press) 2010.

22. James Belich, *Replenishing the Earth: The Settler Revolution and the Rise of the Anglo-World, 1783–1939*, Oxford (Oxford University Press) 2009; Gary Magee and Andrew Thompson, *Empire and Globalisation: Networks of People, Goods and Capital in the British World, c.1850–1914*, Cambridge (Cambridge University Press) 2010.

23. Kenneth Pomeranz and Steven Topik, *The World that Trade Created: Society, Culture, and the World Economy, 1400 to the Present*, Armonk, NY (M.E. Sharpe) 1999.

24. O'Rourke and Williamson, *Globalization and History*; Bordo, Taylor, and Williamson, *Globalization in Historical Perspective*. For a recent theoretical statement, see Kôjin Karatani, *The Structure of World History: From Modes of Production to Modes of Exchange*, Durham, NC (Duke University Press) 2014.

25. William H. Sewell Jr., A Theory of Structure: Duality, Agency, and Transformation, in: Sewell, *Logics of History*, 124–151.

26. Andrew Sartori, Global Intellectual History and the History of Political Economy, in: Moyn and Sartori, *Global Intellectual History*, 110–133. For a critique of this position, see the chapters by Samuel Moyn and Frederic Cooper in the same volume.

27. Sanjay Subrahmanyam, Du Tage au Gange au XVIe siècle: une conjoncture millénariste à l'échelle eurasiatique, *Annales. Histoire, Sciences sociales* 56 (2001), 51–84, quote: 52.

28. Thomas Kuhn, *The Structure of Scientific Revolutions*, Chicago (University of Chicago Press) 1962, 13; Michel Foucault, *The Order of Things: An Archaeology of the Human Sciences*, New York (Pantheon Books) 1970, 168.

29. John W. Meyer, John Boli, George M. Thomas, and Francisco O. Ramirez, World Society and the Nation-State, *American Journal of Sociology* 103 (1997), 144–181; Georg Krücken and Gili S. Drori (eds.), *World Society: The Writings of John W. Meyer*, Oxford (Oxford University Press) 2009.

30. Jared Diamond, *Guns, Germs, and Steel: The Fates of Human Societies*, New York (W. W. Norton) 1997; John Robert McNeill, *Mosquito Empires: Ecology and War in the Greater Caribbean, 1620–1914*, Cambridge (Cambridge University Press) 2010.

31. Sewell, A Theory of Structure, 22.

32. Charles Tilly, *Big Structures, Large Processes, Huge Comparisons*, New York (Russell Sage Foundation) 1984, 147.

33. A prominent work that attempts to work through the overlapping structures of economic, political, military, and ideological networks is Michael Mann, *The Sources of Social Power*, 4 volumes, Cambridge (Cambridge University Press) 1986–2012.

34. Quoted from Ronald Findlay and Kevin O'Rourke, *Power and Plenty: Trade, War and the World Economy in the Second Millennium*, Princeton (Princeton University Press) 2007, 141.

35. Jawaharlal Nehru, *Glimpses of World History* [1934], Oxford (Oxford University Press) 1985, 752. For an impressive work of synthesis that foregrounds exchange and entanglements, see Felipe Fernandez-Armesto, *The World: A Brief History*, New York (Pearson Prentice Hall) 2007.

36. See the special issue "The Global Middle Ages," *Literature Compass* 11 (2014); Oystein S. LaBianca and Sandra Arnold Scham (eds.), *Connectivity in Antiquity: Globalization as a Long Term Historical Process*, Sheffield (Equinox) 2006; Justin Jennings, *Globalizations and the Ancient World*, Cambridge (Cambridge University Press) 2010; Martin Pitts and Miguel John Versluys (eds.), *Globalization and Roman History: World History, Connectivity, and Material Culture*, Cambridge (Cambridge University Press) 2014.

37. For a somewhat euphoric and overly expansive attempt to document globalization already in earliest times, see Jan Nederveen Pieterse, Periodizing Globalization: Histories of Globalization, *New Global Studies* 6, no.2 (2012), Article 1.

38. Siep Stuurman, Herodotus and Sima Qian: History and the Anthropological Turn in Ancient Greece and Han China, *Journal of World History* 19 (2008), 1–40.

Chapter 6

1. Jörg Döring and Tristan Thielmann (eds.), *Spatial Turn: Das Raumparadigma in den Kultur- und Sozialwissenschaften*, Bielefeld (Transcript) 2008; Barney Warf and Santa Arias (eds.), *The Spatial Turn: Interdisciplinary Perspectives*, London (Routledge) 2008.
2. Kenneth Pomeranz, Histories for a Less National Age, *American Historical Review* 119 (2014), 1–22.
3. For global environmental history, see William McNeill, *Plagues and Peoples*, New York (Anchor) 1976; Joachim Radkau, *Nature and Power: A Global History of the Environment*, Cambridge (Cambridge University Press) 2008; John F. Richards, *The Unending Frontier: An Environmental History of the Early Modern World*, Berkeley, CA (University of California Press) 2003; John R. McNeill, *Something New under the Sun: An Environmental History of the Twentieth Century*, New York (Norton) 2000; Edmund Burke III and Kenneth Pomeranz (eds.), *The Environment and World History*, Berkeley, CA (University of California Press) 2009; Corinna Unger and John R. McNeill (eds.), *Environmental Histories of the Cold War*, New York (Cambridge University Press) 2010.
4. Marshall Hodgson, *Rethinking World History: Essays on Europe, Islam, and World History*, Cambridge (Cambridge University Press) 1993; Gagan Sood, Circulation and Exchange in Islamic Eurasia: A Regional Approach to the Early Modern World, *Past and Present* 212 (2011), 113–162; Joshua A. Fogel, *Articulating the Sinosphere: Sino-Japanese Relations in Space and Time*, Cambridge, MA (Harvard University Press) 2009. See also David C. Kang, *East Asia before the West: Five*

Centuries of Trade and Tribute, New York (Columbia University Press) 2010; Shu-mei Shih, *Visuality and Identity: Sinophone Articulations across the Pacific*, Berkeley, CA (University of California Press) 2007. Peregrine Horden and Nicholas Purcell, *The Corrupting Sea: A Study of Mediterranean History*, Oxford (Blackwell) 2000; William V. Harri (ed.), *Rethinking the Mediterranean*, Oxford (Oxford University Press) 2005.

5. Daniel T. Rodgers, *Atlantic Crossings: Social Politics in a Progressive Age*, Princeton (Princeton University Press) 1998; Bernard Bailyn, *Atlantic History: Concept and Contours*, Cambridge, MA (Harvard University Press) 2005; Jeremy Adelman, *Sovereignty and Revolution in the Iberian Atlantic*, Princeton (Princeton University Press) 2006; Jack P. Greene and Philip D. Morgan (eds.), *Atlantic History: A Critical Appraisal*, Oxford (Oxford University Press) 2009.

6. Sugata Bose, *A Hundred Horizons: The Indian Ocean in the Age of Global Empire*, Cambridge, MA (Harvard University Press) 2006; Thomas R. Metcalf, *Imperial Connections: India in the Indian Ocean Arena, 1860–1920,* Berkeley, CA (University of California Press) 2007; Claude Markovits, *The Global World of Indian Merchants, 1750–1947: Traders of Sind from Bukhara to Panama*, Cambridge (Cambridge University Press) 2000; Hamashita Takeshi, *Kindai chūgoku no kokusaiteki keiki: Chōkō bōeki shisutemu to kindai Ajia* [International Factors in Modern Chinese History: The Tributary Trade System in Modern Asia], Tokyo (Tokyo Daigaku Shuppankai) 1990.

7. Paul Gilroy, *The Black Atlantic: Modernity and Double-Consciousness*, Cambridge, MA (Harvard University Press) 1993; and, less sophisticated, Jace Weaver, *The Red Atlantic: American Indigenes and the Making of the Modern World 1000–1927*, Chapel Hill, NC (University of North Carolina Press) 2014.

8. Xinru Liu, *The Silk Road in World History*, Oxford (Oxford University Press) 2010; Christopher I. Beckwith, *Empires of*

the Silk Road: A History of Central Eurasia from the Bronze Age to the Present, Princeton (Princeton University Press) 2009.

9. Dominic Sachsenmaier, Recent Trends in European History: The World beyond Europe and Alternative Historical Spaces, *Journal of Modern European History* 7 (2009), 5–25.

10. For a synthesis, see Markus P. M. Vink, Indian Ocean Studies and the "New Thalassology," *Journal of Global History* 2 (2007), 41–62; Michael N. Pearson, *The Indian Ocean*, London (Routledge) 2003.

11. Denys Lombard, *Le carrefour javanais: Essai d'histoire globale*, 3 volumes, Paris (École des hautes études en sciences sociales) 1990; Charles King, *The Black Sea: A History*, New York (Oxford University Press) 2004; Matt Matsuda, The Pacific, *American Historical Review* 111 (2006), 758–780; Katrina Gulliver, Finding the Pacific World, *Journal of World History* 22 (2011), 83–100; R. Bin Wong, Between Nation and World: Braudelian Regions in Asia, *Review* 26 (2003), 1–45; Sunil Amrith, *Crossing the Bay of Bengal: The Furies of Nature and the Fortunes of Migrants*, Cambridge, MA (Harvard University Press) 2013.

12. Takeshi Hamashita, *China, East Asia and the Global Economy: Regional and Historical Perspectives*, ed. by Linda Grove and Mark Selden, New York (Routledge) 2008; Mizoguchi Yuzo, Hamashita Takeshi, Hiraishi Naoaki, and Miyajima Hiroshi (eds.), *Ajia kara kangaeru [Rethinking History from the Perspective of Asia]*, 7 volumes, Tokyo (University of Tokyo Press) 1993–94; John Lee, Trade and Economy in Preindustrial East Asia, c. 1500-c. 1800: East Asia in the Age of Global Integration, *Journal of Asian Studies* 58 (1999), 2–26; Sugihara Kaoru, *Ajia taiheiyō keizaiken no koryū* [The Rise of the Asia-Pacific Economy], Osaka (Osaka Daigaku Shuppankai) 2003.

13. Some of these approaches have also begun to transform the field of oceanic history: Eric Tagliacozzo, *Secret Trades, Porous Borders: Smuggling and States along a Southeast Asian Frontier*,

1865–1915, New Haven, CT (Yale University Press) 2005; Ulrike Freitag, *Indian Ocean Migrants and the Reform of Hadhramaut,* Leiden (Brill) 2003.

14. George E. Marcus, Ethnography in/of the World System: The Emergence of Multi-Sited Ethnography, *Annual Review of Anthropology* 24 (1995), 95–117.

15. Gregory T. Cushman, *Guano and the Opening of the Pacific World: A Global Ecological History,* Cambridge (Cambridge University Press) 2013.

16. Engseng Ho, *The Graves of Tarim: Genealogy and Mobility across the Indian Ocean,* Berkeley, CA (University of California Press) 2006.

17. David Northrup, *Indentured Labor in the Age of Imperialism, 1834–1922,* Cambridge (Cambridge University Press) 1995; Jan Lucassen (ed.), *Global Labour History: A State of the Art,* Bern (Peter Lang) 2006; Marcel van der Linden, *Workers of the World: Essays Toward a Global Labor History,* Leiden (Brill) 2008.

18. Sidney W. Mintz, *Sweetness and Power: The Place of Sugar in Modern History,* New York (Viking) 1985; Christine M. Du Bois, Chee Beng Tan, and Sidney W. Mintz, *The World of Soy,* Chicago (University of Illinois Press) 2008; Alan Macfarlane and Gerry Martin, *Glass: A World History,* Chicago (Chicago University Press) 2002; Robert Finlay, *The Pilgrim Art: The Culture of Porcelain in World History,* Berkeley, CA (University of California Press) 2010; Sven Beckert, *Empire of Cotton: A Global History,* New York (Knopf) 2014.

19. Steven Topik, Carlos Marichal, and Zephyr Frank (eds.), *From Silver to Cocaine: Latin American Commodity Chains and the Building of the World Economy,* Durham, NC (Duke University Press) 2006; Jeremy Prestholdt, *Domesticating the World: African Consumerism and the Genealogies of Globalization,* Berkeley, CA (University of California Press) 2008. See also Arjun Appadurai (ed.), *The Social Life of Things: Commodities in*

Cultural Perspective, Cambridge (Cambridge University Press) 1986.

20. Charles Maier, Transformations of Territoriality, 1600–2000, in: Gunilla Budde, Sebastian Conrad, and Oliver Janz (eds.), *Transnationale Geschichte: Themen, Tendenzen, Theorien*, Göttingen (Vandenhoeck & Ruprecht) 2006, 24–36.

21. Manuel Castells, *The Rise of the Network Society*, vol. 1: *The Information Age: Economy, Society, and Culture*, Oxford (Blackwell) 1996, 146.

22. Castells, *The Information Age*, 77.

23. Tom Standage, *The Victorian Internet: The Remarkable Story of the Telegraph and the Nineteenth Century's Online Pioneers*, New York (Walker) 1999. See also Dwayne R. Winseck and Robert M. Pike, *Communication and Empire: Media, Markets, and Globalization, 1860–1930*, Durham, NC (Duke University Press) 2007; Daniel R. Headrick, *Power over Peoples: Technology, Environments, and Western Imperialism, 1400 to the Present*, Princeton (Princeton University Press) 2009.

24. For two examples of a broad literature, see Azyumardi Azra, *The Origins of Islamic Reformism in Southeast Asia: Networks of Malay-Indonesian and Middle Eastern "Ulama" in the Seventeenth and Eighteenth Centuries*, Honolulu, HI (University of Hawaii Press) 2004; Gary Magee and Andrew Thompson, *Empire and Globalisation: Networks of People, Goods and Capital in the British World, c.1850–1914*, Cambridge (Cambridge University Press) 2010.

25. E. Natalie Rothman, *Brokering Empire: Trans-Imperial Subjects between Venice and Istanbul*, Ithaca, NY (Cornell University Press) 2012; Francesca Trivellato, *The Familiarity of Strangers: The Sephardic Diaspora, Livorno, and Cross-Cultural Trade in the Early Modern Period*, New Haven, CT (Yale University Press) 2009; Sebouh David Aslanian, *From the Indian Ocean to the Mediterranean: The Global Trade Networks of Armenian Merchants from New Julfa*, Berkeley, CA (University of California Press) 2011.

26. Manuel Castells, Toward a Sociology of the Network Society, *Contemporary Sociology* 29 (2000), 693–699.

27. Bruno Latour, *Reassembling the Social: An Introduction to Actor-Network Theory*, Oxford (Oxford University Press) 2005, 237.

28. Latour, *Reassembling the Social*, 238.

29. Latour, *Reassembling the Social*, 137.

30. For an example of a study inspired by Latour and linking different scales, see Timothy Mitchell, *Carbon Democracy: Political Power in the Age of Oil*, London (Verso) 2011.

31. Donald R. Wright, *The World and a Very Small Place in Africa: A History of Globalization in Niumi, the Gambia,* second edition, Armonk, NY (M.E. Sharpe) 2004.

32. Natalie Zemon Davis, *Trickster Travels: A Sixteenth-Century Muslim between Worlds*, New York (Hill & Wang) 2006, 12–13.

33. For other examples of this genre, see Tony Ballantyne and Antoinette Burton (eds.), *Moving Subjects: Gender, Mobility and Intimacy in an Age of Global Empire*, Champaign, IL (University of Illinois Press) 2009; Desley Deacon, Penny Russell, and Angela Woollacott (eds.), *Transnational Lives: Biographies of Global Modernity, 1700-Present*, Basingstoke (Palgrave Macmillan) 2010; Miles Ogborn (ed.), *Global Lives: Britain and the World, 1550–1800*, Cambridge (Cambridge University Press) 2008; Linda Colley, *The Ordeal of Elizabeth Marsh: A Woman in World History*, New York (Pantheon) 2007; David Lambert and Alan Lester (eds.), *Colonial Lives across the British Empire: Imperial Careering in the Long Nineteenth Century*, Cambridge (Cambridge University Press) 2006; Tonio Andrade, A Chinese Farmer, Two African Boys, and a Warlord: Toward a Global Microhistory, *Journal of World History* 21 (2010), 573–591; Sanjay Subrahmanyam, *Three Ways To Be Alien: Travails and Encounters in the Early Modern World*, Waltham, MA (Brandeis University Press) 2011; Emma Rothschild, *The Inner Life of Empires: An Eighteenth-Century History*, Princeton (Princeton University Press) 2011.

34. Anne Gerritsen, Scales of a Local: The Place of Locality in a Globalizing World, in: Douglas Northrop (ed.), *A Companion to World History*, Oxford (Wiley-Blackwell) 2012, 213–226, quote: 224. See also Anthony G. Hopkins (ed.), *Global History: Interactions between the Universal and the Local*, New York (Palgrave) 2006.

35. Sho Konishi, Reopening the "Opening of Japan": A Russian-Japanese Revolutionary Encounter and the Vision of Anarchist Progress, *American Historical Review* 112 (2007), 101–30; Konishi, *Anarchist Modernity: Cooperatism and Japanese-Russian Intellectual Relations in Modern Japan*, Cambridge, MA (Harvard University Press) 2013.

36. Adam McKeown, What are the Units of World History? in: Northrop, *Companion to World History*, 79–93, quote: 83.

37. For the example of macro-regions, see Martin W. Lewis and Kären E. Wigen, *The Myth of Continents: A Critique of Metageography*, Berkeley, CA (University of California Press) 1997. For the example of East Asia, see Sebastian Conrad and Prasenjit Duara, Viewing Regionalisms from East Asia, *American Historical Association Pamphlet* 2013.

38. Duncan Bell, Making and Taking Worlds, in: Samuel Moyn and Andrew Sartori (eds.), *Global Intellectual History*, New York (Columbia University Press) 2013, 254–279.

39. Arif Dirlik, Performing the World: Reality and Representation in the Making of World Histor(ies), *Journal of World History* 16 (2005), 391–410, quote: 406.

40. Pomeranz, Histories for a Less National Age; Sebouh David Aslanian, Joyce E. Chaplin, Ann McGrath, and Kristin Mann, "AHR Conversation: How Size Matters: The Question of Scale in History," *American Historical Review* 118 (2013), 1431–1472.

41. Roland Robertson, Glocalization: Time-space and homogeneity-heterogeneity, in: Mike Featherstone, Scott M. Lash, and Roland Robertson (eds.), *Global Modernities*, London (Sage) 1995, 25–44, quote: 35.

42. Jacques Revel (ed.), *Jeux d'échelles: Le micro-analyse à l'expérience*, Paris (Seuil-Gallimard) 1996.
43. Quoted in Andrew Zimmerman, A German Alabama in Africa: The Tuskegee Expedition to German Togo and the Transnational Origins of West African Cotton Growers, *American Historical Review* 110 (2005), 1362–1398, quote: 1380. See also Zimmerman, *Alabama in Africa: Booker T. Washington, the German Empire, and the Globalization of the New South*, Princeton (Princeton University Press) 2010.

Chapter 7

1. David Armitage, What's the Big Idea? Intellectual History and the Longue Durée, *History of European Ideas* 38 (2012), 493–507, quote: 493.
2. Daniel L. Smail and Andrew Shryock, History and the "Pre," *American Historical Review* 118 (2013), 709–737, quote: 713.
3. Daniel L. Smail, In the Grip of Sacred History, *American Historical Review* 110 (2005), 1336–1361; Smail, *On Deep History and the Brain*, Berkeley, CA (University of California Press) 2008; Andrew Shryock and Daniel L. Smail (eds.), *Deep History: The Architecture of Past and Present*, Berkeley, CA (University of California Press) 2011.
4. David Christian, *Maps of Time: An Introduction to Big History*, Berkeley, CA (University of California Press) 2004; Fred Spier, *The Structure of Big History: From the Big Bang until Today*, Amsterdam (Amsterdam University Press) 1996; Fred Spier, *Big History and the Future of Humanity*, Oxford (Wiley-Blackwell) 2010; Cynthia Stokes Brown, *Big History: From the Big Bang to the Present*, New York (The New Press) 2007; Michael Cook, *A Brief History of the Human Race*, New York (Norton) 2003; David Christian, Cynthia Stokes Brown, and Craig Benjamin, *Big History: Between Nothing and Everything*, New York (McGraw-Hill) 2013.

5. Jared Diamond, *Guns, Germs, and Steel: The Fates of Human Societies*, New York (W. W. Norton) 1997.

6. William McNeill, Foreword, in: Christian, *Maps of Time*, xv.

7. David Christian, Contingency, Pattern and the S-curve in Human History, *World History Connected*, October 2009, par. 12. Online URL: <http://worldhistoryconnected.press.illinois.edu/6.3/christian.html> [accessed 17 March 2014].

8. Diamond, *Guns, Germs, and Steel*, 26.

9. Quoted in Julia Adeney Thomas, History and Biology in the Anthropocene: Problems of Scale, Problems of Value, *American Historical Review* 119 (2014), 1587–1607, quote: 1587.

10. David Christian, The Return of Universal History, *History and Theory*, theme issue 49 (2010), 6–27.

11. Ian Morris, *Why the West Rules—for Now: The Patterns of History, and What They Reveal about the Future*, New York (Farrar, Straus and Giroux) 2010, 582.

12. Fernand Braudel, Histoire et Science sociales: La longue durée, *Annales ESC* 4 (1958), 725–753; Reinhart Koselleck, *Zeitschichten: Studien zur Historik*, Frankfurt (Suhrkamp) 2002.

13. Kenneth Pomeranz, Teleology, Discontinuity and World History: Periodization and Some Creation Myths of Modernity, *Asian Review of World Histories* 1 (2013), 189–226.

14. Jo Guldi and David Armitage, *The History Manifesto*, Cambridge (Cambridge University Press) 2014.

15. Jürgen Osterhammel, Vergangenheiten: Über die Zeithorizonte der Geschichte, unpublished manuscript.

16. Sebastian Conrad, Remembering Asia: History and Memory in Post–Cold War Japan, in: Aleida Assmann and Sebastian Conrad (eds.), *Memory in a Global Age*, London (Palgrave Macmillan) 2010, 163–177.

17. Christopher L. Hill, *National History and the World of Nations: Capital, State, and the Rhetoric of History in Japan, France, and the United States*, Durham, NC (Duke University Press) 2008, 71.

18. John E. Wills, *1688: A Global History*, New York (W. W. Norton) 2002, 112. See also Olivier Bernier, *The World in 1800*, New York (Wiley) 2000; Christian Caryl, *Strange Rebels: 1979 and the Birth of the 21st Century*, New York (Basic Books) 2013.

19. Erez Manela, *The Wilsonian Moment: Self-Determination and the International Origins of Anticolonial Nationalism*, Oxford (Oxford University Press) 2007. For the range of reactions, compare the glowing review by Ussama Makdisi in *Diplomatic History* 33 (2009), 133–137 to the scathing comments by Rebecca E. Karl in *American Historical Review* 113 (2008), 1474–1476.

20. On this issue, see also Carlo Ginzburg, Microhistory: Two or Three Things That I Know about It, *Critical Inquiry* 20 (1993), 10–35; Siegfried Kracauer, *History: The Last Things before the Last*, New York (M. Wiener) 1969.

21. Spier, *The Structure of Big History*, 18.

22. Janet L. Abu-Lughod, *Before European Hegemony: The World System, A.D. 1250–1350*, Oxford (Oxford University Press) 1989, 12.

23. Kenneth Pomeranz, *The Great Divergence: China, Europe, and the Making of the Modern World Economy*, Princeton (Princeton University Press) 2000, 23, 12, 207.

24. Dipesh Chakrabarty, The Climate of History: Four Theses, *Critical Inquiry* 35 (2009), 197–222; Thomas, History and Biology in the Anthropocene.

25. Anthony Giddens, *The Constitution of Society: Outline of the Theory of Structuration*, Cambridge (Polity) 1984.

Chapter 8

1. Fred Spier, Big History, in: Douglas Northrop (ed.), *A Companion to World History*, Oxford (Wiley-Blackwell) 2012, 171–184, quote: 173.

2. Dario Castiglione and Ian Hamphser-Monk (eds.), *The History of Political Thought in National Context*, Cambridge (Cambridge University Press) 2011.

3. For a typology, see John M. Hobson, *The Eurocentric Conception of World Politics: Western International Theory, 1760–2010*, Cambridge (Cambridge University Press) 2012.

4. Robert B. Marks, *The Origins of the Modern World: A Global and Ecological Narrative*, Lanham, MD (Rowman & Littlefield) 2002, 8.

5. Prominent examples include William McNeill, *The Rise of the West: A History of the Human Community*, Chicago (University of Chicago Press) 1963; Eric Jones, *The European Miracle: Environments, Economies and Geopolitics in the History of Europe and Asia*, Cambridge (Cambridge University Press) 1981; David Landes, *The Wealth and Poverty of Nations: Why Some Are So Rich and Some So Poor*, New York (W. W. Norton) 1999.

6. Arnold J. Toynbee, *A Study of History*, vol. 12: *Reconsiderations*, London (Oxford University Press) 1961, 630.

7. Vinay Lal, Provincializing the West: World History from the Perspective of Indian History, in: Benedikt Stuchtey and Eckhardt Fuchs (eds.), *Writing World History, 1800–2000*, Oxford (Oxford University Press) 2003, 271–289, quote: 283.

8. For an insightful critique, see Sho Konishi, Reopening the "Opening of Japan": A Russian-Japanese Revolutionary Encounter and the Vision of Anarchist Progress, *American Historical Review* 112 (2007), 101–130.

9. Robert Bartlett, *The Making of Europe*, Princeton (Princeton University Press) 1994; Jack Goody, *The East in the West*, Cambridge (Cambridge University Press) 1996; John M. Hobson, *The Eastern Origins of Western Civilisation*, Cambridge (Cambridge University Press) 2004.

10. Jerry H. Bentley, *Shapes of World History in Twentieth-Century Scholarship*, Washington, DC (American Historical Association) 1996, 4–5.

11. Dipesh Chakrabarty, Postcoloniality and the Artifice of History: Who Speaks for "Indian" Pasts? *Representations* 37 (1992), 1–26, quote: 1.

12. For such myth-history, see Gavin Menzies, *1421: The Year China Discovered the World*, London (Bantam) 2003; Menzies, *1434: The Year a Magnificent Chinese Fleet Sailed to Italy and Ignited the Renaissance*, London (HarperCollins) 2008.

13. Andre Gunder Frank, *ReOrient: Global Economy in the Asian Age*, Berkeley, CA (University of California Press) 1998.

14. Chakrabarty, Postcoloniality and the Artifice of History, 3.

15. Larry Wolff, *Inventing Eastern Europe: The Map of Civilization on the Mind of the Enlightenment*, Stanford, CA (Stanford University Press) 1994. See also Dominic Sachsenmaier, Recent Trends in European History: The World beyond Europe and Alternative Historical Space, *Journal of Modern European History* 7 (2009), 5–25.

16. Arif Dirlik, Thinking Modernity Historically: Is "Alternative Modernity" the Answer? *Asian Review of World Histories* 1 (2013), 5–44.

17. Santiago Castro-Gómez, *La Hybris del Punto Cero*, Bogotá (Editorial pontifica Universidad Javeriana) 2005; Walter Mignolo, Epistemic Disobedience, Independent Thought and Decolonial Freedom, *Theory, Culture & Society* 26 (2009), 159–181, quote: 160.

18. Douglas Northrop, Introduction: The Challenge of World History, in: Northrop, *Companion to World History*, 1–12, quote: 4.

19. Dominic Sachsenmaier, *Global Perspectives on Global History: Theories and Approaches in a Connected World*, Cambridge (Cambridge University Press) 2011, 1–10.

20. Arif Dirlik, Performing the World: Reality and Representation in the Making of World Histor(ies), *Journal of World History* 16 (2005), 391–410.

21. Maghan Keita, *Race and the Writing of History: Riddling the Sphinx*, Oxford (Oxford University Press) 2000.

22. Martin Bernal, *Black Athena: The Afroasiatic Roots of Classical Civilization*, New Brunswick, NJ (Rutgers University Press) 1987; Valentin Y. Mudimbe, *The Invention of Africa: Gnosis, Philosophy, and the Order of Knowledge*, Bloomington, IN (Indiana University Press) 1988; Paul Gilroy, *The Black Atlantic: Modernity and Double-Consciousness*, Cambridge, MA (Harvard University Press) 1993; Joseph C. Miller, History and Africa/Africa and History, *American Historical Review* 104 (1999), 1–32.

23. Steven Feierman, African Histories and the Dissolution of World History, in: Robert H. Bates, V. Y. Mudimbe, and Jean O'Barr (eds.), *Africa and the Disciplines: The Contributions of Research in Africa to the Social Sciences and Humanities*, Chicago (University of Chicago Press) 182–216, quote: 198.

24. See Dirlik, Thinking Modernity.

25. Cheikh Anta Diop, *Civilization or Barbarism: An Authentic Anthropology*, New York (Lawrence Hill) 1991; Molefe Kete Asante, *The Afrocentric Idea*, Philadelphia, PA (Temple University Press) 1998; Ama Mazama (ed.), *The Afrocentric Paradigm*, Trenton, NJ (Africa World Press) 2003. For a critical assessment, see Stephen Howe, *Afrocentrism: Mythical Pasts and Imagined Homes*, London (Verso) 1998.

26. Ahmed Ibrahim Abushouk, World History from an Islamic Perspective: The Experience of the International Islamic University Malaysia, in: Patrick Manning (ed.), *Global Practice in World History: Advances Worldwide*, Princeton (Markus Wiener) 2008, 39–56.

27. Ashis Nandy, History's Forgotten Doubles, *History and Theory* 34 (1995), 44–66.

28. Kawakatsu Heita, *Nihon bunmei to kindai seiyō: 'Sakoku' saikō*, Tokyo (NHK Books) 1991.

29. Sachsenmaier, *Global Perspectives on Global History*, 200–206.

30. Sachsenmaier, *Global Perspectives*.

31. Ricardo Duchesne, *The Uniqueness of Western Civilization*, Leiden (Brill) 2011, x.
32. Examples include John M. Headley, *The Europeanization of the World: On the Origins of Human Rights and Democracy*, Princeton (Princeton University Press) 2008; Anthony Pagden, *Worlds at War: The 2,500-Year Struggle between East and West*, Oxford (Oxford University Press) 2008; Toby E. Huff, *Intellectual Curiosity and the Scientific Revolution: A Global Perspective*, Cambridge (Cambridge University Press) 2010.
33. Gary B. Nash, Charlotte A. Crabtree, and Ross E. Dunn, *History on Trial: Culture Wars and the Teaching of the Past*, New York (Vintage Books) 2000; Jill Lepore, *The Whites of Their Eyes: The Tea Party's Revolution and the Battle over American History*, Princeton (Princeton University Press) 2010.
34. George Thompson and Jerry Combee, *World History and Cultures in Christian Perspective*, Pensacola, FL (A Beka Book) 1997. See also Frances R. A. Paterson, *Democracy and Intolerance: Christian School Curricula, School Choice, and Public Policy*, Bloomington, IN (Phi Delta Kappa) 2003.
35. Niall Ferguson, *Civilisation: The West and the Rest*, London (Allen Lane) 2011, preface to the UK edition.
36. For such scholarly cooperation, see Molefe Keta Asante, Yoshitaka Miike, and Jing Yin (eds.), *The Global Intercultural Communication Reader*, 2nd edition, New York (Routledge) 2013. For a historical perspective on the transnational conversations between protagonists of cultural uniqueness, see Dominic Sachsenmaier, Searching for Alternatives to Western Modernity, *Journal of Modern European History* 4 (2006), 241–159.
37. Dirlik, Thinking Modernity, quote: 15.
38. For promising steps in such a direction, see a number of recent attempts to build on early insights of the Japanese philosopher

Takeuchi Yoshimi in his article *Hōhō to shite no Ajia* [Asia as Method], in: Takeuchi Yoshimi, *What is Modernity? Writings of Takeuchi Yoshimi*, edited, translated, and with an introduction by Richard Calichman, New York (Columbia University Press) 2005, 149–165. See, for example, Arif Dirlik, Revisioning Modernity: Modernity in Eurasian Perspectives, *Inter-Asia Cultural Studies* 12 (2011), 284–305; Kuan-hsing Chen, *Asia as Method: Toward Deimperialization*, Durham, NC (Duke University Press) 2010; Wang Hui, The Politics of Imagining Asia: A Genealogical Analysis, *Inter-Asia Cultural Studies* 8 (2007), 1–33.

39. Arif Dirlik, *Culture and History in Post-Revolutionary China: The Perspective of Global Modernity*, Hong Kong (Chinese University of Hong Kong Press) 2011.

40. Jean Comaroff and John Comaroff, Theory from the South: A Rejoinder, *Cultural Anthropology*, March 2012, http://culanth .org/fieldsights/273--theory--from--the--south--a--rejoinder. See also Marcelo C. Rosa, Theories of the South: Limits and Perspectives of an Emergent Movement in Social Sciences, *Current Sociology* 62 (2014), 851–867.

Chapter 9

1. Barry K. Gills and William R. Thompson, Globalization, Global Histories and Historical Globalities, in: Gills and Thompson (eds.), *Globalization and Global History*, London (Routledge) 2006, 1–17, quote: 2.

2. See, for example, the debates triggered by Hayden V. White, *Metahistory: The Historical Imagination in Nineteenth-Century Europe*, Baltimore, MD (Johns Hopkins University Press) 1973.

3. Nelson Goodman, *Ways of Worldmaking*, New York (Hackett) 1978. For the quote, see Goodman, Realism, Relativism, and Reality, *New Literary History* 14 (1983), 269–272, quote: 269.

4. Sanjay Krishnan, *Reading the Global: Troubling Perspectives on Britain's Empire in Asia*, New York (Columbia University Press) 2007, 2, 4.

5. Krishnan, *Reading the Global*, 4.

6. Thomas Friedman, *The World is Flat*, New York (Farrar, Straus and Giroux) 2005.

7. Samuel Huntington, *The Clash of Civilizations and the Remaking of World Order*, New York (Simon & Schuster) 1996; Robert D. Kaplan, *The Coming Anarchy*, New York (Random House) 2000; and from a very different angle: Anna Lowenhaupt Tsing, *Frictions: An Ethnography of Global Connection*, Princeton (Princeton University Press) 2004.

8. Antonio Negri and Michael Hardt, *Empire*, Cambridge, MA (Harvard University Press) 2000.

9. Nathalie Karagiannis and Peter Wagner (eds.), *Varieties of World-Making: Beyond Globalization*, Liverpool (Liverpool University Press) 2007.

10. Wang Gungwu (ed.), *Global History and Migrations*, Boulder, CO (Westview Press) 1997; Patrick Manning, *Migration in World History*, New York (Routledge) 2005; Dirk Hoerder, *Cultures in Contact: World Migrations in the Second Millennium*, Durham, NC (Duke University Press) 2002.

11. This is a general issue of all mobility studies, such as Linda Basch, Cristina Blanc-Szanton, and Nina Glick Schiller (eds.), *Nations Unbound: Transnational Projects, Postcolonial Predicaments and Deterritorialized Nation-States*, New York (Routledge) 1994; Stephen Greenblatt et al., *Cultural Mobility: A Manifesto*, Cambridge (Cambridge University Press) 2009.

12. On the modern "making" of migration, see Adam McKeown, *Melancholy Order: Asian Migration and the Globalization of Borders*, New York (Columbia University Press) 2008.

13. John Darwin, *After Tamerlane: The Global History of Empire*, London (Penguin Books) 2007, 23.

14. Jane Burbank and Frederick Cooper, *Empires in World History: Power and the Politics of Difference*, Princeton (Princeton University Press) 2010, 2–3.

15. Pekka Hämäläinen, *The Comanche Empire*, New Haven (Yale University Press) 2008.

16. Karl Jacoby, Indigenous Empires and Native Nations: Beyond History and Ethnohistory in Pekka Hämäläinen's *The Comanche Empire*, *History and Theory* 52 (2013), 60–66, quote: 63.

17. John Tutino, Globalizing the Comanche Empire, *History and Theory* 52 (2013), 67–74.

18. Gyan Prakash, Subaltern Studies as Postcolonial Criticism, *American Historical Review* 99 (1994), 1475–1490; Vinayak Chaturvedi (ed.), *Mapping Subaltern Studies and the Postcolonial*, London (Verso) 2000.

19. Stefano Varese, Indigenous Epistemologies in the Age of Globalization, in: Juan Poblete (ed.), *Critical Latin American and Latino Studies*, Minneapolis, MN (University of Minnesota Press) 2002, 138–153; Madina V. Tlostanova and Walter D. Mignolo, *Learning to Unlearn: Decolonial Reflections from Eurasia and the Americas*, Columbus, OH (Ohio State University Press) 2012.

20. Republic of South Africa, Department of Science and Technology, *Indigenous Knowledge Systems*, Pretoria (Government Printer) 2006.

21. John Makeham, Disciplining Tradition in Modern China: Two Case Studies, *History and Theory* 51 (2012), 89–104.

22. Benjamin Elman, *On Their Own Terms: Science in China, 1550–1900*, Cambridge, MA (Harvard University Press) 2005. For a provocative position, see also Min OuYang, There Is No Need for *Zhongguo Zhexue* to Be Philosophy, *Asian Philosophy* 22 (2012), 199–223.

23. See for example the work of Wang Hui, *Zhongguo xiandai sixiang de xingqi (The Rise of Modern Chinese Thought)*, 4 volumes, Beijing (Sanlian Shudian) 2004. For a short summary

of the line of argument, see Wang Hui, *China from Empire to Nation-State*, Cambridge, MA (Harvard University Press) 2014.

24. See Arif Dirlik, Guoxue/National Learning in the Age of Global Modernity, *China Perspectives* 1 (2011), 4–13.

25. Dipesh Chakrabarty, *Provincializing Europe: Postcolonial Thought and Historical Difference*, Princeton (Princeton University Press) 2000, 16.

26. C. A. Bayly, The Empire of Religion, in: Bayly, *The Birth of the Modern World, 1780–1914*, Oxford (Blackwell) 2004, 325–365; Tomoko Masuzawa, *The Invention of World Religions: Or, How European Universalism was Preserved in the Language of Pluralism*, Chicago (Chicago University Press) 2005; Jason Ānanda Josephson, *The Invention of Religion in Japan*, Chicago (Chicago University Press) 2012.

27. Margrit Pernau, Whither Conceptual History? From National to Entangled Histories, *Contributions to the History of Concepts* 7 (2012), 1–11; Carol Gluck and Anna Lowenhaupt Tsing (eds.), *Words in Motion: Towards a Global Lexicon*, Durham, NC (Duke University Press) 2009.

28. John F. Richards, Early Modern India and World History, *Journal of World History* 8 (1997), 197–209, quote: 197. For the debate on early modernity in global history, see Lynn Struve, Introduction, in: Struve (ed.), *The Qing Formation in World Historical Time*, Cambridge, MA (Harvard University Press) 2004, 1–54.

29. Dipesh Chakrabarty, The Muddle of Modernity, *American Historical Review* 116 (2011), 663–675, quotes: 672.

30. Christopher L. Hill, Conceptual Universalization in the Transnational Nineteenth Century, in: Samuel Moyn and Andrew Sartori (eds.), *Global Intellectual History*, New York (Columbia University Press) 2013, 134–158; Sebastian Conrad, Enlightenment in Global History: A Historiographical Critique, *American Historical Review* 117 (2012), 999–1027.

31. Arif Dirlik, Is There History after Eurocentrism? Globalism, Postcolonialism, and the Disavowal of History, in: Dirlik, *Postmodernity's Histories: The Past as Legacy and Project*, Lanham, MD (Rowman & Littlefield) 2000, 63–90, quote: 72.

Chapter 10

1. Sven Beckert, The Travails of Doing History from Abroad, *American Historical Review* 119 (2014), 817–823, quote: 821.
2. Friedrich von Schiller, The Nature and Value of Universal History: An Inaugural Lecture [1789], *History and Theory* 11 (1972), 321–334, quote: 327.
3. Haneda Masashi, *Atarashii sekaishi e: Chikyū shimin no tame no kōsō*, Tokyo (Iwanami Shinsho) 2011, 3–16; Jerry H. Bentley, Myths, Wagers, and Some Moral Implications of World History, *Journal of World History* 16 (2005), 51–82; Dominic Sachsenmaier, World History as Ecumenical History? *Journal of World History* 18 (2007) 465–490.
4. Sugata Bose and Kris Manjapra (eds.), *Cosmopolitan Thought Zones: South Asia and the Global Circulation of Ideas*, New York (Palgrave Macmillan) 2010. See also Carol A. Breckenridge, Sheldon Pollock, Homi K. Bhabha, and Dipesh Chakrabarty (eds.), *Cosmopolitanism*, Durham, NC (Duke University Press) 2000; Pheng Cheah and Bruce Robbins (eds.), *Cosmopolitics: Thinking and Feeling Beyond the Nation*, Minneapolis (University of Minnesota Press) 1998; Kwame Appiah, *Cosmopolitanism: Ethics in a World of Strangers*, New York (Norton) 2006; Gerard Delanty, *The Cosmopolitan Imagination: The Renewal of Critical Social Theory*, Cambridge (Cambridge University Press) 2009.
5. Sachsenmaier, *Global Perspectives*, 213–231; Luo Xu, Reconstructing World History in the People's Republic of China since the 1980s, *Journal of World History* 18 (2007), 325–350.

6. Arif Dirlik, Performing the World: Reality and Representation in the Making of World Histor(ies), *Journal of World History* 16 (2005), 391–410.

7. Karen Ho, Situating Global Capitalisms: A View from Wall Street Investment Banks, *Cultural Anthropology* 20 (2005), 68–96, quote: 69; see also Stuart Alexander Rockefeller, Flow, *Current Anthropology* 52 (2011), 557–578; Augustine Sedgewick, Against Flows, *History of the Present* 4 (2014), 143–170.

8. Fernando Coronil, Towards a Critique of Globalcentrism: Speculations on Capitalism's Nature, *Public Culture* 12 (2000), 351–374.

9. Immanuel Wallerstein, Eurocentrism and its Avatars: The Dilemmas of Social Science, *New Left Review* 226 (1997), 93–107.

10. Arif Dirlik, Globalization Now and Then: Some Thoughts on Contemporary Readings of Late 19th/Early 20th Century Responses to Modernity, *Journal of Modern European History* 4, no. 2 (2006), 137–157, quote: 154; Arif Dirlik, Confounding Metaphors, Inventions of the World: What Is World History For? in: Benedikt Stuchtey and Eckhardt Fuchs (eds.), *Writing World History, 1800–2000,* Oxford (Oxford University Press) 2003, 91–133.

11. Jürgen Osterhammel, Globalizations, in: Jerry H. Bentley (ed.), *The Oxford Handbook of World History*, Oxford (Oxford University Press) 2011, 89–104.

12. Dipesh Chakrabarty, *Provincializing Europe: Postcolonial Thought and Historical Difference*, Princeton (Princeton University Press) 2000, 28.

13. Patrick Manning, *Navigating World History: Historians Create a Global Past*, New York (Palgrave Macmillan) 2003; Dominic Sachsenmaier, *Global Perspectives on Global History: Theories and Approaches in a Connected World*, Cambridge (Cambridge University Press) 2011.

14. Stefan Berger and Chris Lorenz (eds.), *Nationalizing the Past: Historians as Nation Builders in Modern Europe*, Basingstoke (Palgrave Macmillan) 2010; Stefan Berger (ed.), *Writing the Nation: Global Perspectives*, Basingstoke (Palgrave Macmillan) 2006; Toyin Falola, Nationalism and African Historiography, in: Q. Edward Wang and Georg G. Iggers (eds.), *Turning Points in History: A Cross Cultural Perspective*, Rochester, NY (University of Rochester Press) 2002, 209–231; Georg G. Iggers and Q. Edward Wang, The Appeal of Nationalist History around the World, in: Iggers and Wang, *A Global History of Modern Historiography*, Harlow (Pearson) 2008, 194–249.

15. Eckhardt Fuchs and Benedikt Stuchtey (eds.), *Across Cultural Borders: Historiography in Global Perspective*, Lanham, MD (Rowman & Littlefield) 2002; Stuchtey and Fuchs, *Writing World History*; Q. Edward Wang and Franz L. Fillafer (eds.), *The Many Faces of Clio: Cross-Cultural Approaches to Historiography*, New York (Berghahn) 2007; Douglas Northrop (ed.), *A Companion to World History*, Oxford (Wiley-Blackwell) 2012, 389–526.

16. Vinay Lal, Provincializing the West: World History from the Perspective of Indian History, in: Benedikt Stuchtey and Eckhardt Fuchs (eds.), *Writing World History, 1800–2000,* Oxford (Oxford University Press) 2003, 271–289, quote: 278–79.

17. Dominic Sachsenmaier, Some Reflections on the Nature of Global History, Toynbee Prize Foundation, http://toynbee prize.org/global-history-forum/some-reflections-on-the-nature -of-global-history/#more-984.

18. Examples for Italy include, Laura Di Fiore and Marco Meriggi, *World History: Le nuove rotte della storia*, Rome (Laterza) 2011; for Belgium, Eric Vanhaute, *Wereldgeschiedenis: Eeen inleiding*, Ghent (Academia Press) 2008; for Germany, Sebastian Conrad, Andreas Eckert, and Ulrike Freitag (eds.), *Globalgeschichte: Theorien, Ansätze, Themen*, Frankfurt (Campus) 2007; for Switzerland, Jérome David, Thomas David and Bar-

bara Lüthi (eds.), *Globalgeschichte/Histoire Global/Global History*, Zurich (Chronos) 2007; for France, Philippe Beaujard, Laurent Berger, and Philippe Norel (eds.), *Histoire globale, mondialisations et capitalisme*, Paris (La Découverte) 2009; for South Korea, Cho Ji-hyŏng and Kim Yong-Woo (eds.), *Chigusa ŭi tojŏn: ŏddŏgge yurŏpchungsimjuŭi rŭl nŏmŏsŏl kŏtinga*, Seoul (Sŏhaemunjip) 2010; for Japan, Mizushima Tsukasa, *Gurōbaru hisutorī nyūmon*, Tokyo (Yamakawa Shuppan) 2010.

19. Benedict Anderson, *Under Three Flags: Anarchism and the Anti-Colonial Imagination*, London (Verso) 2005, 5.

20. John Darwin, *After Tamerlane: The Global History of Empire*, London (Penguin) 2007.

21. Kenneth Pomeranz, *The Great Divergence: Europe, China, and the Making of the Modern World Economy*, Princeton (Princeton University Press) 2000.

22. John-Paul A. Ghobrial, The Secret Life of Elias of Babylon and the Uses of Global Microhistory, *Past & Present* 222 (2014), 51–93, quote: 59.

23. James C. Scott, *The Art of Not Being Governed: An Anarchist History of Upland Southeast Asia*, New Haven, CT (Yale University Press) 2009.

24. For a critique of the flow metaphor, popularized by scholars like Arjun Appadurai and Ulf Hannerz, see Stuart A. Rockefeller, Flow, *Current Anthropology* 52 (2011), 557–578.

25. Valeska Huber, *Channelling Mobilities: Migration and Globalisation in the Suez Canal Region and Beyond*, Cambridge (Cambridge University Press) 2013.

26. Londa Schiebinger, *Plants and Empire: Colonial Bioprospecting in the Atlantic World*, Cambridge, MA (Harvard University Press) 2007; Robert N. Proctor and Londa Schiebinger (eds.), *Agnotology: The Making and Unmaking of Ignorance*, Stanford, CA (Stanford University Press) 2008. See also Anna L. Tsing, *Friction: An Ethnography of Global Connection*, Princeton (Princeton University Press) 2004.

27. Stefan Zweig, *Die Welt von gestern: Erinnerungen eines Europäers*, Frankfurt am Main (Fischer) 1970, 465.

28. Richard Drayton, Where Does the World Historian Write From? Objectivity, Moral Conscience and the Past and Present of Imperialism, *Journal of Contemporary History* 46 (2011), 671–685.

29. For example, John E. Wills, *1688: A Global History*, New York (W. W. Norton) 2002; Miles Ogborn (ed.), *Global Lives: Britain and the World, 1550–1800*, Cambridge (Cambridge University Press) 2008.

30. Anthony Giddens, *The Constitution of Society: Outline of the Theory of Structuration*, Cambridge (Polity) 1984.

31. For "Anglobalization," see Ferguson, *Empire*, xxii. For a more sober analysis of the link between imperial and global links, see Gary Magee and Andrew Thompson, *Empire and Globalisation: Networks of People, Goods and Capital in the British World, c.1850–1914*, Cambridge (Cambridge University Press) 2010.

32. Sujit Sivasundaram, *Islanded: Britain, Sri Lanka, and the Bounds of an Indian Ocean Colony*, Chicago (Chicago University Press) 2013.

33. This is where I differ from Frederick Cooper, even if the general thrust of this section is compatible with his position in Cooper, What is the Concept of Globalization Good for? An African Historian's Perspective, *African Affairs* 100 (2001), 189–213.

34. For overviews, see Patrick Manning (ed.), *Global Practice in World History: Advances Worldwide*, Princeton, NJ (Markus Wiener) 2008; Dominic Sachsenmaier, *Global Perspectives on Global History: Theories and Approaches in a Connected World*, Cambridge (Cambridge University Press) 2011. See also Luke Clossey and Nicholas Guyatt, It's a Small World After All: The Wider World in Historians' Peripheral Vision, *Perspectives on History* 51 (May 2013).

Index

of Eurocentrism in, 50; as the macro-historical alternative to modernization theory, 48; and the notion of a "unified theory," 52

World and a Very Small Place in Africa, The (Wright), 129–30

World War II, 32, 180–81; and the "memory wars" in Japan, China, and Korea, 150–51

World of Yesterday (Zweig), 229

Wright, Donald R., 129–30

Xiamen, 109

Yangtze Delta, 43
Yemen, 122
Yew, Lee Kuan, 178
Yokohama, 109

Zheng He, 168, 208
Zimmerman, Andrew, 137–38
Zweig, Stefan, 229